A volume in the series

Anthropology of Contemporary Issues

EDITED BY ROGER SANJEK

A complete list of titles in the series
appears at the end of the book.

Anthony Leeds

Photo: Eric Almquist

Cities, Classes, and the Social Order

Anthony Leeds

EDITED BY

Roger Sanjek

Cornell University Press

Ithaca and London

First published 1994 by Cornell University Press.

Library of Congress Cataloging-in-Publication Data

Leeds, Anthony, 1925–1989
    Cities, classes, and the social order / Anthony Leeds ; edited by
Roger Sanjek.
        p.   cm. — (Anthropology of contemporary issues)
    Includes bibliographical references and index.
    ISBN 0-8014-2957-9. — ISBN 0-8014-8168-6
    1. Urban anthropology. 2. Cities and towns. 3. Sociology,
Urban. I. Sanjek, Roger. II. Title. III. Series.
GN395.L44 1994
307.76—dc20   93-38934

Contents

Contents

Classes in the Social Order

Localities in Urban Systems

Photographs

Preface

Anthony Leeds was a creative and visionary anthropological theorist. A member of the remarkable post–World War II cohort of Columbia University anthropologists, Leeds shared interests in history,
evolution, and power with fellow students and colleagues Stanley Diamond, Morton Fried, Marvin Harris, Eleanor Leacock, Robert Manners, Sidney Mintz, Sally Falk Moore, Marshall Sahlins, Eric Wolf,
and others. Although less well known than the leading work of these
peers, his intellectual synthesis, still expanding and growing at the
time of his death in 1989, is perhaps most far-reaching of all. Rooted
philosophically in both scientific and humanistic sensibilities, Leeds's
vision of anthropology is of major relevance to the dilemmas the discipline faces today in understanding an intensely interconnected world.

Leeds's thinking tied together grand evolutionary transitions, specific historical sequences, ecology, technology, classes, power, social
organization, individual choice, human creativity, and the epistemology of social thought. Although a coherent vision underlay his writings, it appeared in unified form nowhere in them. It was presented,
or leaked out, in different places, at different times, in his forty published papers written over nearly three decades. Leeds's métier, the
long essay, was not conducive to precise, clipped, unified statements;
no master theoretical treatise brought together all the strands of his
thought. Yet the connections among the intensely theoretical nuggets
that appear throughout his writings, taken as a whole, interlink with
each other, and emerge forcefully as one digests his many-faceted
work.

Until now, locating that work has been no easy task. Leeds published in such a variety of major and hard-to-find journals and in both widely accessible and relatively obscure essay collections that few persons, certainly, have read more than a small fraction of his output, despite his many cross-references to his other writings. Even for those familiar with Leeds through some of his best-known papers, the range and scope of his vision as presented in this book will be fresh and new.

This volume brings together the best of Leeds's work on cities, classes, and the social order, along with introductions to his life and thought by R. Timothy Sieber and myself. Sieber's essay situates Leeds in the liberal New York milieu into which he was born, and describes the personal circumstances of socialist family influences and upstate New York farm childhood that produced his particular blend of political and ecological interests. Sieber delineates Leeds's career trajectory: his research in rural and urban Brazil, the Venezuelan tropical forest, and Portugal; his work on ecological, evolutionary, and epistemological issues; and the highly personal field-research and cooperative-seminar style of his scholarly life in Brazil, Texas, and Boston.

My essay draws on Leeds's entire body of published and unpublished writings to present the significant dimensions of his theoretical vision. Influenced strongly by both Kroeber and Marx, as well as by the ecological-evolutionary strain in American anthropology, Leeds developed an orientation at once materialist, behavioral, and scientific, but also deeply philosophical and committed to the enduring importance of culture, symbolism, and ideology. Leeds's vision saw human evolution as connective—interlinking individual, group, social order, and culture—and responsive to both ecology and power, two concepts he developed in nuanced and ethnographically sensitive fashion.

My selection of the eight essays included in this volume was relatively easy (though other excellent papers more specifically ethnographic in tone could not be included). The nature of Leeds's interlocking views on cities in history, on classes, and on the organization and diversity of urban localities, is relatively clear-cut, as my introductory essay and Leeds's essays themselves make apparent. Leeds's ideas on these topics have been somewhat influential, but not nearly enough. Only one of these essays (Chapter 7) is widely cited, but its place in relation to the others here has not been appreciated. For most readers, the scope of Leeds's thought that these essays reveal will be unanticipated.

What was more difficult than selecting the essays was drawing together the strands and sinews of Leeds's holistic anthropology to reveal the protean vision that underlies his work. This must be an editor's version of that vision and not necessarily the presentation of it that Leeds might have made himself. I met Tony Leeds only once, during the 1970s, and corresponded with him once thereafter. I admired the essays on Brazil that I had read many years ago (Chapters 7 and 8, and Leeds 1964b) and his critique of the culture of poverty concept (1971), and these were deeply influential on my thinking. But I had never made the effort to track down the rest of his writings, and was unaware of the full scope of his ideas until beginning to work on this volume after his death in 1989. During that year I also wrote a review essay on urban anthropology (Sanjek 1990b), and the impact of Leeds's thinking on this field became even more apparent to me. The need for a collection of his work was obvious. After discussing this idea with Tim Sieber, who knew Leeds and his family, and meeting with Elizabeth Leeds early in 1990, I began work on this volume together with Sieber. Tim, Liz, and I also thank Kathleen Logan, Chip Maxwell, and Robert J. Smith for advice that helped shape the volume as our joint effort moved it along.

My own assimilation of Leeds's full body of work was strongly facilitated by the Columbia University Department of Anthropology milieu that we both shared, a generation apart. Leeds was a Columbia anthropology undergraduate major and Ph.D.; his years there spanned the late 1940s to the late 1950s. I hold similar credentials; my Columbia years ran from the early 1960s to early 1970s. Among my major influences then was that same postwar Columbia cohort of which Leeds was a member.

It is our hope that *Cities, Classes, and the Social Order* will serve well a broad spectrum of anthropologists, as well as students of comparative social theory and contemporary urban studies. As anthropologists and other scholars currently grope toward greater intellectual reintegration of past attention to ecology, evolution, history, power, social organization, individual creativity, and cultural processes, the holistic anthropology of Anthony Leeds provides rich ground for ongoing work and reflection, and a sense of direction.

ROGER SANJEK

New York City

Acknowledgments

Chapter 1, which originally appeared in *Cities of the Mind: Images and Themes in the Social Sciences,* ed. Lloyd Rodwin and Robert M. Hollister (New York: Plenum, 1984), is republished here by permission of Plenum Press. Chapters 2 and 8 are used by permission of the Southern Anthropology Society. Chapter 3, from *Peasant Livelihood: Studies in Economic Anthropology and Cultural Ecology,* ed. Rhoda Halperin and James Dow, copyright © 1977, is reprinted with permission of St. Martin's Press, Incorporated. Chapter 4, from *Proceedings of the Expert's Conference on Latin America and the Future of Its Jewish Communities,* 1973, appears with the permission of the Institute of Jewish Affairs, London. Chapter 5, from *Social Structure, Stratification, and Mobility,* is republished with the permission of the General Secretariat of the Organization of American States. Chapter 7, from *Urban Anthropology: Cross-Cultural Studies of Urbanization,* ed. Aidan Southall, appears with the permission of Aidan Southall.

Anthony Leeds:
Life and Work

The Life of Anthony Leeds:
Unity in Diversity

R. Timothy Sieber

I first met Tony Leeds in 1974 when, as a newly arrived assistant professor at the University of Massachusetts Boston campus, I traveled across town to visit the Boston University Anthropology Colloquium series that he organized. That day Leeds's friend and former Columbia classmate Eleanor Leacock, one of my own mentors, was speaking on the status of women in hunting-gathering societies. Leeds's presence was palpable: he was short, stocky, horn-rimmed, intense, intellectually pugnacious, in fine form as the impresario of critical, wide-ranging, and sometimes heated discussion about contemporary anthropological theory. His performance displayed the same qualities of incisiveness, iconoclasm, and passion that I had discovered as a graduate student in his provocative work on cities and on Brazil. My conversation with Leeds began: I became an on-again-off-again member of the "Thursday Night Group" that met at his Dedham, Massachusetts, kitchen table and was fortunate to know him as professional colleague and friend for the next fifteen years.

Any endeavor to sum up a life must necessarily be a selective one—especially when the life is as multifaceted and complex as Tony Leeds's. This biographical account will emphasize the shaping and expression of Leeds's public persona as anthropologist, cultural critic, artist, and keen analyst of society in Europe and the Americas. As Roger Sanjek explains in his overview of Leeds's theoretical ideas, Leeds was first and foremost a broad cultural theorist who principally distinguished himself in three areas of study: urban and complex society, cultural ecology (including technology and agriculture), and the philosophy and history of social science. This biographic essay contextualizes Leeds's work primarily in the first of these areas—the analysis of urban and complex social systems, which is the focus of this volume of his collected papers.

This account will have two parts. The first is a chronological narrative of Leeds's life that moves from his childhood and youth through his years of professional training and attempts to demonstrate their links with his later thinking and writing during nearly thirty years of work as academic, researcher, and theorist. As Norman B. Schwartz has noted, all biography links individual action with "antecedent experiences which dispose the subject to deal with the world in characteristic ways" (Schwartz 1977:94, quoted in Langness and Frank 1981:78), and these links are compelling in Leeds's life. He had an upbringing and family heritage which were deeply multicultural and multilingual and which early on problematized the question of culture and developed in him many sensibilities later reflected in his anthropology. Also significant for his later work in urban anthropology and insightful observations on the integration of urban and rural sectors, he spent his childhood and adolescence alternating residence between country and city. Urbane and cosmopolitan even as a youth, he nonetheless came of age on a family farm and graduated from a small country high school. Strong family traditions of political activism and involvement in the arts similarly shaped not only many of his private passions but also his visions of anthropological theory and practice. As a young anthropologist at Columbia University in the intense milieu of the post–World War II years, he trained as a materialist, neo-Marxist, and Latin Americanist and established lifelong theoretical commitments that shaped his thinking and writing until his death. Both at Columbia and in early faculty appointments at City College of New York and Hofstra University, he trained himself in ancillary fields beyond anthropology and developed his characteristically broad interdisciplinary approach to the study of complex society.

The chronology then traces the course of Leeds's mature professional life at the Pan-American Union and at the University of Texas, and I explain how during these years Leeds broadened his studies of Brazilian society and of Latin America to include proletarian sectors as well as elites, and how he contributed significantly to the growth of urban anthropology as a new field in the United States as well as in Brazil. Later, at Boston University, Leeds shifted toward broader, synthetic, more theoretical treatments of complex society. He also

[4]

developed new research interests in European labor migration, carried out fieldwork in Portugal, and began to experiment with new genres of anthropological writing, including poetry.

In the second half of the essay, I focus on several important overarching themes that characterize Leeds's identity and work as student of complex society and examine each in some detail. First to be considered is his open interpersonal style and his commitment to study groups, which dramatically extended the reach of his influence inside and outside of anthropology. Next treated is the distinctive lifelong integration of rural and urban in Leeds's personal history, which was reflected not only in his research agenda and theoretical ideas, but also in his everyday political commitments and residences. Leeds's political activism, the next topic, was also deeply rooted in his family history and shaped his identity and commitments as intellectual and citizen of the United States and the world. The final section examines Leeds's experimentation in later life with "multiple epistemologies" of cultural understanding and, in particular, with his anthropological uses of poetry and photography. The essay's conclusion reflects on the broad scope of Leeds's complex intellectual project and its inherently expanding and visionary qualities.

Cradled in an Urbane, Cosmopolitan World

Anthony Leeds was born on January 26, 1925, on New York City's Lower West Side, "then a solidly bourgeois part of the city, brownstone and brick houses, maids, 'nurses,' and all" (Leeds 1984c:1). His parents were both of Jewish extraction, intensely secular or "apostate" as Leeds said. His mother's family migrated to the United States from Germany and his father's family, with distant Sephardic roots, from England. The young Leeds grew up in a cosmopolitan, urbane world with strong ties to Europe, especially Austria, Germany, and Britain. As a child he interacted regularly with extended kin, both in the United States and in Europe. He was exposed early to German and French, as well as to English, and he became fluent in all three languages (and, later in life, in Portuguese and Spanish as well.) Leeds spent four years (1929–33) of his early childhood in Vienna, where his mother had moved to study psychoanalysis at Freud's Psychoanalytic Institute, and for part of this time he attended boarding school in Switzerland. Political events in Europe led to his family's return to

New York City in 1933. Leeds maintained throughout his adult life that, because of these early experiences in Europe and his international family background, he never fully identified himself as an American or felt completely at home in the United States.

All the time he was growing up, Leeds's parents, his wider senior kin, their associates, and visitors to the household were deeply "enmeshed in all the major social, political, and cultural movements of the time: modern art, music, poetry, theater, architecture, psychoanalysis, science, civil liberties, socialism" (Leeds 1984c:8). His mother, Polly Leeds Weil, was an actress, translator, and psychoanalyst, and his surrogate mother and aunt, Anita Block, was a theater critic. His father, Arthur Leeds, who died when Tony was only three, was a businessman and lawyer involved in civil liberty causes. Leeds's stepfather, Edmund Weil, a sculptor, musician, and political activist, became the major father figure of his childhood. His maternal grandfather, Herman Cahn, a silk manufacturer in Passaic, New Jersey, was also a socialist, economist, and writer. Leeds's only sibling, Winifred, seven years his senior—who became an influential leader of Farm and Wilderness Quaker summer camps in Vermont—completed the family circle of his childhood.

Many of Leeds's most enduring traits were formed during these early years: his intense intellectualism, cultural cosmopolitanism, love of the arts, and broad political commitments. All later guided his approach to anthropology. His childhood environment was filled with books, play and delight in literary language, discussions over the leading cultural and political issues of the day, and progressive education at the Walden School on Manhattan's Upper West Side, which he attended for four years (two years of preschool and third and fourth grades). Intellectual, studious, and intensely curious, he early garnered the nickname "professor" from his classmates. He was also continually immersed in the world of the arts, particularly in the grand European bourgeois tradition. He later became active in musical and artistic circles himself: he sang, played cello and piano, and eventually became a poet and photographer as well. Leeds also credited the remarkable cultural diversity and flux of his upbringing for propelling him on a lifelong search for discovery, as anthropologist and human being, to understand and incorporate new cultural meanings into his ever-evolving, complex self. Indeed, the leitmotiv of Leeds's intellectual life—the drive to mediate diversity by incorporating it into frameworks of ever increasing scope—first appeared in his childhood struggles to fix identity in this richly textured multicultural world.

From City to Country and Back

Heir to a rich cosmopolitan, urbane tradition drawn from Western Europe, Leeds also displayed a consistent involvement with things rural, agricultural, and land-related. He spent nine years of his adolescence, from ages ten to nineteen, on a working farm in Clinton Corners, Dutchess County, New York, where his mother moved in 1935. The farm, which his mother operated until 1954, mainly produced chickens and eggs but also dairy products and vegetables. Leeds did farm work throughout this period, and for two years after his high school graduation in 1942 his labor alone sustained the farm. During the late Depression era, he experienced rural development firsthand when Roosevelt's Rural Electrification Administration brought electricity to the family house and barn. A veteran of Swiss boarding schools and the cosmopolitan Walden School, he experienced sixth grade in a one-room schoolhouse, then attended a small town high school and participated in square dancing and other communal functions in nearby village centers. In reflecting on his rural and small town years, he wrote of the "profound and pervasive experience of community in a rural setting, including even the central school, school bus, scouts, Christian Endeavor, Community Day, [informal] groups at the stores, etc., even despite my own sense of partial alienation as a city boy with the entire weight of the background which found no counterpart among my rural networks. That kind of experience . . . has most deeply affected both my fieldwork and my understanding of rural settings studied as an anthropologist" (1984c:33).

Columbia University and Early Intellectual Formation

Leeds's study of anthropology began during his undergraduate years at Columbia, when he took a first course at the suggestion of his stepfather. He graduated Phi Beta Kappa, with honors in Anthropology and a minor in German in 1949 and proceeded directly into graduate studies at Columbia, which he later described as a "cauldron of innovative thought," in anthropology and related fields in the 1940s (Leeds 1984c:53). In his 1984 draft autobiography, Leeds credited a number of figures at Columbia as major mentors, teachers, and influences on his thinking: Professors Charles Wagley, Alfred L. Kroeber, Morton Fried, Elman Service, Joseph Greenberg, Conrad Arensberg, William Duncan Strong, Gene Weltfish, and Karl Polanyi, and fel-

[7]

low student Anne Chapman (Leeds 1984c:50–52). Although he had
courses with Julian Steward, he denied any serious influence from
Steward (Leeds 1984c:52). He also cited the influences of others who
had recently been students at Columbia and still actively circulated
there, such as Eleanor Leacock, Stanley Diamond, Sidney Mintz, and
Eric Wolf. His immediate peers and fellow students in the program
included Andrew P. Vayda, Marshall Sahlins, Robert Murphy, Muriel
Hammer, Sally Falk Moore, and Marvin Harris. Harris has noted that,
throughout these years, Leeds's classmates marveled at his voracious
intellectual appetite—in class he "always sat in the front row of class
furiously taking notes" (Harris 1989), and outside of class he organized
incessant study groups and tutored his peers. He was a demanding
student, as well, who continually posed challenging questions for his
professors and often argued with them. He also did not hesitate to
offer irreverent commentary—including paper airplanes sailed to the
front of the room—when he found the pacing and content of professors' lectures particularly wanting (Osmundsen 1991).

Leeds's dissertation research was a 1951–52 study of the political
economy of cocoa production in Bahia. It was one of four Bahia investi-
gations supervised by Charles Wagley and Brazilian anthropologist
Thales de Azevedo and carried out by, in addition to Leeds, Marvin
Harris, Benjamin Zimmerman, and William Hutchinson. Completed
in 1957, Leeds's dissertation, entitled *Economic Cycles in Brazil: The
Persistence of a Total-Cultural Pattern: Cacao and Other Cases*, was
"essentially a Marxist analysis of the base and superstructure of cocoa
production, amplified by a very strong ecological bent and . . . some
innovative analysis of the ideological systems of the two major classes"
(Leeds 1984c:54). Vast in scope and never published, the dissertation
study took into account international, national, and regional markets,
banks, law, the courts, class stratification, and localities, all as interacting levels of a single multilevel system. Leeds's study propelled him
into a lifetime of additional work, mainly in Brazil but also elsewhere,
on such issues as the relations between elite and proletarian sectors,
internal migration, and the interactions between localities and supralocal institutions.

During his years at Columbia from 1947 to 1957, the university was
the "generating milieu of the major works in Marxist Anthropology
since World War II" (Leeds 1984c:52), and Leeds belonged to two
Marxist social science study groups. Like the Marxism of many in
anthropology who became professionally active during the McCarthy

and early Cold War eras, Leeds's Marxism was central but submerged. Throughout his early career, Leeds saw his own work as substantively Marxist without explicitly identifying it as such, although by the 1970s he increasingly did so. Leeds criticized studies that purported to be Marxist without thoroughly documenting the materialist domain. Citing a "life-long profound skepticism of theology of any sort" (Leeds 1984c:26), Leeds also distinguished his own pragmatic Marxism from more doctrinaire varieties connected to particular political programs —these he termed "ideological Marxism"—and from highly self-conscious theoretical schools, especially French structural Marxism. These latter he criticized for their "intellectualist posturing . . . , each claiming sanctity by use and exegesis of the proper ritual words, while the substantive treatments—and sometimes the issues as well—are thinly dealt with" (Leeds 1984c:61, n.12).

Leeds continued to live in New York until 1961, four years after finishing his doctorate, and held his first university teaching positions during this period. For three years he taught at Hofstra (1956–59), and subsequently for two at City College. He expanded the scope of his theoretical understanding of complex societies and began to develop the hallmark interdisciplinary approaches that characterized his teaching and much of his writing about cities through the rest of his life. During this time, he taught the interdisciplinary course, Introduction to Social Science, created by Hofstra's historian and philosopher of social science, Benjamin N. Nelson, whom Leeds considered one of his greatest mentors. As part of the faculty seminar attached to the course, Leeds received what he called a "vast in-house training in economics, political science, history, and particularly sociology" (Leeds 1984c:60).

He remained a lifelong critic of anthropological parochialism and narrowness, particularly in relation to urban studies; he advocated an interdisciplinary approach to urban analysis. Leeds always maintained that no single discipline alone could study or understand urban society, and in this vein he was an early and persistent critic of the very concept of "urban anthropology": he argued, "I consider such a field a spurious and retrograde one in that it tends to make an excuse for maintaining a subject matter within a discipline which cannot and should not handle it" (1972:4). When Leeds first moved to the University of Texas in 1963, he insisted on calling his basic urban course, "Principles of Urban Analysis" (1972:5), but later at Boston University he finally applied the label "Urban Anthropology" to his course (Leeds 1986). In both places, however, his teaching—like his research—drew

[9]

deeply from sociology, economics, geography, history, and systems theory.

Leeds's New York years were also marked by a brief 1958 field trip to Venezuela, where he studied the Yaruro of the southern Llanos (e.g., Leeds 1960, 1961c, 1964d). Through his entire New York period and beyond, from 1948 until 1966, Leeds was married to artist and teacher Jo Alice Lowrey, with whom he had the first three of his five children. These New York years were also the heart of his fourteen-year involvement with the Cantata Singers, an early music choral society whose president he became in 1958. For six years during the 1950s, in addition, Leeds underwent psychoanalysis, an experience he termed "one of the profoundest of my life . . . that helped me tremendously both in field work and in teaching and working with students" (Leeds 1984c:75, n.7).

Washington, D.C., and the Pan-American Union:
Extending Horizons in Latin America

Leeds spent the next two years (1961–63) as chief of the Program of Urban Development at the Pan-American Union (PAU) in Washington, D.C., forerunner of today's Organization of American States. Under their auspices he returned to Brazil to complete research for his classic study on careers and social structure (1964b) and to finish other work on analysis of class and class structure in Brazil (e.g., Chapter 5). Still mainly an analyst of elites, Leeds first became acquainted with squatter settlements and broader urban proletarian issues and envisioned doing research on these matters during this trip. He also broadened his familiarity with Latin American cities as representative of the PAU, traveled widely to monitor the "Four Cities Study" (supervised by Luis Costa Pinto), and focused on Rio de Janeiro, Montevideo, Santiago de Chile, and Buenos Aires.

At the PAU he was hired by and worked under Mexican Marxist anthropologist Angel Palerm, one of his most significant mentors. An insightful analyst of Mexico, Italy, Iberia, and Israel, Palerm did much to guide Leeds's work during this time, encouraged his study of class structure and first directed him to *favelas*, Brazilian squatter settlements. Leeds's admiration for Palerm was frank and direct, and he recognized similarities between himself and Palerm. When he described Palerm, for example, not as an urbanist, but as a "Marxist

[10]

anthropological political economist, dealing with complex societies, which necessarily have cities/towns/villages in them" (1981b:2), he might well have been talking about himself.

The University of Texas: Deepening Involvement in Brazil

Leeds's next nine years (1963–72) were based at the University of Texas. These years represent, in many respects, his time of most intense urban research, particularly in Latin America. In returning to Brazil, Leeds began the second decade of one of the first genuinely long-term research projects in anthropology—his nearly forty-year study of Brazilian urban society. During his Texas years, Leeds made five field trips to Brazil and initiated his first research on squatter settlements in Rio de Janeiro and São Paulo. Later he made additional field trips to Bogotá, Lima, and Santiago de Chile to study "squatments" in those comparative locations. Never particularly oriented toward microethnography, Leeds also sought formal training at Texas in general systems theory and incorporated it, as well as large-scale survey methods, into the design for his favela research. Unlike most of his anthropological contemporaries, Leeds actively sought to meld quantitative and qualitative approaches in his fieldwork and analysis.

The core of Leeds's research on Brazilian favelas took place during 1965–66, when, under Social Science Research Council and Ford Foundation funding, he studied the social and economic organization of communities in Rio de Janeiro. During this fieldwork, he established one of his most legendary seminar groups—Peace Corps volunteers, Brazilian and foreign academics, local community workers, and favela residents—who together researched, analyzed, and critiqued conditions in twelve of the city's favelas. As might be expected, it was not simply data and understanding that emerged from this seminar, but also strategies for local action in community development and other arenas.

This community-based seminar also generated Leeds's major collaboration, one that lasted twenty-two years until his death, with Elizabeth Plotkin Leeds. In Rio as a U.S. Peace Corps community action worker, Plotkin was the daughter of a journalist and a sophisticated social and political observer in her own right. She later became a political scientist and specialized in popular political movements, particularly in urban Latin America, and the politics of southern Eu-

[11]

ropean labor migration. Plotkin joined Leeds as a research associate in 1966 and actively collaborated in planning and carrying out their favela research, including a survey of over 300 Rio favelas and a later, broader cross-national comparative study. Plotkin and Leeds married in 1967, produced two children (Leeds's fourth and fifth), coauthored several central favela studies (e.g., Leeds and Leeds 1976) and their now classic work in Brazilian urban studies, published in Portuguese as *A Sociologia do Brasil Urbano* (Leeds and Leeds 1978). They later carried on related lines of independent research in Portugal in the late 1970s and in Brazil in 1988, and Liz Leeds continued to influence Tony's thinking, particularly in analysis of popular political movements and in general political structures and processes in complex societies.

Tony Leeds's attention was not exclusively focused on Latin America during this time. While in residence at the University in Austin, Leeds also found time to analyze Texas itself. He taught a course on the history and political economy of the state, directed Peace Corps trainees in a study of ethnic stratification in sixty-three Texas settlements (Leeds, ed. 1965) and eventually completed his own systems analysis during 1971–72 of the ecological, social, and urban aspects of the Texas hill country (Leeds 1980a).

The Boston Years: Striving for Broader Intellectual Synthesis

After leaving Texas, Leeds spent a transitional year in England at the Latin American centers at Oxford University and the University of London, on his way to Boston University, which would be his academic home for the last sixteen years of his life, from 1973 to 1989. In Boston he concentrated on writing synthetic, comparative, and theoretical overviews based on more than two decades of Latin American research of complex urban systems (e.g., 1979, Chapters 1–3).

Leeds's accumulated impact on Brazilian urban studies became profound during these years, both before and after the 1978 publication of his and Elizabeth Leeds's work, *A Sociologia do Brasil Urbano*. At various points, Leeds had affiliations with the Museu Nacional of the Universidade Federal do Rio de Janeiro, the Centro Nacional Pesquisas Habitacionais, and other Brazilian institutes. Beginning in the late 1960s, Leeds introduced the newly emerging idea of "urban anthropology" to Brazilian social science. At the Museu Nacional, he was a profound inspiration and mentor to young Brazilian scholars—such

[12]

as Gilberto Velho—who began to study the country's burgeoning urban zones at a time when most North American anthropological activity at the Museu Nacional, from Harvard and other quarters, was focused exclusively on indigenous peoples in the interior. Leeds promoted interdisciplinary dialogue and debate among specialists from many disciplines, and between academics and policymakers, and helped build urban studies into one of the most advanced areas of Brazilian social science (Velho 1991). He fostered intellectual development not only through his publications (many published originally or solely in Portuguese), but through "always creating a healthy climate of discussion and excited interest" (Velho 1991:1) in the dialogue between thinkers and actors from very diverse positions in the nation.

His work in Brazil, of course, was the counterpart to his formative involvement in the field of urban anthropology in the United States. Leeds was an original founder of the Society for Urban Anthropology and an early editor of its newsletter. He was a passionate, vocal participant in the early debates over the boundaries and aims of the field and often filled the role of gadfly in the loyal opposition. He contributed key essays (Chapters 2, 7, and 8) to a number of seminal early collections in the field, such as those edited by Elizabeth Eddy (1968), Aidan Southall (1973), and Thomas Collins (1980). During the years 1982–83, he also served energetically as president of the Society for Urban Anthropology.

At the same time, Leeds's scholarly interests began to diversify into new areas, both substantively and methodologically. Before and even more after a serious heart attack in 1980, Leeds increased his involvement in creative, professional, and political activity both inside and outside academic anthropology. These efforts did not always receive the support or understanding of his anthropological colleagues, especially those in his own university department. Writing in 1982, Leeds referred to this period in his life as a "macro-transition": "I seem to be both in one of those macro-transitions from one major domain of interest to another . . . ('urban' to 'agriculture'—a false dichotomy, but different focus) and in a grand-scale life transition ('mid-life crisis') from formal anthropological (alienated?) analysis and theory building to something more deeply immersed in praxis, dealing with the humanity and anguishes of everyday life, using my anthropology" (1982d:1).

Through most of the 1970s, he and Elizabeth Leeds pursued independent lines of research—involving seven field trips—on the political economy of Portuguese labor migration, from rural villages to cities within Portugal and within a broader Western European regional context. It was in this work that Leeds experimented with new methodologies and genres of ethnographic presentation and began to use more poetic forms. For example, his unpublished book *Minha Terra, Portugal: Lamentations and Celebrations—the Growth of an Ethnography and a Commitment* (1984b) contains a long analytic essay on political economic context and issues related to the epistemology of fieldwork, photographs, and a series of extended poems. He saw these poems as "ethnographic—they register conversations, events, situations, conditions, histories. They do so with the tonalities of human feelings" (Leeds 1984c:71). Leeds's poetry and photography, and their relation to this work and his broader intellectual aims, will be discussed below.

No account of Leeds's career or many years at Boston University would be complete without mention of graduate student research that he supported there. As at Texas, he always supervised many graduate students. Never provincial academically, he supported students not only at Boston University but, more informally, from a variety of New England universities, and he particularly aided those who felt adrift in their own departments. He was a generous and demanding mentor who responded honestly, incisively, and passionately to students' work. Many of those he mentored later said that no one else had ever read their work so closely. Sometimes it took strength and patience to absorb the multiple pages of single-spaced commentary and suggestions for revision that he commonly pounded out on his ailing, manual Smith-Corona typewriter or, worse yet, wrote on manuscript margins in a nearly illegible scrawl. His demands and perfectionism often made his students suffer, but none ever doubted that he cared deeply about their work (Bray 1989; Maxwell 1991).

At Boston University, the geographical and topical range of his students' doctoral dissertations was impressive. Whether set in communities large or small, in the United States or abroad, most of the dissertation projects took broadly ecological and systems approaches and showed strong concern for political economy and class issues. Many of the projects focused on Boston or other areas of the United States: the organization of the Chicago court system; gentrification in changing neighborhoods of Boston; history and political economy of New England mill towns; popular political and community movements related to such issues as school busing, hazardous waste, and industrial sitings; Haitian migration and family adaptation. Other projects dealt with similar issues in areas geographically farther afield: urban architecture in Botswana; the informal economic sector in urban Indonesia; coffee growers in Colombia; the political economy of the Nigerian truck spare parts business.

In 1987–88, the year before his death, Tony and Liz Leeds returned to Rio de Janeiro under Fulbright and SSRC support, respectively, in order to complete restudies after a quarter-century, Tony of Brazilian careers and Liz of favela politics. Their year in Brazil was a full and productive one, and Leeds returned home with plans to use the newer Brazilian data to update and expand his earlier careers study and to complete a comparative study of race relations in Brazil, the United States, and South Africa. Unfortunately, this and much other work-in-progress was left unfinished when Leeds died less than six months after his return from the field. While socializing with family and friends in the kitchen of his farmhouse in Randolph, Vermont, on the evening of February 20, 1989, Leeds was stricken with another heart attack and died within minutes. He was sixty-four.

Leeds as Interpersonal Human and Facilitator of Groups

One of the important themes that animated Tony Leeds's entire life was his intense intellectual sociability. In this respect, his skill at analysis of informal groups in complex, fluid social situations (e.g., 1964b) reflected his own social adeptness and versatility on the practical level. A deeply gregarious person throughout his life, he became an enthusiastic participant and facilitator of groups of all kinds, especially those dedicated to the intellectual dissection of complex society. Leeds relished honest, engaged, impassioned debate on intellectual issues and usually fostered a critical stance toward received anthropological wisdom. This did not always endear him to those who did not share his passionate convictions or direct style of intellectual engagement and argumentation. These traits, coupled with his strong streak of cynicism and irreverence toward established authority and procedures, made Leeds a demanding, if not difficult, person to deal with professionally. Paradoxically, these same personal traits—intensity, commitment, iconoclasm, excitement—that served to isolate him professionally in some quarters also made him the magnet, wherever he was, of an intense network of loyal followers and eager interlocutors.

[15]

Seen as impolitic by some, he was welcomed as a rare example of intellectual honesty and incisiveness by many others. Leeds was a border crosser and boundary breaker who never fit comfortably in the established center, yet never was isolated: his conversations extended into the terrain of the vast anthropological margins, and far beyond, linking him with multitudes.

It was in the context of his nearly lifelong series of study groups that the quality and the reach of Leeds's dialogue were especially evident. Through these groups, he established a reputation as generous supporter and caring mentor of countless researchers from many disciplines, and as someone who could always be counted upon to offer engaged, insightful criticism. Through the professional networks so often catalyzed through his groups, Leeds exerted a profound interpersonal influence that extended far beyond his research and teaching, strictly defined, and the walls of any university that employed him.

He joined his first study group, on world history and current events, as a high school student in Clinton Corners. At Columbia he hosted study groups of fellow students in his apartment, and he later belonged to two broader faculty-student groups on Marxism and yet another on cultural ecology. Indeed, wherever he was—New York, Texas, Brazil, or Boston—he spawned a seminar whose scope typically was the broad, multidisciplinary investigation of contemporary society. What Susan Eckstein termed "perhaps the longest running kitchen seminar in late twentieth century academic history" (Eckstein 1989) had its final incarnation in the Thursday Night Group that for fifteen years met regularly over coffee in the Leeds's kitchen in Dedham, Massachusetts, often late into the night. Though its core included Boston-area academics, students, and independent scholars from many disciplines, the Thursday Night Group drew broader participation from dozens of universities throughout the northeastern United States and from locations further afield. At these gatherings, Leeds was typically the driving force, inspired deeply participatory "exhilarating brainstorming on all matters great and small," and he always focused on "comparative and cross-cultural" inquiry into the "evolution of local, national, regional and world systems" (Saint-Louis 1989).

Leeds's groups were quite diverse in their composition, disciplinary approaches, and professional status of participants. As in Rio, where favela residents, community organizers, and social scientists engaged in common discussions, in Leeds's later groups academics of all ranks, graduate students, practicing anthropologists from nonacademic settings, and independent scholars shared insights in a spirit of honest exchange. Anthropologists predominated, but political science, history, sociology, economics, folklore, and other fields were also well represented. Through their catholic composition—the result of Leeds's own personal efforts to reach out and include diverse people—his groups were intended as models of the interdisciplinary inquiry, and integration of theory and praxis, that he consistently championed in all his work on complex society.

It is interesting to note that Leeds's involvement in professional associations mainly focused on interdisciplinary groups, such as the Society for the History of Technology. His most intense involvement was with the multidisciplinary American Association for the Advancement of Science (AAAS). Leeds served as AAAS Section H (Anthropology) secretary for eight years (1965–73) and during this time organized meeting symposia on widely ranging themes, including meaning systems, cultural evolution, human emotions, and dry lands management. For nine years Leeds was also active in another group that mixed natural and social scientists, the New England–based Sociobiology Study Group, which developed and issued critiques of the sociobiological paradigm (e.g., Leeds 1977c; Leeds and Dusek 1981–82). Except for his formative service as an early president of the Society for Urban Anthropology, Leeds spurned active involvement in most strictly anthropological groups and even for a time withdrew his membership in the American Anthropological Association in protest over what he saw as its academic provincialism.

Country and City in Leeds's Life

What was probably the most profound theme in his thought—the organic interconnection between the urban and rural sectors in complex societies—was for Leeds not only an academic issue or a matter of theory and research. His own life and professional experience exemplified the integration of these sectors that, Leeds consistently argued, convention had too falsely dichotomized. Things rural and things urban always mixed deeply in his life. The experience of growing up on his family's working farm in Clinton Corners "unscaled my eyes," he

[17]

wrote, "to citycentric social science looking at rural areas as somehow 'simple,' 'backward,' and alien" (Leeds 1984c:34). On the farm, he also gained a firsthand understanding of land, plants, and animals that profoundly informed his extensive work in cultural ecology. He credited his farm experience tending pigs and cows, for example, as the source of insights incorporated into many of his cultural ecological analyses, such as the one he coauthored with A. P. Vayda and D. B. Smith on Melanesian pigs (Vayda, Leeds, and Smith 1961).

Even as a rural child and adolescent, however, Leeds was a former urbanite with continuing cultural ties to New York City and Europe and thus in an especially opportune position to perceive the close systematic linkages between rural areas and larger institutional and urban centers. Brazil later became the main context for his mature analysis of such matters as urban hierarchies, the interpenetration of urban and rural in complex societies, and the rural as a subsystem of urban society. Leeds made his first observations on these matters, however, in Clinton Corners and on occasion used illustrations from this locality in discussions of broader theoretical issues (e.g., Chapter 2).

The integration of rural and urban in larger multilevel systems and the links between agriculture and state systems are reflected in many of his professional involvements. His dissertation was a study of the political economy of cocoa agricultural production in Brazil. Later, at the University of Texas in the early 1970s, he collaborated in a study of hill country ecology (1980a), including the political economy of agriculture and rural-urban linkages. While at Boston University in the 1980s, Leeds' was active in the Massachusetts Food and Agricultural Coalition and did research, public education, and advocacy work to enhance urban gardening, preserve small family farms in the state, and establish direct marketing networks between farms and cities. In his published and unpublished work on Brazil, Portugal, and South Africa, as well, he was preoccupied with demonstrating the place of rural elements in urban systems. For the last five years of his life, he also owned a farm in Randolph, Vermont, leased fields out for active dairy farming, enjoyed interacting with locals, and participated in the life of a community that, he often noted, reminded him of Clinton Corners. However cosmopolitan, Leeds always highly valued his own and others' strong attachment to place, an attachment he had experienced in Clinton Corners, in Vermont, and in his fieldwork sites.

Political Activism

Although very much the scholar, intellectual, and proponent of thoughtful reflection and analysis, Leeds believed that not just truth, but also praxis related to "a real ongoing world" (Leeds 1984c:50), was the proper concern of anthropology. Political activism was a part of all that he did professionally and personally, and he viewed much of his anthropological thinking and writing as a sort of cultural criticism of dominant and emerging trends in Western thought. As Leeds himself recognized, he was born into a "world of political and social awareness and commitment" (Leeds 1984c:3), descended from a long line of socialist activists and intellectuals, including his parents and grandparents on both sides. His mother, Polly Leeds Weil, and maternal aunt and surrogate mother, Anita Block, had both been active suffragists, and his father had run for elective office as a Workers party candidate in New York City. As genealogical charter for his own commitments, Leeds often noted with some humor that among his pacifist manufacturer grandfather Herman Cahn's three books was a 1918 edition, entitled *The Collapse of Capitalism*.

Taking unpopular, critical postures toward conventional institutions and practices came early to the young Leeds. After graduating from high school in the midst of World War II, he became a conscientious objector and eventually served for nearly two years in civilian work assignments, first in a labor camp in Bay Flats, New York, planting trees, and then as a patient care attendant at the Pennhurst State School for Mental Defectives in Spring City, Pennsylvania. At Pennhurst, he helped expose administrative graft and patient abuse by reporting the problems to investigative journalists, who eventually exposed the scandal. For the rest of his life, Leeds maintained an active involvement in questions of war and peace, and he left a series of anthropological publications on these issues (e.g., 1963, 1975). Much of his criticism of sociobiology, in addition, focused on its biodeterministic explanations of aggression.

Eschewing political sectarianism, Leeds continued his family's long history of participation in a variety of progressive causes. In Texas, he participated in teach-ins and other antiwar activities during the Vietnam era. As a researcher in Brazil, he informally trained Peace Corps workers and supported favela organizing. During his Boston years, his involvements were extensive: Middle East politics, especially concerning Lebanon; farm policy; antiapartheid and other South Africa work. He was a leader of the Massachusetts Food and Agricultural Coalition, and he lobbyed for more progressive farm and produce marketing laws. In addition to his regular teaching duties, he twice taught anthropology courses to prisoners in Massachusetts correctional institutions. At Boston University, finally, he became a union activist, helped to organize the faculty union and strike activity, and suffered reprisals for years to come—in the form of restricted pay and benefits from the university administration.

Multiple Epistemologies and Leeds's Poetry and Photography

As the essays in this volume indicate, Anthony Leeds showed great insight and distinction in his analyses and theorizing on the structure of complex urban and national systems. This work was systematic and formal in approach, built upon high levels of ethnographic, historical, and political synthesis and abstraction, and focused heavily on the structural domain and its dynamics. Leeds never published any microethnographic studies, and while he frequently handled the ideological domain within his systems framework, his published anthropological work—particularly his urban studies dating from 1964 to the late 1970s—seldom touched on issues of symbolism, expressive culture, or everyday life.

This limitation was paradoxical, since his private life and other nonacademic domains of his professional life were richly immersed in the arts and expressive culture. For the most part, Leeds accommodated these diverse strands of his own life situation by keeping them segregated from one another or, at least, from anthropology. On his anthropological vita, for example, Leeds did not list his poetry readings, musical involvements, or photographic exhibits, even though he maintained that they furthered ethnographic truth. He always acknowledged that he led a complex and "multi-faceted" life (Leeds 1984c:71).

Throughout his career, as he grew more interested in issues of meaning and aesthetics, Leeds became disenchanted with the limitations of what he finally labeled a "dualist," "scientistic, 'objectivist' social science" (Leeds 1984c:49). He thought that this sort of social science, first, resulted in "knowledge loss and, thereby, distortion and bias" (Leeds 1984c:49) in the attempt to perceive social realities, and was thus a flawed approach to discovery of cultural truths. More aes-

[20]

thetic approaches, including "both poetry and photography," he suggested, "probably undo the selection/abstraction, thereby making possible epistemologically firmer truths" (Leeds 1984c:48). Second, he believed that the traditional social scientist becomes—as he admits he was early in his career—"the split-apart person which our career/occupation institutionalizes, although the role occupants are largely unaware of this" (Leeds 1984c:48).

Leeds had written poetry from adolescence on, most of it on political and cultural issues, and continued writing during the early years of his career. In his mid-twenties, while completing dissertation fieldwork, for example, he wrote the poem, "Cities," which contrasted the aesthetics and sense of place in United States and tropical cities. ("Cities" and all other poems mentioned here are reprinted in this volume.) In grand European intellectual style, Leeds wrote verse in English, German, Spanish, and Portuguese. He also participated in poetry groups outside academia. Yet it was not until his later years, when he questioned the boundaries of anthropological methodology and expression, that Leeds's poetry began to inform his anthropological work, and he envisioned a role for the form in his own anthropological writing. While he never ceased writing in traditional scholarly styles, Leeds came to believe that poetry was a more reliable vehicle for reaching firmer truths about human life and culture, especially the realm of emotions. His efforts bespoke a career-long interest in broader issues in the epistemology of anthropology and the study of emotions, which he addressed in published (e.g., Leeds 1974c) as well as unpublished writings.

Minha Terra never saw publication, but some of Leeds's other poetry did, including thirteen pieces in Ian Prattis's collection, *The Anthropological Muse* (Leeds 1985a). For someone writing in a strongly cultural ecological tradition, poetry provided an arena in which Leeds could connect his more reflexive, interpretive impulses with the other strands of his work. In poetry, Leeds registered an early response to the broad shifts toward more interpretive methodology and exposition that were beginning to characterize anthropology more generally. In the last decade of his life, Leeds even defined interpretation of meaning as the central theme of his anthropological project.

Leeds's poetry was an integral part of his attempt to understand and articulate the nature of complex social and cultural systems, their connection with lived culture, and his own place as anthropologist and human being within them. In this sense, Leeds grappled with the

[21]

same major intellectual issues in his poetry as in his more scholarly prose writings: relations between structure and agency, economy and culture, history and the present, and especially supralocal socio-economic organization and everyday human experience and feelings. He recognized the power of poetry to deal with complex truths in compressed form and—not surprising for an anthropologist—its facility to draw broader meaning from the particular. Poetry also allowed Leeds to consider, as part of the whole, the subtler aspects of human feeling, both his own and his informants', that were often lost in his grander treatments. Through his verse, he also ventured into analysis of face-to-face situations populated by particular persons, for him an unusually "micro" level of analysis that he referred to as "ethnographic."

His characteristic sense of critique, irony, and pathos infused poetic treatments of large-scale forces and their impact on ordinary people's lives and well-being. In his "The F.M.I. Helps Portugal," for example, which he mockingly described as a "paean celebrating the agreement between Portugal and the International Monetary Fund, May 1978," Leeds bitterly faults the bank's "efficiency," and "purely technical" and "impartial" considerations for increasing the unemployment, impoverishment, and hunger of ordinary Portuguese. He also anguishes over the issue of art and whether it is an adequate and intellectually and morally responsible vehicle for analysis and critique of the workings of such large-scale systems. He repeatedly asks in refrain, "How do you write a poem about the F.M.I.?" and further, "Can . . . " and "Should one write a poem about the F.M.I."?

Leeds's poetic writing also contextualized his own activity as person and fieldworker. Poetry was the juncture where Leeds allowed his self, and his history, to most self-consciously intersect with his anthropology. He usually located himself in the situations he described, as in his sardonic "The Green Eye of Xerox in the Tropics," which he wrote at the 1984 International Congress of Anthropological and Ethnological Sciences in Bogotá. Here as "another gringo bringing the best to the unruly tropics," he is keenly aware of the intruding "I Bring More giant from the north," to whom even *he* has to pay dues. Sometimes he makes it clear that his presence is a minor note in scenes of high drama. In "Casal Ventoso, Meeting of the Directoria of the Residents' Association, June 13, 1978," for example, Leeds evokes the rhythm and uncertainty of a tense community meeting. The dialogue recounts how the history of imperialist wars in the waning Portuguese empire shaped the political imaginations of urban proletarians and their openness to revolutionary ideologies. Leeds's poem clarifies how his own and his local assistants' attempts to help the group with their "questionnaire" hinged on the resolution of these interconnected local and global political issues.

In poetry from his Portugal trips between 1978 and 1982 especially, Leeds attempted to capture the texture and vicissitudes of social relationships with informants in the field and what he was able to understand through the personal feelings he had for them as people. In "When the Gulls Fly, the Tempest Comes," he describes the growth of trust and caring with a family, becoming "deepest friends" in the "shacks of Lisbon," and the compassion he feels for their social and economic trials. "São Martinho" describes a quiet reunion with old friends, after three years away from the field, and the patient, simple reassurance of fresh bread and wine. His "Betrayals" stings with the disappointment of rejection, the failure of friendship, as he asks, "in the last hour, you closed from me. Why?"

During this same transitional period, Leeds also deepened his involvement with audiovisual documentation and exposition. Always an accomplished photographer, he had collected photographs from childhood, received expert technical training, and was a member of the International Photographic Society, the Friends of Photography, and the Photographic Resource Center of Boston. By the 1980s he had accumulated thousands of images and produced several professional exhibits, mostly of field photographs. His last was a 1982 exhibit at Bentley College in Massachusetts, entitled "A Sense of Wonder." He conceived of photography as "both documentary and expressive," (Leeds 1982d:2), as tapping emotion and conveying meaning—like poetry—through aesthetic channels closed to other types of perception and exposition. Art, he believed, helps to reveal culture more fully, rather than to obfuscate documentation of culture. He argued against understanding vision—as well as photography—"as 'objective,' somehow 'external' to our feeling, thinking, knowing selves. It is itself immediately immersed in meanings—meanings rooted in our feeling-thought-knowledge" (Leeds 1982b:1).

In his experimentation with visual documentation, during the 1980s Leeds developed and produced extensive multimedia slide presentations based on his fieldwork in Portugal, and later, on a two-month 1986 consulting trip to South Africa to study rural and urban development projects. He sometimes referred to these presentations as "anthropological photo-essays" (Leeds 1985b:2). Frequently his slide shows were accompanied by music and poetry. He described one of his three-hour-long multimedia presentations in this way: "epistemological in intent, called 'Portugal Perceived.' The slides are not arranged according to any standard anthropological categories but by line, color, form, texture. By the time one has seen all 160, some of which associate directly, others free-associate, with certain music (from . . . Portugal), and others with some of the Portuguese poems I wrote, one has been to all parts of Portugal, all sectors, through all sorts of expressions of Portuguese culture and institutions. What started as foreign has become familiar, even internal and unforgettable" (Leeds 1982d:2).

Despite all these explorations in poetry and photography, Leeds never rejected traditional inductivist approaches completely and indeed never stopped using them methodologically in his own work. He simply refused to be bound by their conceptual limitations. Instead, he advocated, as in his unfinished poetic ethnography *Minha Terra* (1984b), using "multiple epistemologies" for data collection and understanding. He strove to be more inclusive, to encompass greater complexity in his methodological net, rather than to replace earlier models with wholly new ones.

The arena in which Leeds developed these ideas and goals was, of course, broader than traditional scholarly publication. It also included, as noted, the art studio and the poetry reading. Teaching was yet another key area in his professional life that reflected a rich integration of materialist and symbolic elements, and "multiple epistemologies," in analysis of cultural systems. Even when he taught science for two years during graduate school at New York's Baldwin School for learning disabled adolescents, Leeds integrated theater and humanities into the curriculum. Beginning early in his university teaching at City College, and extending to Boston University, many of his courses, such as his "Comparative Meaning Systems," were "multimedia" events. Leeds used film, architecture, literary and oral texts, photographs, graphic arts, and music—as well as more strictly socioeconomic data and ethnographic texts—to teach his students comparative cultural analysis.

"Continuous Diversity as an Escape from Categories to Unity"

Leeds's conception of anthropology appears to have been shaped, if not constrained, by his 1940s and 1950s materialist training, especially

[24]

the cultural ecological paradigm, and by early forms of neo-Marxist analysis that granted little scope to symbolic domains of culture. If he had lived longer, had more time to absorb and react to contemporary intellectual developments, and had been able to resolve some of his own methodological strivings, Leeds may well have achieved the kind of synthesis—on the professional academic level, with attendant peer recognition—that he seemed to be seeking. He may have been able to discover more ways to incorporate diverse epistomologies within scholarly discourse.

On another level, however, it is not surprising that Leeds's synthesis remained unfinished. His project was destined to be unfinished by its nature, since it was—like him—a thing of process, not product, and aimed at greater and greater levels of inclusion. As Leeds suggested in the subtitle he gave his unfinished autobiography, "Continuous Diversity as an Escape from Categories to Unity," the more encompassing and diverse his project became, the more unified he considered himself to be, and the truer his analysis.

At every juncture, Leeds sought to contest conventional boundaries and mediate them by reaching for ever wider circles of inclusion. He understood that his drive for inclusion began with his youthful efforts to integrate the swirling multicultural diversity of his family and childhood. The drive for inclusion later extended to efforts to integrate diverse peoples into his study groups, multiple disciplines into a synthetic social science, urban studies and rural studies into a single theory of complex society, and, finally, aesthetic and scientific inquiry into a single approach to human truth. As from a stone thrown into a quiet pond, the scope of Leeds's project rippled ever outward. After his death, even more than before, his vision seems ahead of its time—and, as Aidan Southall (1989) has remarked, "We have hardly caught up with him yet."

Note on Sources and Acknowledgments

The main source of written information available on Leeds's life is his own draft autobiography, "Through Selfethnography to Human Nature: Continuous Diversity as Escape from Categories to Unity." This is an unfinished 83-page manuscript that he prepared in 1984 for inclusion in a planned volume of autobiographies by anthropologists. For reasons that are unclear, the volume never appeared. Interviews with Tony's wife and collaborator, Elizabeth Leeds, also supplied important information and insights. Elizabeth Leeds, in addition, furnished other miscellaneous letters, audiotapes, and documents bearing on Tony's life and career. For her generous and active assistance throughout, I give her great thanks.

I am also grateful to Loretta Saint-Louis and Andrew "Chip" Maxwell, friends and former Boston University students of Leeds, for enlightening conversations that supplied important insights. Lita Osmundsen's careful reading of an early draft of the manuscript greatly sharpened its sensitivity to Leeds's complexities as intellectual and person. Winifred Feise, Leeds's sister, also read the manuscript and offered useful corrections and information, particularly about his childhood and family history. Anthropologist Gilbert Velho, of the Museu Nacional in Rio de Janeiro, read the manuscript and gave pointed testimony on Leeds's contribution to Brazilian urban studies. Alan Sieber provided illuminating advice on the complexities of biographical writing and about Leeds's life in particular. Alan also suggested several central interpretive metaphors, which I have freely and gratefully used here. Susan Reverby offered important editorial advice and a critical reading, as did Roger Sanjek, Leonard Plotnicov, and M. Estellie Smith. Other members of the Thursday Night Group not already mentioned, especially Nancy Sempolski, Bette Denich, Lou Carreras, and Catherine Lugar have also helped me understand Leeds's life and work.

Another valuable source of oral historical information and more thematic insights, as well, were voice transcripts and observations from the three major memorial services held after Tony's death. These were held at Boston University in March 1989, at the American Anthropological Association in Washington, D.C., in November 1989, and at the Latin American Studies Association in Miami in December 1989. More than forty family members, colleagues, and friends offered observations and remembrances about Leeds's life and career at these events. I have also relied on my own personal recollections and impressions accumulated from fifteen years of colleagueship and friendship with Leeds, during the years 1974 to 1989.

Anthony Leeds's personal papers are now part of the collection of the Archives of American Anthropology at the Smithsonian Institution, Washington, D.C.

The Holistic Anthropology
of Anthony Leeds

Roger Sanjek

For those who continue to find comfort in choosing between "science" and "humanism," or "explanation" and "interpretation," to best characterize anthropology, Anthony Leeds's vision of the discipline may present an anomaly. I suggest, rather, it is a way out of this impasse. Anthropology, as well as growing segments of the social sciences and cultural studies, is now searching for transcendance of materialist-symbolist debate, unification of cultural analysis and political economy, and integration of ethnographic and historical interests. Leeds's legacy of work, I am convinced, can be extremely useful in moving forward this theoretical agenda.

Leeds always remained a materialist and a scientist, a man deeply interested in tools, soils, crops, and animals (1957, 1965a, 1980a, 1982a, 1982c). His significant contributions to ecological anthropology are well known (Leeds 1961b, 1962a; Leeds and Vayda, eds. 1965; Vayda, Leeds, and Smith 1961). Yet in essays written in each decade of his published career (1961a, 1962b, 1962c, 1974a, 1974c, 1981–82), culture reappeared as a focus for Leeds, culture as the emergent, meaningful, relational, imposing product of collective and individual human activity. Moreover, culture to Leeds was the object of anthropological study that dissolved the collective-individual dichotomy. Culture, as he understood it, demonstrated that the collective was always implicated in the individual and the individual always implicated in the collective.[1]

[1] Andrew Maxwell, a student of Leeds's, commented to me, however, that in his teaching Leeds did not dwell on culture and had no patience for those who did to the neglect of

Leeds's view of culture, in my view, is the essential bedrock upon which he built his anthropology. Here is where he reconciled his deep humanistic commitments with his ecological, political, and scientific ones. With these connections established, his writing flowed along several more specific channels—ecological, historical, epistemological, urban—and into specific research venues—Brazil, Yaruro, urban settlements worldwide, Texas, Portugal. These areas are where Leeds applied most of his intellectual energy, including that reflected in his essays in this volume. But before we take a closer look at his major work on cities, classes, and social order, it is instructive to examine his formative statements on culture.

Leeds's thoughts on the individual/culture nexus were developed in some of his earliest publications. In a response to George Gaylord Simpson's review of Theodosius Dobzhansky's *Mankind Evolving* (1962) in the journal *Science*, Leeds (1962b) sought to clarify the relationship between human biology and culture. Denying that anthropologists ignore genetic variability within or between human populations, Leeds asserted that whatever adaptive values such biological diversity may impart, it relates merely to local environmental conditions that are always mediated by culture and that many of the ancestors of today's human populations left long ago. Culture, moreover,

> involves symbols whose form and content are independent of individual genetics and can be transferred from one individual to another regardless of their individual genetic constitution. Further, it involves symbol *systems*, or higher orderings of symbols which are still more remote from the genetic foundations of biological individuals. . . . The history of culture traits, indeed of whole cultures, is such as to prove again and again the independence of cultural evolution from any definable population, distinguished on genetic grounds alone. [1962b:914]

The rejoinder to propositions about biological determinants of cultural expression was one Leeds would mount again in his critiques of sociobiology (1977c, 1981–82; Leeds and Dusek 1981–82). But in his early papers, what concerned him more was the relationship of indi-

materialist concerns. The consistency of his thinking about culture in essays spanning two decades suggests that this concept was one he had resolved in his own mind; clearly he felt the need to move on, yet his views on culture remained firmly a part of the evolving synthesis he continued to pursue. I thank Kathleen Logan and Chip Maxwell, as well as Liz Leeds and Tim Sieber, for their comments on this essay.

viduals to the systems of symbols constituting culture. As he saw it, "the individual and the culture are partially autonomous systems, that is, the form, characteristics, and dynamics of one system, are, at most, only partially causal of the . . . other. This implies that, with respect to each other, there is a considerable degree of freedom, although this does not entail any conception of indeterminacy or non-determinacy" (1961a:136n).

Leeds explained that culture presents the individual with "thinkable choices," but that beyond these, an individual may acquire "liberating knowledge" through education or intercultural exposure (which elsewhere he saw as intrinsic to human history). This cultural openness of human beings is one root of historical and evolutionary change: "The less knowledge a person has of cultural possibilities or alternatives, the smaller the range of possible cultural choices which can be conceived of as responses to social and cultural situations, and consequently the less the range of the individual's freedom of self-determining choice, or [of] action that might transform that system" (1961a:136).

The ways in which individuals do act upon and transform their cultural circumstances became the subject of another essay (1962c). Leeds there set out a framework of varieties of "microinvention" that dealt with the problem that "humans encompass past and potential situations in cultural formulae or norms . . . that inherently overlook the unique characteristics of each occurrence of a given kind of situation. Situational variation is woven into human experience as a continual process and requires constant minute adjustive behavior" (931). Microinvention may result in choices between existing cultural alternatives or in innovations. Some of these episodes affect the behavior and life-chances of groups, and thus become the source of social and cultural change. "In short, the cultural process of adaptation through microinvention is continuous and permanent as well as universal" (939).

Leeds was clear that microinvention included innovation in material culture, social organization, and ideas (940), but he later criticized this framework as, not wrong, but too narrow and too Darwinian (1974a). The focus on variation and selective retention at the individual level was useful only "in certain limited spheres . . . only for some problems" (473–74). "The significant units of analysis are . . . much more importantly various types of superorganic, supraindividual orders, such as groups, agencies, bureaucracies, institutions, polities, economies, ecosystems, societies or clusters of societies, and units of multi-society organization, which do not lend themselves to . . . Darwinian models" (474). Leeds felt that change and evolution operate at four levels: the individual, groups (or "nodes"; see below and Chapter 5), and the two supragroup levels of "the social order" (also see below) and culture. These last two "are interlocked across all the varieties of human experience ('cultures') by diffusion and acculturation processes which are specifically human" (475).

Much more about the social order follows in this book. Let us focus here a bit more on culture and how Leeds saw its evolutionary importance as an "emergent" level of human organization. Leeds endorsed the philosophy-of-science conception of "emergence," which stresses the unique properties of levels of natural phenomena that cannot be explained by "reductionism" to lower levels (1981–82). Just as the sociobiologists whom he opposed affirmed that animal behavior could not be explained by chemistry or biophysics, but had its own emergent properties ("success," "altruism"), so Leeds affirmed that culture had its own emergent properties not reducible to individual practice or cognition (and certainly not to human genetics). He noted that anthropologists have grappled with concepts like pattern, theme, configuration, semantic domain, and meaning system to describe the supraindividual, emergent nature of symbol systems that impose upon individuals, but that also may be imposed upon and altered by them.

Perhaps the nature of cultural emergence becomes clearer when we understand that Leeds saw science itself, to which he was dedicated, as a cultural product, not a pure form of knowledge standing apart from any or all cultures. "I do *not* wish," he wrote, "to be taken as saying that there are no relatively firm, persisting objects in the universe, but rather that human *formulations* about these *tend* to change in greater or lesser degree in varying sociocultural contexts because human knowing . . . is inevitably also profoundly culturally shaped" (1981–82:163).

In science as in anything else cultural, "liberating knowledge," and therefore change, might come with intercultural exposure. Here the brief is entered for an anthropology based in fieldwork, with the study of culture as one of its objects. Leeds developed this position in a paper on "'Subjective' and 'Objective' in Social Anthropological Epistemology" (1974c). He stressed that the unique events observed in fieldwork are not equivalent to the repeatable lab experiments or measurement procedures appropriate to the sciences of physical, chemical, and biological levels of emergence. We cannot see and measure symbol systems or social orders, but must construct them from our fieldwork observations. The study of culture and social orders within the flux of history and evolution requires interpretation, contextualization, and comparison. "*All* descriptions of societies and cultures are necessarily interpretations. . . . they are, in fact, complex hypotheses" (1980a:107).

Anthropologists study processes—the connections and sequences among events—not isolates and fixities. Rather than reliability, or repeatable results, what is desired in anthropological research is validity, the formulation of "rules of correspondence for empirical propositions . . . to establish [the] truth value of assertions" (1974c:358–59; cf. Sanjek 1990a, 1991). From this standpoint, Leeds had no reluctance in identifying anthropology as a science and urged that it be even more of one. "Scientists at least *claim* to make their theories explicit, thereby, ostensibly, subjecting them to general review and criticism from many different perspectives. One result . . . is the uncovering of implicit views which are essentially myths and the discovery of error and falsehood, both theoretical and factual" (1982b:1).

Leeds's life work in this regard concerns more the social order than culture, as Sieber points out and the essays that follow demonstrate. Yet his early interests in culture remained a part of the holism that he affirmed as giving his anthropology meaning and purpose (1981–82). A rich statement of this holistic perspective is embodied in his study of the history of ecological and political change in the Texas hill country (1980a). Here Leeds concluded that a concern for history, ecology, or power is incomplete without acknowledgment of the mutual effects among these three terms. And with this accomplished, we arrive at an even more overarching viewpoint—"a general paradigm of sociocultural evolution[:] decreasing localization, increasing detachment of variables from local feedback, and greater and greater linkage into trans- and supralocal systems. . . . Evolutionary . . . perspectives help sort out unique events from general processes" (1980a:135–36).

Still, Leeds's far-reaching theoretical linking of individual behavior, group (or node), social order, culture, ecology, power, process, history, emergence, and evolution was never, to his satisfaction, fully accomplished. "I have not been wholly successful in developing a consistent language for the paradigm, some of which, in my thinking, remains visual and some much like musical counterpoint" (1980c:3). The elements of his holistic anthropology remain scattered among his published and unpublished papers, yet inescapably one reads these works with the sense of the larger scheme looming just behind. Before we turn to the portion of Leeds's vision developed in the themes of this volume, I quote from one of his last formulations of general theoretical outlook.

> In earlier years, I thought of society . . . as a structure of positions, roles, statuses, groups, institutions, and so on, all given shape . . . by the cultures on which they draw. Process, I saw as "forces," movement, connection, pressures, taking place in and among these loci or nodes of organization, peopled by individuals (see Chapter 5). Although this still seems largely true to me, it has also come to seem a static view—more societal order than societal becoming. . . . Since it does not seem inherent in nature—although possibly, in some still unexplored way, in human nature—that these loci exist, it seems unacceptable simply to take them as axiomatic; rather we must search for ways to account for their appearances and forms.
>
> More and more, the problems of becoming—evolution, dialectics, emergence, system amplifying or positive feedback, conflict, disaggregation, disintegration—have led me to look at society as continuous process out of which structure or order precipitates in the forms of the loci listed above and their almost infinite variation due, in large part, to cultural and geographical variability. Such precipitates—structures—themselves affect process, limiting it (or them), setting directions, governing rates, in complex systems of feedback. . . .
>
> For instance, cities centralized in terms of earlier stages of capitalist accumulation, still using a transportation technology from earlier times, create physical city structures that cannot accommodate the kind of transportation system needed by present-day centralization of cities engendered by contemporary capitalist accumulation and production. Boston provides an excellent example in the recurrent conflict about putting in superhighways and thruways, disturbing residential communities, the use of streets in the central business districts for vehicles or for pedestrians, and so on. This is also an example of change being limited by the very structure precipitated by process. [1980c:1–2]

We see here the unity of abstract conception and concrete instance that marks the anthropology of Anthony Leeds. "Structure," "process," "connection," and "feedback" recur in his writing, but Boston, or Brazil, or Portugal, is at the same time always on his mind.

We may now turn to the essays in this volume. They are organized in three sections—"Cities in History," which sets his urban anthropology in a broad historical and comparative perspective; "Classes in the Social Order," which develops his approach to class and his more encompassing concept of "the social order"; and "Localities in Urban Systems," which presents his thinking on the spatial and class dimensions of power, the internal organization of cities, and the combination of evolutionary, historical, and ethnographic approaches that marks his overall theoretical stance.

Cities in History

As we have noted, Leeds was keenly aware that the analytic terminology of social science, anthropology included, was rooted in the culture of its users (see Leeds 1981–82). At times, he advanced new usages to break this hold (1976a, Chapter 5), but more often he probed and questioned the commonsense meanings of familiar terms, as he does for "urban" in "City and Countryside in Anthropology," Chapter 1. Here he cautions that too much discussion of "the urban" or of "the city" depends upon the historical experience of cities as they developed under Western capitalism during the past few hundred years. Earlier forms of urbanism had different patterns of organization, and to demonstrate this he contrasts the spatial and class organization of European feudalism with that of recent capitalist society.

"Urban society" for Leeds is some 10,000 years old in its earliest appearance. As an analytic term, "urban" should stand for the interlocking of specialized localities (food-producing, mining, administrative, etc.), specialized technologies, and specialized institutions. What is urban is the systemic linkage among places and technologies, achieved through institutions like government, priesthoods, taxation, and trade. Consequently, only total societies or states are urban, and not particular places within them. The view that only the cities are truly urban, which Leeds associates with Max Weber and Robert Redfield, betrays the centralizing viewpoint of the city-centered elites of recent world history. The free and fixed laboring classes of capitalist and feudal European societies are equally urban, if many of their members are located outside the localities deemed "cities."

In Chapter 2, "Towns and Villages in Society," Leeds continues this argument. He notes that the process of "aggregating specialities,"

[33]

which certainly marks capitalist urbanism, "helps maximize *predict-ability* and favorable . . . desired outcomes of exchanges of all sorts." An example of this would be the location in a "world city" like New York of so many corporate headquarters, business services (such as law, finance, printing, advertising), and private clubs, restaurants, and cultural facilities that cater to the corporate elite. Leeds also questions the substantive usefulness of population size–based typologies of city, town, and village; he prefers to see all localities on a continuum and focuses on their specialization, interlinkage, and exchanges rather than on size alone.

In this chapter Leeds also blasts the attitude in anthropology that has narrowed study of "communities" to what is internal to them (see also Chapter 7). He argues that much is then left out, even for such nonurban societies as the Nuer cattle-herders and farmers of the Sudan, or the !Kung food-gatherers and desert hunters of southern Africa (or the Yaruro horticulturalists of Venezuela's tropical forest, see Leeds 1964d). Many items flow in, chiefly through trade and individual exchanges, and other items flow out. For "rural" communities in urban society, such as Andean "peasant" villages, and for poor and working-class city neighborhoods, the outward flow of labor, cash, and commodities is unequal to the inward flow of the necessities of social reproduction. The life of an urban society is not played out fully in any community, but rather, as Leeds illustrates for Portugal, involves flows of people, information, food, money, and goods that cross locality, regional, and even national boundaries. In the contemporary world, these external influences shape the internal life of all localities; Leeds argues that we should look for similar influences in each of the cultures that anthropologists study.

The interplay of external influences and internal organization was the focus of Leeds's early essay on Indian "ports-of-trade" before and during the early stages of European contact (1961c). This was written during 1957–58, just after Leeds completed his Ph.D. dissertation, for a seminar on the history of economic institutions organized at Columbia University by economist Karl Polanyi and anthropologist Conrad M. Arensberg. Earlier work by the seminar had resulted in the volume *Trade and Market in the Early Empires* (Polanyi, Arensberg, and Pearson, eds. 1957), which gave impetus to the emerging field of economic anthropology. One of the major themes of the volume was the identification of distinctive administrative features of transregional trade in such historically unconnected locales as the ancient Near East, pre-Columbian Mexico, and Dahomey during the slave trade era. Though later work has modified some of this book's claims about ports-of-trade (see Curtin 1986:13–14, 70, 86n, 134n; Johnson 1980; Law 1977, 1986), themes raised in *Trade and Market* and in Leeds's essay have remained significant in anthropological and historical research (Adams 1974; Curtin 1986; Fisher 1972–73; Geertz 1980:87–97; Goody 1971; Schneider 1977; Wheatley 1975).

After summarizing the major points of agreement as to what constitutes a port-of-trade (clearly an institutionally and technologically specialized urban locality, as Leeds later phrased it), he presented a wealth of historical evidence for India. This covered foreign-local merchant interaction, local political oversight, taxation, and the exchange of elite and luxury commodities, including precious jewels and metals, spices, fancy cloths and woods, and animals of military use—horses and elephants. Through this exchange, the Indian coastal ports-of-trade linked the interior and overseas centers around the Indian Ocean, from east Africa to China, with a medley of traders leaving and arriving in ports throughout this wider domain.

Leeds emphasized the role in statecraft of imported luxury items like gold and horses (cf. Schneider 1977), and tied this to his explanation of the conditions under which ports-of-trade rise and fall. These specialized localities link states that control different but each relatively homogeneous ecological zones, a point the Polanyi group had established. Leeds suggests that ports-of-trade appear historically when one such state begins to expand into the territory of another, or when states of similar ecological endowment come into conflict. The inflow of luxury goods then fuels internal elite requirements for military expansion or defense. When one of the interacting states, or the port-of-trade as a state on its own, achieves technological advantage (as European interlopers eventually did in the Indian Ocean—Curtin 1986, chap. 6–8; Leeds 1975), the port-of-trade has seen its heyday, and disappears.

As in other of his works, Leeds's use of the term "technology" in this examination of medieval Indian urban settlements implied much more than implements: technology as a cultural system comprehends tools, techniques, resource availability, and social relations (1965b). As Leeds argued in his Ph.D. dissertation (1957) on Brazil's stagnant cocoa regime, even when tools, favorable ecological conditions, and

[35]

markets were available, and techniques known, the social relations of production could inhibit the full productive potential of a given material technology.

Classes in the Social Order

Leeds's approach to class is a highly ethnographic one. Rather than accepting postulated social science concepts like "middle class" or "elite" or "peasant," and then finding persons to put in them, he begins with palpable fieldwork experiences—"the daily observations of events and situations" (Chapter 5). He then sorts and arranges these into a description of an overall social order, one bounded by the city, the region, or the state (or one overlapping the state, as in the case already mentioned of Portuguese city-dwellers in Chapter 2).

Leeds's approach to agrarian social orders is the subject of Chapter 3, "Mythos and Pathos: Some Unpleasantries on Peasantries." He first excoriates the tendency to search for the essence of "the peasant," or to epitomize "peasant society." He points out that little agreement has been achieved in this quest anyway, and that rural society always is more socially complex, including social actors other than peasants, no matter how peasants are defined. "Peasant" is basically a role persons occupy in agrarian social orders, one that comprehends freeheld land, subsistence and market production, and taxation. Through taxes and market exchange, peasants contribute to the maintenance of state administrative and military operations, organized priesthoods, and city and town provisioning. Their society is urban, hardly peasant in its entirety, and clearly includes others playing nonpeasant roles.

These others in the nonagrarian portion of the total social order are the subjects of later essays. But here, in Chapter 3, Leeds presents a framework for analyzing agrarian labor roles that contrast with peasant in terms of land rights, freedom of movement, and access to subsistence. These roles include rural proletarian, farmer, tenant, squatter, job contractor, serf, and slave. The scale of agricultural enterprise in which any of these laborers work is determined not by them, but by landowners and urban classes who control capital and credit. Thus the particular agrarian social order in any time or place is part of the larger social order. Leeds illustrates his approach by sketching the social history of the Brazilian cocoa (or cacao) region he studied first in 1951-52. He shows how rural proletarians, job contractors, squatters, and peasants coexisted, and how the quantitative mix of these types of agrarian labor has shifted over time.

In Leeds's best-known paper, "Brazilian Careers and Social Structure" (1964b), he turned to the city-centered national upper class. There was simply no ethnographic study of elites like it when this essay appeared, and very few have appeared since (see Cohen 1971, 1981, on Sierra Leone's urban Creoles; Weatherford 1985, on the U.S. Congress). Leeds later repudiated the unilineal viewpoint in this paper's beginning section (see Chapter 4); by the 1970s his evolutionism became more open and historically nuanced (see Leeds 1974a, 1975, 1980a).

What most concerned him about Brazil were the ongoing changes there and in other Third World societies (see also Chapter 8, n. 10). Leeds observed that as new urban positions in Brazilian government and business opened, recruitment was not based on professional credentials, training, or merit alone. A variety of "personalist" means was evident—kinship, patronage, social connections—and, in addition, self-trained persons, and occupiers of multiple jobs and positions, appeared in frequent numbers in high places.

That such a situation was more than the subject of newspaper columns and gossip (which it was in Brazil), and might be examined systematically, was the rationale for Leeds's path-breaking investigation. He uncovered a colorful vocabulary for the career machinations of Brazil's upper classes—*cabide* (a job "hanger," the multiple position-holder); *trampolim* ("springboard," those actions that launch and build a career); *igrejinha* ("little church," a budding careerist's boosters and gofers); *panelinha* ("little saucepan," the mutually supportive informal group of influentials a successful careerist joins); and *cupola* ("turret," the uppermost circle of Brazil's elites). Only a few rose through local, to state, to national panelinhas, and even fewer to the national cupola. Yet, it was the constant pursuit of such careers, and the numerous hopefuls, supporters, and beneficiaries at each level, that animated the public and private sectors of Brazil (see also Leeds 1964a).

Still, this remained in key aspects a closed system. It was open to "the classes," the literate city and town dwellers who staffed and controlled Brazil's public and private bureaucracies. But it was closed to "the masses," both the agrarian laborers, whom Leeds had studied in the 1950s, and the urban poor, to whom he turned later during the 1960s and 1970s (see Leeds 1981a; Chapter 7). Leeds ended his careers essay by hazarding that similar social orders marked many Third World nations.

In Chapter 4, prepared for a conference on Jewish communities in Latin America, Leeds used the occasion to contrast his "two-class" model for Brazil (and elsewhere) with the three-class social order of the United States and Western Europe. (He locates Latin American Jews among the classes, not the masses, in the final section of the essay.) Typically, Leeds turns to questioning received wisdom, here about the middle class concept. He separates the notion of "middleness" as intermediate in terms of income and rank from "middleness" as the "lubricatory" functions of exchange and information processing that occur between elite and working classes. The first notion implies no necessary *social* coherence in the sense of a class of persons who associate predominantly with each other, and minimally with those above or below them in income and rank. It is more valid, Leeds cautions, first to determine ethnographically whether such a middle grouping indeed exists than to award it existence merely on the basis of income and rank divisions. (These can as easily be broken into four, six, or ten income groups or prestige ranks as into three.) It must be in their actual association memberships and interpersonal ties, Leeds argues, that such a middle class can be identified operationally in three-class social orders like the United States.

In the United States, this socially coherent middle class performs the middle lubricatory functions between similar socially coherent upper and working classes. In two-class Brazil, these functions are absorbed by the classes, with no separate national middle group arising between the classes and the masses. In the United States there *are* three "delimitable groups." In Brazil there are two. Overall, Leeds predicts that the two-class systems will endure through "expansion of ranges of positions, roles, types of organization, rankings, and functions" *within* the upper half of the social order. As he argued elsewhere (1957, 1964c), education in Brazil operated to maintain the classes/masses boundary, and not to enhance mobility from the working class into the middle class, as it does in three-class systems.

Chapter 5, "Problems in the Analysis of Class and the Social Order," is a more abstract and theoretical presentation of Leeds's approach to class. It merits close attention, despite some demanding passages, because it is the key to his ethnographic insights and underpins his processual view linking human action, social order, history, and evolu-

tion. It was presented at an international seminar that Leeds organized, and which included Michael Banton, Robert Bierstedt, Marvin
Harris, Octavio Ianni, Renate Mayntz, Rodolfo Stavenhagen, and Al-
ain Touraine, among others (Leeds ed. 1967).

Taking the viewpoint that higher level divisions of the social order
like classes are socially constructed, Leeds argues that we must begin
with what they are constructed of, with the observed behavioral situations described in an ethnographer's fieldnotes. This approach moves
classes from the realm of ontology—something assumed to exist out
there—to epistemology—the research procedures and logic by which
we come to identify and describe classes. In a footnote, Leeds associates the ontological view of class with Marx's dichotomy of producers
and controllers of surplus labor value (proletariat and capitalists), and
the epistemological with Marx's analysis of the groupings and relationships observable in concrete historical settings. Delineating class in
this second sense is the object of the theoretical framework Leeds
develops (see Leeds 1978; Chapter 6).

The framework begins with "nodes," the observable groups that
appear in sequences of events (for an even more rigorous view see
Harris 1964; cf. Sanjek 1995). The notion of nodes is one that draws
upon the many kinds of behavioral groups (not categories) that anthropologists have described in ethnographies, if usually without the epistemological self-consciousness that Leeds brings to bear. Nodes include households, kin groups, associations, cliques, friendship sets,
firms, organizations, and government agencies. Higher-level components of the social order that are not *directly* observable in themselves
—like localities, ethnic minorities, classes, or the state apparatus—
are ensembles of nodes.

Nodes have their internal compositions (statuses, roles, charters),
but it is the concept of "nexuses," or links between nodes, that leads us
to the structure of the social order. Nexuses are of four kinds: genealogical, personal, customary, and contractual. A social order consists of many diverse nodes, linked through various kinds of nexuses,
into a series of nodal networks. "In describing the nodes and nexuses
of a given society, we would be bound to describe ever more inclusive
social alignments, with more and more inclusive boundaries, up to the
level of the polity itself and, in some respects, beyond it to interpolity
networks such as cartels and intergovernmental bodies. All these
alignments are built up from the minimal loci of organization, or

[39]

nodes, present in the society." These arrangements change through political conflict as well as ecologically adaptive and individually creative processes; they also change through time in historical sequences; and in evolutionary terms, they emerge in patterned arrangements of band, kin-based, expansive-agrarian, static-agrarian or feudal, industrial-capitalist, and neocolonial-capitalist types of society (see Leeds 1964b, 1975, 1976a, and Chapter 4).

Hierarchy and control are present in all state-level social orders. In Leeds's view, the multiplicity of nodes and nexuses in such complex social orders can include both: (1) nodal networks that tie together groups varying widely in power—thus reinforcing an open, vertical-continuum, columnar image of the social order—and (2) nodal networks of different degrees of power that oppose and maintain few links with each other—affording a closed, class-stratified, layered image of the social order. Sorting out which of these two images is the more telling requires careful empirical study—first, of those nodes that control strategic resources, wealth, productive labor, and military force, and, second, of their permeability to persons in less powerful nodes.

When decisive political and economic control by particular nodal networks does exist, Leeds is ready to speak of classes. "Doing so can serve as a kind of shorthand, so long as we have already described the underlying structure of the system and so long as we know that class is not an entity existing merely by definition or by postulation" (Chap. 5, p. 186). Critical questions of social ideology and individual cognition remain, approachable as well through ethnographic fieldwork. Still, in Leeds's view, the actions of individuals are governed principally by the nodes in which they interact. Whether the norms of their daily nodal experience are class-conscious, and how they become so, are questions that anthropology must seek to answer about each particular social order.

Chapter 6, "Marx, Class, and Power" (in effect, an appendix to Chapter 5), reprints Leeds's statement of the strengths and weaknesses of Marxist approaches to class. Leeds appropriates the more ethnographically rooted of Marx's own writings on change in the Europe of his day from what Leeds saw as a philosophical dualism obscuring Marx's more abstract writings. This piece formed the first half of the introduction to Anthony and Elizabeth Leeds's collection of essays on Brazil published in Portuguese (1978), and has never been published in English.

[40]

Localities in Urban Systems

People live in places. Place has long been central to anthropological fieldwork, so much so in Leeds's opinion that anthropologists have made unwarranted generalizations about the wider social order on the basis of what they observe and record in the specific places they study. Even worse, normative theoretical models of "community," of close-knit and cooperative relationships, have skewed studies of particular localities by prescribing what to look for and by screening out both ephemeral and conflictual local relationships and external contacts and influences. The larger urban, regional, and state-level social orders have emergent properties and forms of organization that involve more—bureaucracies, taxation, labor markets, power relationships—than merely the neighborhoods and communities (better, localities) they comprise on the ground.

This viewpoint sets the terms of the argument of Chapter 7, "Locality Power in Relation to Supralocal Power Institutions," written just as Leeds was beginning his extensive 1960s' research in Rio de Janeiro's *favelas*, the self-built squatter settlements of its masses. More detail on the life and politics of these localities is found in other essays (Leeds 1969, 1971, 1973c, 1974b, 1977a; Leeds and Leeds 1970, 1972, 1976), several of which were republished in Brazil in the volume coauthored with Elizabeth Leeds (1978). Here, in Chapter 7, Leeds uses his first encounters with favela life to formulate a model of the locality in opposition to those "supralocal" institutions of the urban and national social order that impinge upon it. In using "locality" rather than "community," Leeds attempts to purge normative notions of what to find and allow description of ephemeral, close-knit, cooperative, and conflictual relationships to emerge as the result of ethnographic fieldwork.

He catalogues a general range of potential cooperative social forms for localities (and many specific such forms for Rio's favelas), but here, in my view, betrays some of the optimism of the 1960s era. As we saw during later decades in the United States, and certainly during the Reagan years, with recession and withdrawal of federal aid to cities, many localities could *not* muster "a wide range of responses to an almost infinite variety of events, contexts, and exigencies," or achieve "rapid mobilization of . . . social and economic resources for different ends and in diverse forms . . . under the most extreme stress." Still, to understand the ravages of plant closings, homelessness, and health and social service cutbacks, certainly it is to the external "supralocal power institutions" that Leeds directed us, and not merely to internal characteristics, that we need to turn to explain the experiences of these localities (see Baxter and Hopper 1980; Bookman and Morgen eds. 1988; Lamphere 1987; Mullings ed. 1987; Nash 1989; Pappas 1989; Sanjek 1984; Williams 1988).

These "supralocal" institutions display power in two forms: in the control of material resources, principally by an upper class and its elites in strategic government and corporate positions; and in the organizational control of bureaucratic, technical, and legal procedures, and information, lodged in a middle class (or the lower strata of the classes in two-class social orders). The power of the working class and the poor (or the masses) is primarily in their mobilizable numbers, though here dispersal among many localities defuses potential power and requires organization, a resource most usually controlled (and applied) by interests outside these localities. Conflict in complex social orders thus arises repeatedly between the power of emergent forms of cross-locality organization at the bottom and the opposing organizational, and ultimately police and military, power of the state and the classes it serves (see also Leeds 1957, 1975).

In terms of Rio's favelas, Leeds applies this perspective to explain the seemingly rural patterns of association and intense interaction that these localities contain. Such social forms, he argues, operate to redistribute locally the resources that are earned externally or created internally by favela residents. They also obviate expropriations by supralocal classes and fend off or oppose organizational power that would reduce them. What at first looks like rural persistence is in fact better understood as adaptive behavior under intensely urban conditions. (Even in mainland China, briefly discussed at the end of Chapter 7, the erosion of locality power by imposed commune organization was less than Leeds then suspected; see Skinner 1964–65.)

In one of his last essays, "Lower-Income Settlement Types: Processes, Structures, Policies" (1981a), Leeds took a look back at Rio's favelas, and at other poor and working class urban localities worldwide. Written with the hindsight of Tony and Elizabeth Leeds' joint six years of fieldwork in Brazil, research experience in Peru, Colombia, and Portugal, and visits to many cities elsewhere, this essay offered a typology of housing forms, contrasting most broadly new housing (and localities of such housing) created by or for the urban masses, with "used" housing, or slums.

[42]

Favelas fall into the worldwide category of squatter settlements. This form of housing is erected and later improved by its occupants, who squat on unused land owned by others, frequently government agencies. These organized "invasions" result from the relative dearth of new or affordable housing provided by supralocal power institutions —the state or the private market. Other forms of newly built housing for the working class and the poor offer them much less autonomy in altering or adding to the original construction, and usually are more available to them to rent, unlike squatter settlement housing which its builders own (if they may later rent out to others).

In contrast to the peripheral urban location of most of these newly built lower-income housing types, slum housing is located in the inner city and is inhabited predominantly by renters. The sizes and forms of slums vary (Leeds discussed several subtypes), but they too must be understood in terms of the supralocal public and private interests that structure the housing market. These interests create the conditions under which crowding and deterioration become both unavoidable and profitable.

An intriguing section of this essay of Leeds focused on the Boston housing situation. As he made clear elsewhere, Leeds felt strongly about this: "I live in a city with acute racism, . . . major residential red-lining, heavy incidence of large- and small-scale arson, slum land-lordism, areas of major infrastructural and constructional decay and collapse, large numbers of people in extreme poverty, . . . an inhumane transportation system, an abandoned and unproductive countryside, and a class system that supports this entire structure. . . . The specific form of city system [is] not necessary [or] something we need to accept as being in the nature of things" (Leeds 1979).

Leeds (1981a) went on to relate the ever-increasing squeeze on lower-income housing, and its overuse and deterioration, to the wider political economy of the city. Large sections of Boston are occupied by private institutions (universities, medical centers) that do not pay property taxes. As the city reaches the limits of the property taxation of its upper and middle classes—the point at which they move elsewhere, or threaten to—it turns to urban renewal projects and policies that increase land value, and therefore property taxes, by replacing lower-income housing with higher-income housing or commercial uses. This enriches the nodal networks that staff and run the city. It also increases density in lower-income localities as their housing resources shrink, and their population grows when those displaced from the "renewed" areas move in. The supralocal real estate interests benefit in two ways: first, their renewed property is more valuable; and second, so is their remaining slum property, now occupied by an augmented renter pool which, most often, is accommodated in newly subdivided (and more profitable) units that their owners have less and less incentive to maintain.[2]

From today's perspective, we know that urban renewal also results in homelessness, as does the "gentrification" of slum housing by new, middle-class owners who improve and remove it from the lower-income housing stock. Leeds's views on the dilemma of rent control (1981a) also need amendment; this institution can serve various class interests under different conditions (see Gilderbloom 1980; Gilderbloom and Friends 1981; Marcuse 1981). But just as appropriate now as when he wrote it is Leeds's conclusion that "housing is not mere shelter, but part of a complex hierarchy of social organizational systems, involving various kinds of strategizing social units" (1981a:58).

The last essay in this book, Chapter 8, "The Anthropology of Cities: Some Methodological Issues," is written from and for the perspective of the urban fieldworker, whom Leeds argues must also be a scholar of comparative urban social orders. This role requires not only attention to evolutionarily emergent types of cities, but also to the history of the particular city in which one studies a selected locality. Leeds criticizes anthropological studies of urban kinship or associations or neighborhoods for being studies "in the city," but not "of the city." By this he means neglect of the effects that a particular city's social order has upon the expression of kinship ties, the form and purpose of associations, or the composition and location of neighborhoods. We must ask, he says, how "*this* city" and its history affect the social forms we study.

Leeds holds that only through understanding the specific history of each city's migration and growth patterns, class structure, labor market, and transportation network, can we understand the "molding effects" of these institutions on any particular locality's social life. To illustrate this he contrasts the place of favelas in Rio de Janeiro and São Paulo, Brazil's two largest cities, but cities that differ markedly in their institutional histories (for a similar approach see Southall 1967). As a consequence of their contrasting historical pathways, much of everyday social life, even interpersonal and sexual ambiance, differs in the two cities. "The point

[2] For an analysis of such processes in New York City, see Caro 1974. For further studies of Boston consistent with Leeds's approach, see Maxwell 1988, Sheehan 1984, and Sieber 1990, 1991.

is that the highly differentiated roles in the nation of these two cit- ies . . . seen as total systems . . . affect what happens to the specific variables or entities under study."

To make this kind of sense, urban anthropology must be equal part history, ethnographic fieldwork, and social and evolutionary theory. The holistic anthropology of Anthony Leeds points us in no other direction.

Cities [1952]

We come from the cities of America
with their dun drab dreariness
of grey-brown houses
and asphalt streets.
We come here from the towns of beige America
with the brownstone houses
and the Victorian melancholia
of architecture
scabby on the land

Have you ever seen
Bucyrus of Ohio
or been in Tennessee to Cookeville,
the Home of Southern Hospitality?
Have you ever shaken hands
at Trenton
or speeded with a parting gust
Away from Jersey's Camden
or soot-sunk Pittsburgh?

Yes we come from the sorespots of America
where people live
and say
"I have no own, no native town!"
We come to cities in the sun
in pastel calcimines
gleaming in the sun.
We come to brilliant cities of Brasil
which do not dirty in the sun
with soot and smoke and smog
Cities with a feel for light
and air and sun
for space and colour

Cities unafraid to splash
in colour and design
to spatter decoration
on every lintel, every eave.

Fine backward cities
unencumbered by the laws of modern speed
trotting at a dog-trot
or blasting through the ox-carts
in a fish-tailed Cadillac
or cobbled-stony streets
or in the mud

Fine lusty growing cities
joined by the corrugated clearings
colloquially called roads
Cities unplanned, unsuited
and always running second
to their work

The Cities are the fathers
of a surging life of splashes
of colour and of light
fresh and different
in the sun
where people live
and say
"I am a son of *this*, my native town!"

Cities in History

Callao (port city of Lima), Peru, 1969. Maker of plaster casts creates images of past splendor and greatness. (photo by Anthony Leeds)

[1]

Cities and Countryside
in Anthropology

Misconceptions about the Urban—Broader Perspectives

Most current discussion of "urbanism" and "urbanization" can be shown to be ethno- and temporocentric and based on a historically particular class of urban phenomena and urban forms of integration. Exegesis of text after text—whether produced by persons ostensibly doing "pure," "objective," descriptive, or "basic" science, or engaged in some form of application—shows systematic orientations whose axiomatic presuppositions and logical consequences can be clearly laid out as emanations of a specific world view.

Briefly, to summarize the world view underlying this ethnocentrism, the fact that some form or another of urban society has existed for between 8,000 and 10,000 years in the Old World and in the New World for some 3,000 years or more is forgotten entirely. Generalizations are then made about "urbanism" and "urban society" based essentially on the urban experience of the past few hundred years, apparently without the realization that all urban phenomena of the past 500 years have been ineluctably affected by the expansion of the capitalist system, in short by the development of what Wallerstein (1974) calls the "World System." The generalizations are, then, in fact, not about "urbanization" in general but about a single form of "urbanism" or "urbanization," its evolution, and its acculturational byproducts.

That there are other forms of urban structure, or urban phenomena, of urban society is practically universally forgotten, except perhaps by persons, mostly anthropologists, involved with broad understandings of societal evolution (see Adams 1966; Braidwood and Willey, eds. 1962; Childe 1942, 1948, 1950; Fox 1977; Hardoy and Schaedel, eds. 1969, 1975; Leeds 1980b; Nutini 1972; Redfield 1947, 1955, 1956; Schaedel 1972; Schaedel, Hardoy, and Kinzer eds. 1978), or historians concerned with comparisons of urban civilizations, and architects or art historians concerned with comparisons of urban form (see Hall 1966; Hardoy 1964, 1968; Kraeling and Adams eds. 1960; Morse 1973a, 1973b, 1974; Mumford 1938, 1961; Sjoberg 1960; Weber 1921). The fact of such variants of "the urban experience" is uniformly obliterated by persons concerned with "development" and "modernization." Their programs and plans are invariably built on premises derived from the single, historically recent form of urban experience—the capitalist city in urban capitalist society. As will be seen, this is not entirely surprising since much of such developmentalism is rooted in the discipline of economics, itself a specific Western and capitalist form of thought and ideology.

Even anthropologists, however, have failed to view specific urban forms in the wider perspective. Doing so would have permitted them to sort out what was generic to urban structures and what was specific to only a class of such structures. The properties of the latter have often been taken as properties of the former, with the result that erroneous generalizations are drawn about urban form and process. Failure to see the temporal and spatial specificity of these properties is failure to see immensely broader alternatives of organization of urban societies, failure to see the relationship between, on one hand, a specific historical sequence and, on the other, general evolutionary aspects of the progression of urban societies, and the failure to see drastically different possible "solutions" to the "problems" of urban societies through policy, plans, and political action. A problem derived from seeing urban phenomena in terms of only a single class of urban societies is that of getting bogged down in conceptualizations formulated in terms of that single experience. Such conceptualizations, as I have shown elsewhere (Leeds 1968a, 1968b, 1971, 1976a, 1976d, 1981a, Chapter 2; Leeds and Leeds 1970, 1976), have produced systematic distortions of understanding, systematic omissions in description (e.g., of urban agriculture) (1973c, 1974b, Chapter 7; Leeds and Leeds 1970), and systematic imposition of misbegotten policies and plans (1974b).

The major misconceptualizations involved are those which oppose "urban" to "rural" and "urban society" to "rural society" or "peasant society"; those which identify "urban" with "city"; those which conceive of "communities" as some sort of largely closed, localized nucleation of persons, houses, and institutions; or those that conceive of localities as communities (Leeds 1973c, Chapter 2).

At a most general level, *all* human nucleations, from the smallest "tribal" villages to the largest megalopolises, have the same functions with respect to an inclusive society: facilitation of all forms of exchange, transfer, and communications, while linking the nucleation or locality both with other localities and with the society at large.

Within that generality, at some point in societal-cultural evolution, an interrelated, threefold specialization appeared in society. One form of specialization is that of localities—sometimes for ecological reasons, sometimes for sociocultural reasons, sometimes for both. Such specialization, even without the other two described below, is found incipiently in simple societies. The result of such specialization is that the societal system, as such, comes to be characterized by the internal *differentiation of functions* of localities, superimposed on the *universal functions* of all localities just mentioned.

Another form of specialization is that of the components of technology—tools, materials, techniques, housings, tasks, activities, labor/skills, and knowledge (Leeds 1965b, 1976c)—whose result is differentiation in the structure of labor and of the ecological determinants of its ordering.

The third form of specialization is that of institutions—the separating out by function of more-or-less autonomously ordered and chartered ways of doing things (Leeds, 1976c, Chapter 5), ranging from large-scale orders such as government, church, and education, to small-scale institutions such as roles.

Each of these forms of specialization is in some measure independent and in some measure a resultant of the other. Thus, a certain degree of locality specialization can occur—minimally, to be sure—in the absence of any significant technological or institutional specialization, while the development of these latter forms of specialization tends to generate an increase in locality specialization. Considerable technological specialization may occur without significant locality specialization. However, further increases of specialization, especially in the domain of materials, necessarily governed by the ecological variation of resource location, induces locality differentiation, for example, by generating production activities of one sort in one locality and of a different sort in another, with specialized trade activities of different kinds within each and between them.

I define *urban* as the interacting confluence of all three of these specializations, a definition quite in line with *implicitly* presupposed attributes in most standard definitions of *the urban*.[1] By definition, then, that which is urban is *always* a matter of degree, and degree of urbanness is measured not by the size of nucleations (which may be profoundly affected by ecology, institutional structures, and policies), nor by density (which may be profoundly affected by locality and technical specializations, as well as by policy), nor, *generally*, by the classical measures of "urbanization" effectively derived from recent Western experience, but, rather, by an interaction index of the three forms of specialization (to a large extent, these govern size and density).

Justification for such a definition is worth presenting. First, in anthropology, despite a long-standing tradition of studying so-called communities in isolation, everyone except the most gung-ho ideologist of community studies knows that any given locality chosen for such a study is variously linked with other localities. This is quite as true for "simple" primitives as for modern states, as for example, Birdsell (1953) has shown.[2] When one looks beyond the anthropologists' model of the self-sufficient isolated community into the actual data of description in the monographs, such ties are always evident, if unsystematically described. Systematic attention would clearly have shown the network relations of localities to, and in, larger systems as well as identified the types of flows, however intermittent, among them. It would also have helped define societal boundary conditions, to which we have given almost no attention in anthropology—a serious problem

[1] See Childe 1948, 1950. The endings *-ism* and *-ization*, added to the root *urban*, both have specific sets of connotations, none of which mean precisely "having the properties of being urban." *Urbanism* sometimes seems to mean that, but it also means rather unclearly defined things such as "attitudes about cities," "policies with respect to cities," etc. *Urbanization* means, usually, "the process of city population growth" or, sometimes, much more widely, "the process of becoming citylike or graced with towns and cities." I use *the Urban* here to indicate "that which is urban, having the properties of being an urban society,") borrowed from the Spanish *el Urbano*, which is fairly commonly used with the meaning I define.

[2] See also !Kung Bushmen material or Leeds 1964d.

since network ties exist over these boundaries as well as internally, though, I would propose, with markedly less density over the boundaries than internally.

By extension, any city or town is part of a total system—a *societal* system of localities, each of which has some function in the total system. Where localities are specialized and as locality-specialization increases, their functions are differentiated and the linking ties become more critical or more tightly coupled and also more hierarchic. They also *tend* to become more multistranded, although this is not a necessary consequence.

Second, all anthropologists know that one specialty requires another. Specialization means, necessarily, a *structure* of interrelated differentiations. Indeed, one cannot properly describe one specialty by itself—whether that specialty be a technological one, a role, or an institution. They come in sets. Most descriptions tend, or have tended, to focus on one or a reduced number of specialties, but a more-or-less discomforting awareness of their relation to others not being described is almost always nagging us. The implication of these considerations may be summarized in the assertion that the greater the degree of either or both of these forms of specialization (aside from their interaction effect), the more complex and differentiated the total societal order, including nonchartered—that is, noninstitutional— forms of organization such as networks, rank, and class.

The interaction of the three forms of specialization—seen as an evolutionary process creating ever-greater differentiation—involves ever-greater complexity of order characterized by, on one hand, translocal, differentiated structures (e.g., the classes of a class system), represented also in localities, and, on the other, specialization of localities as such, all linked to each other. It may further be noted that the internal specialization of localities subtends such derivative properties as density and population size, properties standardly given as criteria of "urban."

The interaction effect of the three forms of specialization is a very complex problem involving all sorts of ecological dimensions. Suffice it to say, here, that once they start interacting, the degree and rate of differentiation increase. More important is the ultimate comprehensive inclusion of all aspects of society in the total structure of specialization: all people, all action, all culture, all social organization, all technology become specialized. Hence, insofar as such systems dis-

[55]

play those properties conventionally designated as "urban" we are *obliged* to regard the *entire* society as urban and cities merely as concentrations of more-or-less large ranges and arrays of certain types of specialties (Leeds 1980b).

Elsewhere, I have pointed to the utility of looking at agriculture, mining, lumbering, fishing, and the like as specialty sets subordinate to the total structure of specialization in a society (Leeds 1980b). They are linked into the latter by complex systems of exchange moving in all directions among all kinds and levels of locality and all kinds and levels of institutional structure.

Given the general proposition presented above—the general model —and this intimate linkage of these particular specialty categories and sets with the total specialty system, it is evident that "a peasant is an urban man" (Leeds 1976d), as is also a miner, a lumberjack, and a fisherman. They are all operators or actors within systems of locality, of labor, of technical, institutional, and informal social organizational specialties. Further, they *comprehend* such complex specializations with a cognitive *model* of society which recognizes its complexity, including the structure of its urban centers and their hierarchical relations.

It is no accident that we have numberless descriptions of "successful" "adaptations" of supposedly "unskilled" and "unspecialized" "peasants" to cities. My argument, represented in all the quotation marks, is that social scientists have consistently misread the *meaning* of this phenomenon. They have failed to see that the participants are *already* urban people because the observing anthropologists have interpreted the "rural" as *tribal*, that is, as nonspecialized in any significant degree in any of the senses I have defined, and as largely isolated from the "urban" (i.e., city) society as a result of some inherent property of rurality (see comments on Redfield below), while sociologists have treated the "rural" as some sort of converse of the city—the opposite of density, large size, anonymity, secondary relationships.

All of these conceptions are demonstrably and drastically false. Put another way, once a significant interaction of the three kinds of specialty develops, all rural people are urban people. It is necessary to understand *rural* as referring simply to a subset of specialties of an urban society and *rural people* as referring to part or subsocieties of urban societies, as in effect, Kroeber, speaking of peasants, said thirty-five years ago (Kroeber 1948).

[56]

So far, the discussion has delineated two subclasses of all human societies: primitive and urban societies. Doing so has already posed a dilemma for those holding the ethnocentric view of the Urban, or at least for me, in that the idea of the "social urbanization" of agricultural personnel must necessarily also apply to *all* urban societies if agriculture is to be regarded as urban, as I propose. It is logically wrong to see "social urbanization" as a historically recent phenomenon if we hold any *generic* theory about the nature of urban society.

The conception of "social urbanization" as being recent and as being a property of a certain subclass—I would say subsubclass (see below)—of societies is itself a product of a certain intellectual history, chiefly of anthropology. Not only did this intellectual approach tribalize "peasants," reify "peasant societies," and hermetically seal off "peasants," "peasant societies," and even "peasant economics" from the larger societies of which they were parts, but it even reformulated the supposed trajectory of sociocultural evolution either to place "peasants" at a "stage" of evolution intermediate between "tribal" or "folk," on one hand, and "urban," on the other, or practically to assimilate them to "folk" culture.

The chief offender (and offender he was) was Robert Redfield, building out of his Mexican experience. In publications between 1930 and 1956, he created a thoroughly formalistic model of the trajectory of sociocultural evolution. This model was constructed on an idealized conception (Redfield 1947) of a moral tribal society (practically devoid of pragmatics, choice, or strategy), a reified and idealized "peasant society" operating as a closed system, and a misapprehended and ethnocentric conception of city life derived from Robert E. Park, Ernest W. Burgess, and especially Louis Wirth, who generalized the Chicago of the 1910s or 1920s as a world model not only of cities but of the urban in general (Redfield 1930, 1941, 1953). Fortunately, most of this sorry metaphysics has not stood the test of time and criticism; most of it has disappeared. However, some still lingers, especially in conceptions, still prevalent in anthropology, about "peasants." The reformulated way of looking at this evolutionary problem appearing in the following pages fits into a general theory of the Urban, thereby permitting, or better, *requiring*, us to look at several different kinds of society at once. That is, it forces us to do the theoretical work of comparison, differentiation, structural and processual analysis, and generalization at one and the same time.

[57]

Differential Integration of Urban
Societies through the Class System

As the three forms of specialization interlock and interact, social orders themselves differentiate. Such differentiation *inherently* leads to class differentiation in society—using any of the currently standard social science usages of the term *class*, but most especially one form or another of the Marxian conception of class. In oversimplified form, all urban society and all urban societies are class societies, as V. Gordon Childe pointed out long ago (Childe 1942, 1948, 1950). This follows, too, from the general theory proposed above. That they are also state societies likewise follows but need not be pursued in detail here, except to say that the theory of specialization requires the emergence of specialized coordinative and administrative functions, hence government.

What is critical is our universal recognition that these specialized, urban, state societies present a great array of drastically different forms of organization; that, within this variety of expression, rather similar forms often appeared which we tend to classify together. We therefore speak of feudal Europe, of feudal Japan, possibly of feudal early China, of a possibly feudal-like phase in early Indian history, and, as we get confused about the critical criteria, we slither off into argument whether this or that African state or chiefdom was feudal or not, and even whether the first centuries after the Iberian conquest of South America were feudal or not.

What are the critical criteria? They are the criteria that we, as analysts—historians, anthropologists, political scientists, etc.—consider most relevant in analyzing what holds the society together, what links its specialized pieces, or "parts," into a "whole," providing the routes of exchange, transmission, and transfer. One common way of talking about the question of linkage—or of what holds society together—in practically all the social science disciplines is the idea of *integration*. This term, however, has also come to take on an ethnocentric sense in the context of the temporo-and ethnocentric development models which have infused all the social sciences, especially the essentially noncomparativist ones like economics and political science. It is this latter, ethnocentric sense of *integration* which carried over into the formulation of the problem of "social urbanization" which I am using as example here.

The general proposition that I wish to forward is: different forms of urban society involve different forms of societal integration. These forms of integration are expressed through the structures of class relations. The structures of these class relations determine what the forms of integration of the "rural" specialty sets with those of the urban centers—that is, with the "towns," "cities," *and other nodal points*—will be. In fact, they also determine what the very characteristics of all the urban centers will be. Thus, medieval European urban centers—towns, abbeys, castles, manors[3]— not only were quite different from capitalist ones but lay out for us major features of the class organization and the societal specialization to which it was attached. The urban centers themselves were specialized according to major institutional features and class orders of the society. This feature of medieval urbanism led that great ethnocentric, comparative historian and sociologist Max Weber (1921) to say that medieval society did not yet have "true" cities—that is, they were not like those he knew from capitalist society which provided his model of Truth not only for cities but for bureaucracies as well. Put another way, using our everyday terms in the way I have redefined them here, the characteristics of both rural and urban ("country" and city) areas of an urban society and the relation between them are defined by the interaction of the structure of specialties of the society and its class relations. The major implication, for present purposes, is that *every* urban society has its characteristic form of "social urbanization." We can even *predict the properties* of the social urbanization and its processes, actions, and events from the form of integration of the society.

Capitalist Integration of Urban Society

For this purpose, it suffices here to compare and contrast two equally "valid" forms of societal integration, say, feudal and capitalist. I turn to the latter first because it is the most familiar and, simply by putting the key properties in the context of the discussion, immediately illu-

[3] These are clearly urban centers, at least in the sense of this chapter. Each is a central place, with a central administration. Each has a remarkable array of specializations and specialists. Each is itself a specialized nucleation with a specialized function in the larger society, and a nodal point for exchange and transfer, as of taxes and foodstuffs. Each is hierarchic, class-divided, and institutionally complex. Each has its literate system of complex record keeping, ranging from censuses to production and tax figures. Each is a substate of a more inclusive state. See, in this connection, Abbot Irminon 1946; Louis the Pious 1946; Mundy & Risenberg 1948; Pirenne 1925.

minates the contrasting type of social urbanization in feudal society. These sketches are brief and incomplete, dealing only with a few relevant, illustrative variables.

Capitalist society revolves about the centralization of the productive process ("integration," in the popular ethnocentric jargon of the social sciences). Even under the putting-out system, there was a centralization of management and handling. The centralization, on one hand, involves concentrating numbers of specialties and specialists and, on the other, developing new forms of flow of wealth (i.e., capital), as well as organizing its concentration. Such tasks can be and have been carried out in a number of different ways, but in the West, a specific form of so doing was invented beginning 500 or more years ago and became the integrating form not only for the West but, more recently, largely for the world. This form we call *capitalist accumulation*. One of its chief properties is capital accumulation in private or quasi-private hands, controlled largely by individual or small-group entrepreneurial decision-making, all with the goal of making not merely recompensatory but cumulative profits. These profits are not directed chiefly to consumption ends but to continuous reinvestment in order to make more profits.

Although primitive capital accumulation can be carried out in other ways (although this is not recognized in Western economics because it is overwhelmingly concerned with raising capital within the framework of *preserving* the capitalist system), the chief means used in capitalist development have been, on one hand, the appropriation of the means of production, as in the enclosures in sixteenth-century England and in the expropriations of common lands (*baldios*) in twentieth-century Portugal and, on the other hand, the generating of a cheap wage-labor supply. *Cheap* means "paid much less than the value of its product," that is, exploited. Since the capital accumulation, primitive or otherwise, in great measure excludes the producer of the value concerned from its use, two exclusive categories of persons are generated, that is, two major classes.

It is in the interest of one of these two classes to make sure that the capital keeps flowing to it, but not back, in any significant proportion, to the other. This requirement, over time, leads to the generation of forms of control to preserve such a system of flows. Accordingly, we find emerging the typical forms of the capitalist state and the correlated informal structure characterized by invidious individualism even where, later in this development, corporate structures are developed. We see the emergence of what comes to be known as "liberalism" both as a structure and an ideology: minimum intervention of a state which acts as a handmaiden to the economy, and so on.

It should be noted that primitive capital accumulation could have been or could be carried out by the state or by private and public corporations while still not being integrated around some major participation by the value producers in the value produced, nor around a major redistributional system (i.e., some form of socialist integration). Such societies have been organized around continuous private and quasi-private accumulation operating *through* the state, as in several Latin American countries at various times and as in Portugal and the various fascist states of Europe in this century (Poulantzas 1976).

Neither concentration of productive resources and the means of production, nor continuous private accumulation of profits and wealth, nor even a labor paid in money wages, exists in nature or society by necessity. It is not the case that increasing specialization requires geographical concentration of multiple specialties and specialty sets on a grand and increasing scale. My argument is that that process which our current temporo-ethnocentric literature calls "urbanization" is a product of a historically particular orientation toward the means of production, labor, and value produced by labor; one which eventually produced its characteristic ideology, even its characteristic science— called neoclassical economics—and, even more, its diagnostic catch-phrase to summarize all this, namely, "cost–benefit analysis." This phrase can be translated as "a procedure for reducing costs of inputs (e.g., labor and raw materials) and increasing profits"—the general program of capitalists and capitalism. It is interesting to note that materialist anthropologists living in capitalist societies have widely adapted the use of this (folk) concept to the analysis of primitive societies and how they handle, say, their gardens, cows, and pigs.

Let us turn briefly to labor needs under such a system. As the properties of the system become increasingly defined and increasingly dominant, a labor supply is needed which is increasingly detachable from geographical contexts. It must be movable from localities of origin to points of concentration of capital. It must also be detachable from social contexts of origin, specifically from community and family, and, later, also from associations (e.g., unions), for at least two reasons. The first is to detach it from any sort of social group which might act in

[61]

a corporate way against the interests of capitalist encroachment (e.g., in England of the sixteenth century, the struggles against enclosures; in the nineteenth century, the Luddites; in the twentieth century, various community resistances to being wiped out by the encroachment of the European economic community's forty-ton trucks and the roads to carry them). The second is to create a free-flowing supply of the minimal labor unit, the single person, especially men, in order to create maximal adjustability of the labor force needed in any given enterprise at a minimal cost. The cost is reduced by having to support only the individual worker. Where one has, in addition, to support, say a family group—as, for example, by providing housing or other services—costs go up in proportion to benefits. That is, profits decrease. The maximal adjustability is achieved, of course, by hiring or firing the minimal possible labor unit, that is, just one person at a time.

By the same token, the characteristic "cost–benefit analysis," as a social process operating in the context of private property for private profits, generates a much greater degree of geographical concentration of specialties than in other forms of societal integration with similar levels of specialization. Note the geographical redistribution of specialties and the population stabilization of Havana in postrevolutionary Cuba (Acosta and Hardoy 1972). In cases such as the latter, the development of transportation systems is directed at the relative *dispersion* of clusters of specialties instead of their continuous concentration. Note the Red Chinese effort to develop backyard steel production in the earlier years. What is involved, here, using the sloganistic capitalist metaphor, is a drastic redefinition of what is costly and what is beneficial, especially the widening of what is referred to by both terms to far vaster ranges of human interest, endeavor, and personnel.

The capitalist cost–benefit concentration of specialties generates the characteristic structure and process of urban centers (of villages, towns, cities, mine heads, farmsteads, lumber camps, etc.) which we are so familiar with from our daily lives and which so many take to be paradigmatic of the Urban and hence label with such terms as *urbanization*. We are, in fact, continuously living in, experiencing, and looking at *capitalist* forms of urbanization. Some of the chief features of capitalist urban structure and process have already been adverted to: concentration, including that of labor, as a necessary capitalist consequence of specialty and capital concentration, and labor detachment from geographic and social contexts of origin. Great density, large population agglomerations, and increasing population size are necessary symptomatic results but, as diagnostic traits of the Urban in general, are of limited value since they describe only the cities—and then chiefly capitalist cities—of urban society and not urban societies as wholes, especially noncapitalist ones.

Given these basic conditions of capitalist urban structure and process—a historically particular set of phenomena—the *particular* phenomena of "social urbanization" *necessarily* follow. They follow whether encountered in Latin America or, for that matter, in the United States, internally, and, at the turn of the century, between the United States, and the rural areas of half of Europe and parts of Asia, especially China, as well. It is necessarily the case that capitalist interests generate models of connecting "peasant" areas more tightly to the areas of concentrated capital resources (i.e., cities) and the corresponding systems of control in order to generate flows of labor and capital, as well as at least part of the markets on which profits depend. The capitalist interests establish the structural channels by which labor concentration, capital flow, and marketing can be facilitated. The whole procedure is justified by science—specifically the capitalist science of economics, which today endlessly discusses the relative merits of "generalized development" as against "growth poles" and "trickle down," most commonly opting for the latter two, not surprisingly. It even has a label for the entire procedure just described: *integration.* It will be noted that *integration* here means the capitalist form of linking agricultural hinterlands to cities and labor to capital, and only that form.

Feudal Integration of Class Society

To turn now to another form of society: feudalism clearly did not look like this at all. Profits, as a structural and institutional aspect of the political economy, as in capitalism, simply did not exist. The capitalist form and process of profit making should *not* be confused with making some amount over cost and value (in medieval public discourse, the problem of "just price"), which is *hoarded* as personal wealth or some portion of which is paid in taxes or tribute to an overlord in a personalized payment for public functions (Pollock and

[63]

Maitland 1895). The hoarding of wealth is not carried out in a competitive market with N players striving to get into the profit and reinvestment system but by a largely jurally restricted set of players to accumulate hoards for sumptuary and other consumptional purposes *and* for utilization in *public* duties and functions.

Such a system required relatively *fixed* labor, including a very large range of specialists both in the agrarian sector and in the production of sumptuary goods and the goods needed for maintaining the whole system, especially relatively personalized military equipment.[4] The whole structure of feudal society was institutionally directed at nonmobility of a geographical or social sort. (This nonmobility was strengthened by serfly rights to land and their jural tie with it— drastically different from the detachability by sale of slaves in a capitalist system.) Monetarization was deliberately suppressed (e.g., "peasants" were not allowed to hold gold and silver or their money forms). Note, in this connection, "peasant" awareness of the problem reflected in any number of, say, the Grimms's fairy tales about finding lumps or hoards of gold or, in the opera *Boris Godunoff,* the symbol of the idiot who finds a kopek. Put another way, demonetarization of agrarian producers is a deliberate *class* policy of control and wealth accumulation. It is one which has persisted even in certain capitalist contexts until quite recently (e.g., in parts of Portugal until the 1950s and 1960s). In this case, the contradiction between a coexisting wealth accumulation based on a nonmonetarized fixed labor force and capitalist accumulation based on a mobile labor force reflected itself in a very striking form of internal migration, at least from the 1930s until the end of the 1960s, referred to as *ranchos,* followed by an equally striking explosion of emigration from the same area of origin as the *ranchos,* which immediately disappeared as the area in question monetarized by means of migrant remittances sent from abroad. The suppression of monetarization is itself directed at making mobility difficult, hence at its suppression or control.

But the structure and process of urban centers are also shaped by this entire order. Labor needs inside the medieval urban center (city, town, castle, abbey, manor) are very much restricted by the class interests themselves—largely to specialists who can handle the sumptuary, housing, and subsistence needs of the controlling class. It is a

---

[4] See n.3.

major interest to keep others than these *out* of the towns, fixed in their own agrarian, mining, or other extractive areas. There is no *labor* need for masses of "unskilled" and "semiskilled" workers, to use the capitalist classifications serving to categorize large numbers of people and to cheapen their labor. At the same time, there was every *political* reason not to want restless masses of people right in the locales of the public display of pomp and wealth. In fact, jural restrictions on residing in towns and penal sanctions for doing so illicitly existed throughout medieval society. The urban centers, therefore, tended to remain small. They tended to be fairly sharply separated in social and functional terms from the agrarian hinterlands. The connection between urban centers and country was intermediated by the taxation system and its administrators—church, military, royalty, nobility—and largely (and sometimes formally, as historically particular forms of integration) by socially and jurally restricted subclasses of persons, the merchants (a special caste in India and an almost castelike order in China and Japan before capitalist encroachment).

Another feature of medieval society which it is of utmost importance to recognize is that the societywide specialized institutions of church, military, public administration, commerce, and agrarian production—the very separation and specialization of which are themselves diagnostic of urban society generally—were geographically segregated into distinct and distinctive urban centers: the abbey, the castle town, the commercial town, and the manor, respectively, although the first two also had their own agrarian bases. The abbey, like the castle town and the manor, aside from its religious specialization, was also a very complex, internally differentiated, hierarchic, and specialized system of quasi-public administration, labor allocation, production, and social and political controls—in short, a statelike order with an administrative center, the abbey itself. Abbey records much resemble those of a state or a very large industrial corporation (Abbot Irminon 1946; Louis the Pious 1946). In a nonethnocentric view, such a description of an abbey indicates an urban place or center (quite corresponding to Mayan temple communities or Cambodian Angkor Wats and Thoms, and many other examples, as well as to forms of urban place more familiar to us), one treatable by central place theory. In a parallel manner, the castle town was the urban central place for the military aspect of public administration and the manor for large-scale agrarian production (Louis the Pious 1946). (To generalize this last piece of the argument,

[65]

any farmstead is an urban central place, characterized by a minimum range of specializations of a certain type, but including production, exchange, and managerial functions.)

Just like in "capitalist" or "Asiatic" societies, in medieval society "peasants" learned models of town life. They learned jural norms about their relation to urban places and experienced specific institutional relations to representatives of and from urban places, for example, taxation and the rights of the first night (*jus primae noctis*). All of these constituted aspects of one kind of social urbanization—or urban socialization.

The medieval European system, just like the capitalist system, had its characteristic ideology and science. Medieval people lived in a world of fixed species, created in the beginning by God for *all* generations. Species existed in a fixed hierarchy, the *scala naturae* or Great Chain of Being (Lovejoy 1937), which, of course, applied not only to interspecies ranking but also to intraspecies ranking. Accordingly, human society had its fixed ranks as well as "species" differences, that is, class differences (e.g., the estates or castes or castelike orders). Each of the classes or estates had its species characteristics, that is, its own proper societal functions, not to be aspired to by members of other classes. Since these societal tasks came, *ab origine,* from God, they were also Good. This entire science and ideology was broadly reflected, in Western medieval society, in Catholic ideology (and brought to a peak by a Catholic theologian-scientist, Saint Thomas Aquinas), which consistently reinforced the idea that it was God's will for each type of person to fulfill his proper calling, to live in his proper station in life, to do Good by accepting the Good of what he was by God's Providence. Further, the ideology was even encapsulated in an image of society as body[5]: the prince was the head; the heart was the senate; the eyes, ears, and tongue were the judges and governors of provinces; the hands ("arms"!) were the officials and soldiers; stomach and guts were the financial officers (!!); and the feet (of clay, presumably!) were, of course, the husbandmen or "peasants" (John of Salisbury 1949). The model is one of fixity and immutability of relationships, though the parts might go through the cycle of birth, growth, and aging (i.e., the reproduction of labor in its proper place).

[5] See residues of this conception in the idea of 'the body politic' and in British functionalism's organicism; cf. "On the Concept of Function in Social Science," in Radcliffe-Brown 1952.

Conclusion

Several critical conclusions are to be drawn from the above discussion. First, *clearly,* all the "pieces" of feudal society were tied together, or in current terminology, the "variables" were "tightly coupled." In short, *medieval society was highly integrated,* just as "integrated" as capitalist society. The point is that the medieval form of integration was drastically different from the capitalist form of integration. It was built on the fixity of labor, fixity of class membership, restricted uses of the forms of competition, the geographical as well as social *distancing* of classes, and separation physically of their functions in the productive and sociopolitical processes.

Second, correspondingly, the structures and processes of urban places look quite different from those of capitalist society: in one instance, practically fixed sizes of rather small urban centers differentiated by major societal functions; in the other, Weber's "true"—no more "true" than any other—city, in which occurs the superposition of all societal functions in single urban places characterized by continual and virtually uncontrollable growth to create, ultimately, "world cities" (Hall 1966), metropolises (and "metropolitan sprawl"), "megalopolises" (Gottman 1961), and so on. Each has its characteristic local and regional land use and internal ordering, for example, in capitalist cities, substantial confusion and contradiction between formal and informal ordering and enormous stress over zoning, community versus private interests, residential location and process, etc., and in capitalist circum-city regions, decline of agrarian uses to be replaced by abandoned areas, wastelands, reforestation, or industrial uses, as in the New Jersey area around New York and in the environs of Boston. The breaking of the boundaries of medieval urban places can be seen in any city over 400 years old in Europe, while the accompanying, capitalism-induced landscapes just described are also immediately recognizable (perhaps its most recent and most visually striking symptom is the car mortuary on the edges of towns).

Third, the different forms of integration and the different systems—structures and process—of urban centers entail different forms of "social urbanization." Medieval societies had their characteristic forms, just as capitalist societies—or, better, each of the rather different structures of evolving capitalist society (Leeds 1975)—have theirs. The contemporary Latin American case of "social urbanization" is one characteristic of a relatively late or recent phase of capitalist evolution, undoubtedly a special subcategory of the latter rooted in the structures of neocolonial dependency.

Fourth, bits and pieces of modifications of late medieval forms of "social urbanization" were integrated into the colonial mercantile- or commodity-capitalist organization of Latin American society from 1500 on. As capitalism itself evolved, both the forms of social urbanization attached to mercantilist-commodity capitalism and the still older, epifeudal forms became increasingly less useful and more poorly adapted to the needs of the new forms of industrial, finance, monopoly, and transnational capitalism. Also, the fixity of labor had to be broken down by formal and informal means: by legislation, military action, institutional reorganization, indirect economic penetration, encouragement of intra- and international migration, planning (especially by economists), elite revolutions, invention of new forms of organization, and the utilization of social networks. The older forms of social urbanization have been caused largely to disappear, to be replaced by the kind of social urbanization discussed in Margolies and Lavenda 1979.

Placing the ethnocentric version of "social urbanization" in a general theoretical framework of urban societies leads to the recognition that there is nothing inherent or inevitable about the form of social urbanization in question. The *theory* implies that other choices and alternatives are possible. Contrary to the implicit position of nineteenth-century evolutionism and to practically all Western developmentalist thought today, societies need not inevitably become capitalist. Not only are alternative models actually present, enjoying essentially like degrees and forms of specialization, but others are both thinkable and, at least in principle, institutionally feasible. Alternative models of societal integration mean alternative models of social urbanization.

With alternative models of societal integration and social urbanization at hand, questions of choice become critical. At such a juncture, we can no longer be mere analysts and theorists but necessarily must also be citizens and creatures of values since we are forced to decide on action (including inaction). We must decide on what our values are, collectively and individually, and, accordingly, make choices, that is, plans and programs at all levels of societal organization from international to personal.

Finally, I wish to urge that we should always formulate our problems in terms of more general, comparative, and contrastive theory. If we do not, we always run the danger of the ethnocentric formulation of problems. Just as strong theory—at least, societal theory, if not also theory in the physical sciences—has political implications, so, too, does an ethnocentric formulation of a theoretical problem. Inevitably, it serves certain interests. Just as ethnocentric economics and ethnocentric economists almost universally serve certain interests, social urbanization, as somehow inevitable or in the nature of things, serves certain interests, especially when translated into various forms of ameliorative and cooptative planning and policy.

Favela Macedo Sobrinho, Rio de Janeiro, 1966. Removed in the early 1970s. One of many sites of Leeds's favela research. (photo by Anthony Leeds)

[2]

Towns and Villages in Society:
Hierarchies of Order and Cause

No Towne Is an Islande of Itselfe:
Specialization and Linkage

The nucleated human settlement (village, town, city) has consistent-ly been treated as an isolate in anthropological studies, as in "commu-nity" studies and such few studies as have tried to describe large settlements (towns or cities) as a whole. Even more or less neatly discernible subnucleations, as "neighborhoods," squatter settlements, shantytowns, wards, and the like, have been treated largely as isolates. The general argument of this chapter is that in human settlement patterns in general all aggregations or nucleations ('localities'), from "tribal villages" to "megalopolises," can only be fully understood if looked at as nodal points within societal systems or between hierarchic levels of such systems. The specific location of any nodal point, or locality, with respect to one or more systems in a hierarchy, along with specified ecological conditions, largely delineates the characteristics of the nucleation (including such categories as "tribal villages," "peasant villages," mining towns, fishing villages, industrial towns, ports, "cen-tral places," and so on).

In 1976, I presented a very synoptic sketch of a theory of urban society which provides the basis for the extended argument developed in this chapter (Leeds 1976a). Briefly, it asserts that any society which has in it what we commonly call "towns" or "cities" is in *all* aspects an "urban" society, including its agricultural and extractive domains. In both these spheres all major transactions respecting them are carried out in the "central places," either local or supralocal, while both agriculture and extraction, including fishing, are merely sets of specialties within the urban society, just like industrial, commercial, bureaucratic, intellectual, and other sets of specialties mostly located in agglomerations we call 'cities' and 'towns.'

A series of reexaminations of our conceptual apparatus flows from this argument. First, at a generic level, "villages," "towns," and "cities" all have the same *functions* in society, including nonurban "tribal" villages in so-called "primitive" societies.[1] They function as nodal points of exchange and transaction for those specialties which are not *necessarily* tied to any given geographical territory ('space-intensive specialties') as well as those that are·('space-extensive' or 'space-linked specialties,' e.g., extensive large-scale cropping as of wheat and corn, trawler fishing, forestry, etc.). Regardless of the character of the specialization, whether as crude as the very simple specialization of mere male/female divisions of labor or as complex as the microspecialization of modern industrial society, exchange takes place and is facilitated by more or less consistent localization—that is, a "locality," a "central place," even if it be only a "tribal village."

The exchanges suggested in the above are primarily those of mate-

---

[1] The whole problem of what constitutes a "tribe" and what is meant by 'primitive' is very vexed. There is a great deal of evolutionary, Western ethnocentrism in the terms. A brief case makes the point clear and, indirectly, illuminates the discussion of similarity of function of villages, towns, cities. Nucleations in what is now Botswana are systematically called villages in the anthropological literature (for example, the various publications of Schapera). Some of these were quite large, such as Mochudi and Serowe, etc., which reached up to several tens of thousands of people (see Hardie 1980). Further, they were run by persons called, in the literature, 'chiefs.' The "chiefs" administered civil functions such as land redistribution and jural functions such as court hearings, *not* merely for their kin but also for all sorts of nonkin. In short, they patently were officials in a civil system of a society with nucleations with specialized functions of government, politics, social organization, and economy. Athens, the largest Greek nucleation, at its *peak*, had a maximum population of about 40–50,000 including helots, not even a difference of one magnitude from the larger Botswana nucleations. It was run by various sorts of figures variously called "kings," "tyrants," et cetera, who carried out civil and jural functions—obviously a *civil* system of a society with nucleations with specialized functions of government, politics, social organization, and economy. But Africans are black and were (and have) colonials, so I suggest, they had "tribes," "villages" or "tribal villages," and "chiefs," while Greeks, the "fathers" of our intellectual tradition—*and* white *and* European—had "states," "cities," and "kings."

The entire set of terms is ethnocentric to Western culture and ought to be excised from the social sciences. Much thought, for example, by people like Morton Fried, has been given to the conception of 'tribe,' with some salutary movement toward dropping the concept as one that does not fit our facts. 'Primitive," especially as used as an adjective for nouns such as 'religion,' 'art,' 'music,' etc., has little discernible right to life (itself a "primitive" term in certain cult groups).

rial goods and of services connected with them. But by virtue of their localization, other services aggregate about them, in turn generating other exchanges of goods. Further, by virtue of all of these activities the exchanges necessarily generate localization of a more or less stable population and physical apparatus (houses, other buildings, and infrastructure) for their maintenance. Over time, these in turn breed new aggregations of exchanges of goods and services, but also of exchanges of other sorts (social, religious, recreational, and purely personal) all revolving about specialized aspects of social existence.

Exchange among all of these sociocultural specializations, even in the simplest forms known to anthropologists, are facilitated by the proximity afforded by aggregating them in a locality, by "nucleating" them and the appropriate personnel. Aggregating specialties helps maximize *predictability* and favorable (i.e., desired) outcomes of exchanges of all sorts, for example, by reducing unpredicted or unpredictable delays involved in long-distance transport (e.g., due to snow) or over long periods of time (physical, sociopolitical, etc., perturbations). Aggregation in localities to create a nucleated settlement reduces the problems of coordinating interdependent specialties due to separation in space and time. In other words, it is easier to get things done and the outcomes are more certain when people are close together, a truth for all human societies and all seasons.

Second, the terms 'urban' and 'rural' come to stand to each other not as opposites and equivalents. Rather, the inclusive term describing the whole society is 'urban' while the term 'rural' refers only to a set of specialties of an urban society characterized by being inherently linked (under any technology known) to specific geographical spaces—that is, "space-linked." The set of specialties concerned are, in fact, merely subsets, however complex, of the entire *structure* of specialties of an urban society. (The reader may want to consult Appendix A in order to follow the discussion more closely). The inherited dualism crystallized in the terms 'rural' and 'urban' indeed obfuscates what are, in fact, much more complex structures. The dual terms reflect essentially urbanite world views ("whatever is not urban, that is, city, is rural"). Labor structures, institutional features, jural dimensions, et cetera, of agriculture, mining, lumbering, fishing, et cetera, often differ among themselves drastically within a single society, and cannot be homogeneously subsumed under the single rubric, 'rural.'

Chart A attempts to clarify technical ('. . .') and general colloquial (". . .") usages as to their referents. The classification obviously falsi-

[73]

fies actual structures; for example, commerce, administration, education, and even some aspects of industry are found in agricultural, mining, lumbering, and fishing areas, even outside towns and villages. If the reader tries another classification he will also encounter such difficulties. The problem lies in trying to reify cities as something *separate* from the societal structure as a whole. Obviously, the divisions are entirely arbitrary as well as nonparallel, one set of terms having to do with economic activities, another with settlement patterns, but neither set sharing the other. In short, the colloquial of folk-theory terms, which are still being used by social scientists, simply will not work.

A consistent interpretation is, however, given in Chart B where each of the subsidiary categories involves a set of specialties or several such sets, with considerable institutional and organizational autonomy, one from the other, but also with necessary or at least important interlockings as well as spatial overlaps. The more the overlaps, the greater is the density of aggregation of specialties and hence the larger the scale of the nucleations. On the whole /h/ through /k/ are "space-extensive" although intensive agricultural techniques such as horticulture (for example, in *chinampas* in the Valley of Mexico) can be fitted into very reduced space such as one finds in city interstices (urban agriculture).[2] /a/ through /d/, in particular, and to a large extent /e/

[2] Actually 'horticulture' would be better since most of the instances involve primarily gardening, although there is also much small-animal raising. I first noted it while doing squatter settlement studies in Rio de Janeiro. We did house-to-house surveys that included censusing all vegetable and fruit crops cultivated and animals raised. According to our calculations, there must have been in Rio about 200,000 pigs in squatter settlements *alone,* then (1967). To this one may add pigeons, chickens and other fowl, rabbits, some goats, and so on. In Lima, we saw cows in squatter settlements as well as rabbits, guinea pigs, ducks, chickens, et cetera, gardens for various crops, and even some corn and potato fields. We have not calculated the estimates for total squatter settlement crops for either place, but we know that they are significant in household economies as a kind of import substitution. We even found corn and manioc *fields* in Rio. There were also sections of Rio devoted to (Japanese?) truck gardening and a great deal of small-scale backyard vegetable planting in lower- and middle-class sections of town of various kinds. The total contribution to the gross national product has never been thought about, much less calculated.

Later I spent a year in Oxford, England, already sensitized to the phenomenon. Oxford, a dense, closely-clustered settlement of about 125,000 people, must have nearly 500 acres in "allotment gardens." In addition, practically everyone in a separate house (most of Oxford) has backyards also gardened. The latter are more devoted to flowers than the former, while the former are mostly for vegetables (the endless English cabbage, God help us!). Every city in England has allotment gardens in at least part of the city. No one has thought to calculate their aggregate contribution to the gross national product.

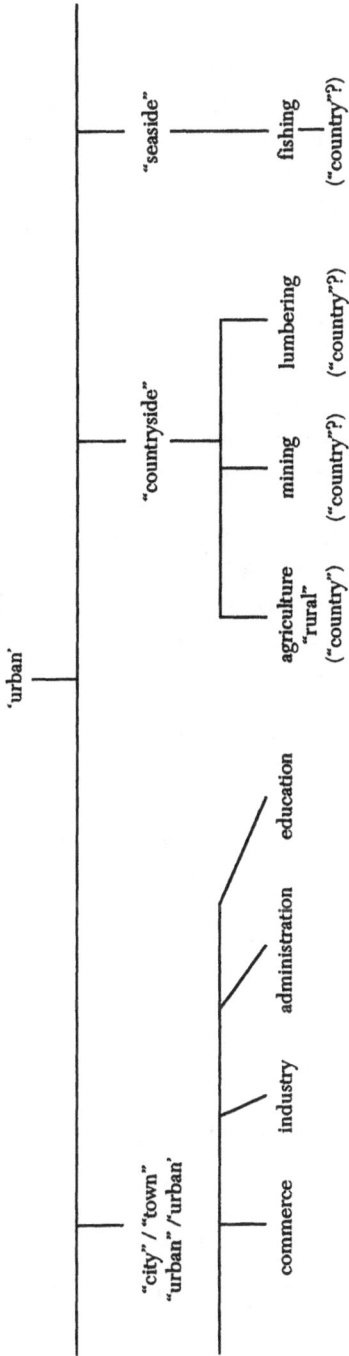

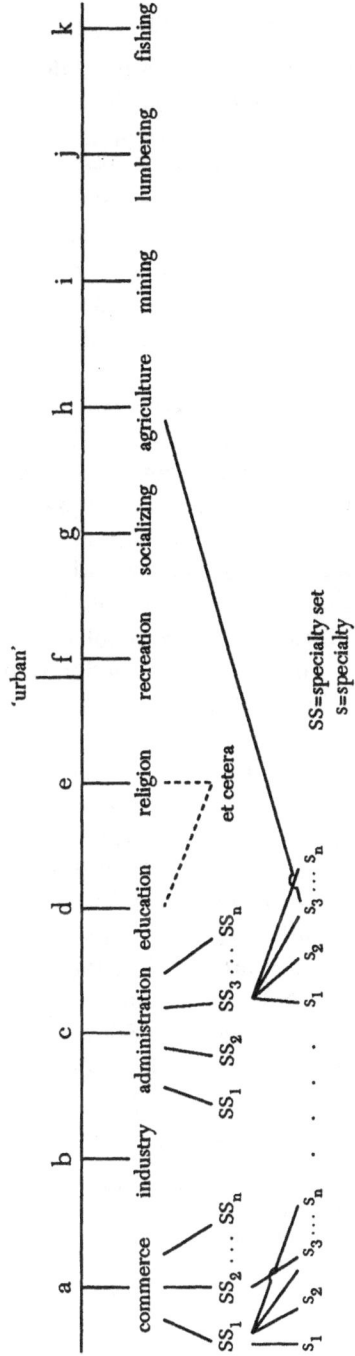

Chart A
'urban'

"city" / "town"
"urban" /'urban'

commerce   industry   administration   education

"countryside"

agriculture   mining   lumbering
"rural"
("country")   ("country"?)   ("country"?)

"seaside"

fishing
("country"?)

Chart B
'urban'

| a | b | c | d | e | f | g | h | i | j | k |

commerce   industry   administration   education   religion   recreation   socializing   agriculture   mining   lumbering   fishing

SS_1 $SS_2 \cdots SS_n$ SS_1 SS_2 $SS_3 \cdots SS_n$ et cetera

s_1 s_2 $s_3 \cdots s_n$ s_1 s_2 $s_3 \cdots s_n$

SS=specialty set
s=specialty

[75]

and /f/, are "space-intensive," that is, not inherently linked to a given geographical territory. Not being so linked they are *movable,* but must nevertheless be located for relatively long periods of time (by reason of their "housings" and/or materials used) in some locality, that is, in villages, towns, or cities—in nucleations, or for present purposes, in "urban centers." But all of the domains overlap or interlock, hence the whole society participates in some characteristics of specialization, exchange, institutionalization, jural norms, et cetera. Therefore, again, the total society is best conceived as "urban."

Third, the foregoing argument suggests the *intrinsic* character of linkage not only between any given nucleation (composed of space-intensive specialties) and space-extensive specialties external to it, but also among various kinds of space-extensive specialties, among the nucleations, and between them and nodes at other higher levels in the hierarchy of nucleations. If one merely looks, say, at the equipment needs of agriculture and the food needs of people occupied in mining, this is immediately obvious. All nucleations, localities, or "communities," then, are involved in and responsive to externalties.

Fourth, the distinction between "town" and "city" is not sociologically meaningful.[3] That the latter conventionally means something large and the former something small is sociologically practically useless. In any case, even this usage is inconsistent (for example, a New York or Boston suburbanite says "I'm going to town," meaning New York or Boston; he does *not* say "I'm going to [the] city").[4] Often 'city' is merely a jural term (for example, "the City of New York," not "the Town of New York," as the jural name; or, in Portugal and Brazil, 'cidade' as a legal descriptor). In this usage, it points only to the jural array of attributes of the nucleation.

What is important is not the term used for, but rather two descriptive aspects of, these nucleations looked at comparatively. In such a perspective, both aspects are ranges or continua, making any real

---

[3] Note, in this case, Jane Jacobs's wholly abortive attempt (1969, appendix) to distinguish between 'town' and 'city.' The town she tries to designate as smaller places with stagnant economies and the city as larger places with growth economies. Thus Lowell or Leominster, Massachusetts, were cities in the nineteenth century and are now towns. If one of them develops a boom, it becomes a city again. Obviously this is absurd as well as nonhistorical and nonsociological.

[4] Note the term 'town house,' referring to a city dwelling par excellence. If I recall correctly from my childhood, there were also "town cars," the most expensive elite automobiles (Packards, Mercedes, Daimlers, etc.) for in-city driving, with chauffeurs, of course.

separation between supposed "types" practically impossible and intellectually obfuscatory because nucleations overlap widely in content of specialties. The first of these aspects is the diversity of specialties present, which could be represented as an index. This is governed by several factors for all of which measures can be given: (1) the degree of specialization present in the society as a whole; (2) the immediate ecological specialization of the locality; and (3) its relative geographical accessibility or isolation. The second is the scale or size of nucleation, measured not only in population, but also in urban infrastructure and apparatuses, both fairly easily measurable by various means. This second aspect is also largely dependent on the factors just listed. A number of other features of towns tend to vary with scale, for example, number and variety of educational and recreational institutions (for example, Archer City, Texas, with its *Last Picture Show* versus Wichita Falls with its several movie houses and intriguing parties).

Fifth, as noted, the model sees societies as structures of specializations, while nucleations are seen as nodal points in the flows of exchanges and transactions, demands and supplies, that link specialties. Explicit in the model is the argument that nucleations (villages, towns, or cities) can *never* be looked at in isolation, as closed systems, as tightly bounded entities. A corollary to this argument would be that all studies of localities such as those we still call "community studies" must have major omissions or even falsifications insofar as they failed to consider the extra-community linkages in detail. Take, as an example, the systems of national or subnational taxation existent in all urban ("state") societies whose effects on localities have practically never been systematically described in anthropological community studies.

The model permits us to generate a series of theorems including some respecting the evolution of urban societies and others regarding ecological determinants of settlement. I present only a few here, by way of exemplification.

Theorem One

The size of the largest nucleation and the range of sizes of the nucleations in a hierarchy will vary more or less in proportion to the degree of specialization of the society. In effect, this theorem is compatible with central place theory in geography.

[77]

Theorem Two

The greater the specialization, the greater is the proportion of population living in central places at various hierarchic levels and the smaller is the proportion of the total population living in villages and outlying locations.

Theorem Three

The greater the aggregation of individuals and ("space-intensive") specialties, the tighter and more elaborate must be the linkages between towns and the space-extensive specialties. This is compatible with the economists' notion of economic integration.

Theorem Four

The greater the degree of specialization, the more complex the system of coordination among specialties must be.

Corollary 1. The more complex it becomes, the more hierarchic it must be.

Corollary 2. The more complex and hierarchic it becomes, the more it must be crystallized as an autonomous set of specialties ('coordinative specialties'), namely, institutionalized administration such as public and private bureaucracies, courts, executives, et cetera.

Theorem Five

The more complex the overall system of specialization, the more sensitive is the system as a whole to disturbances in any major interspecialty flows of the system (e.g., breakdowns of oil supply to any number of industrial and private users in our society).

Corollary 1. The increasing sensitivity of the complex system of specialties and their linkages to perturbation generates improvements in transportation and communications ('space-linking specialties') directed at reducing entropy and increasing predictability of flows.

Many other theorems and propositions can be generated including some very interesting ones about "primitive" societies and their evolution with respect to settlement patterns. (This specialization model or theory applies to, and includes, "primitive" societies as well as "complex" and "urban" ones.)

No Towne Is an Islande of Itselfe:
External Connectedness

From the foregoing, especially the theorems, it is overwhelmingly clear on theoretical grounds that any treatment of villages or towns as isolated or closed or autonomous necessarily misrepresents, distorts, or falsifies. We are compellingly led away from treatments of localities as being marked by closed boundaries, inwardly focused even, perhaps, from being "communities" (at least as an a priori; see Chapter 7). We are compellingly driven *to* look at certain aspects which have been consistently neglected in anthropological works.[5]

That the theory and its derivatives force us in this direction does not deny the patent fact that most aggregations or nucleations have certain degrees of closure, especially if incorporated, that is, defined *legally* as territorial bodies with specified rights of government over that territory and its population and their socioeconomic apparatus. What territory is so defined varies from society to society (e.g., in Portugal and Brazil, the *cidade* or seat of a *freguesia* or *município* in the respective countries includes both the nucleation and its hinterland, usually but not necessarily agricultural, *not* separated conceptually *or* legally as is the practice in the United States). Such jural boundaries, however, apply only to certain domains or sets of specialties present in the settlement, while other sets of specialties and their subtended role relations, possibly not even recognized by the State as existing, exhibit exchanges and transactions that flow freely across the jural boundaries.

---

[5] It is striking that practically none of the papers either in Southall, ed. 1973 (publishing a collection of papers written for a conference in 1964) or Eddy, ed. 1968 deals systematically or systemically with linkage between the place studied and other places or domains of the society. Even the studies of hometown associations (Mangin 1959; Little 1973) or of rural-urban migration (e.g., Banton, Mitchell, Mangin, Bradfield, Bruner, etc., in Southall 1973; Gugler & Flanagan 1978; Kemper 1977; and thousands of others) have either been focused on the towns with very brief venturings to the country localities or on both the towns and country localities, but *only* these, to the exclusion of the rest of society as it encompasses those two localities linked by migration or by remittances and other resources from hometown associations. In neither case is the focus on the *general* linkage of the town with the society insofar as such linkages have causal effects on the town itself.

For example, in American towns, practically no connection exists between their jural boundaries and, say, kinship networks. By the same token, only the haziest relationship exists between the jural boundaries of a locality and the federal income tax. Even in societies where the role of the state in closing town boundaries may include control over who comes and goes, or even their class, ethnic, caste, and perhaps kin connections, the closure is not complete because of the necessary flow of fundamental supplies (not only of foods but of those materials, tools, and implements needed by the State to maintain itself, as well as the relatively closed boundaries). Thus, although wards in classical Japanese cities may have been kept under tight bureaucratic control and merchants constrained by status limitations, yet the latter linked the wards inside the cities with larger political economy outside them.

In this connection, it is interesting to ransack anthropological monographs describing examples of that popular category, "the closed corporate community," for evidence of nonclosedness. Take, for example, William Stein's monograph (1961) on a supposedly "closed corporate community" in the Andean highlands. One extracts from it a whole roster of goods which are obviously, and in some cases must *necessarily* be, trade goods. Yet there is no discussion of the extent or significance of the trade articulation with the larger Peruvian society.

Take an example from "primitive" societies, one that is treated almost wholly as self-enclosed both in its classic monograph (Evans-Pritchard 1940) and in an ethnographic movie (*The Nuer* 1968). Yet, in the former, mention is made of, and in the latter one actually sees such items as guns, bullets, white cotton shorts, other kinds of cloth obviously not locally made, razor blades, steel used for spearheads, safety pins, cold chisels, and several others which are all trade goods. Neither the film nor the monograph discusses trade or its significance at all. I shall not elaborate on the fact that this tribe—"isolated," "self-enclosed," in a kind of geographical cul-de-sac more or less in central Africa—raises maize and tobacco: both New World crops! This fact is also not discussed in either source.

These examples remind us that this closure model is general to anthropology and to its monographs. One might well claim that it has even been actively sought, as in the formulation of the concept of the "closed corporate community." I do not assert that external linkages are *never* mentioned; they are even sometimes rather well described. Rather, the dominating *view* is of boundaries, closure, self-maintaining systems, autonomy, and so on, with respect to which external linkages are mostly seen as incidental.[6] This model was transferred, in this history of anthropology, first from tribal studies to "peasant communities" where it was intensified by the invention not only of the conceptions of the "closed corporate community," but the equally closed "peasant society," whence it was then transferred to the understanding of "communities" in "nonpeasant societies" (e.g., West 1945), and thence to towns and parts of towns such as neighborhoods.

True, "closed corporate communities" have forms of governance applying to the locality, that is, various kinds of "town government." So, too, do large cities like Boston, Lisbon, London, Rio, et cetera. So, too, do incorporated New England villages. So, too, did medieval French towns. So, too, in the form of the *mir*, did Russian peasant villages. So, too, does the Brazilian *município*. So, too, do even certain kinds of neighborhoods *in* towns, for example, the so-called *bairros de lata* ('tin-can-neighborhoods') of Lisbon and many of the *barriadas* ('squatter settlements,' now called *pueblos jovenes* or 'new towns') of Lima. Admittedly, the relationships between the territory of the nucleation and its surrounding territories and the populations of both vary among these, but, nevertheless, each is a form of bounded, jurally defined or delimited system betokening a degree of closure—"village" or "town governments" in short.

But the point here emphasized is that the closure in each ease is relative. Take any American town and consider just the federal income

---

[6] Note, in this connection, the use of the word 'the' as in "the" Arunta, "the" Yaruro, even "the" Americans. What it does is reify some attribute—in the first two cases particularly language, in the latter language and citizenship—into representing a whole socio-politico-economico-cultural system. We then *describe* "the" Yaruro, or "the" This or That as if they were a closed system for all aspects of sociocultural life, despite the fact that many or most of these aspects have non-coterminous boundaries and some are not even closely related to the linguistic boundaries. There *is*, for instance, no entity "the" Yaruro. There are relatively autonomous villages; there are groups of weakly interacting villages; there are no interactions at all for the population-as-a-whole of Yaruro-speakers. There are some very weak interactions today, though stronger in the past, with speakers of other, unrelated languages in the same general territory, including somewhat stronger ones with Venezuelans of European background. Many culture *traits* are shared across several different populations (that is, speakers of different languages, including unrelated ones). If I took a culture trait perspective or one of trade, of intermarriage, of the sustenance of everyday life, my sociocultural units will be *quite* varied and different. The same argument goes for "the" Americans: city-dwellers? Southerners? "ethnics"? capitalists? I can safely assert that there is *no* attribute shared by all residents in the territorial space called the United States except that residence itself and perhaps the institution of the income tax discussed in the text—and, for citizens, *only* the attribute of citizenship and its consequences, but even these are unequally shared (for example, taxation and military service).

tax, as an example. No village, no town, no locality, even an unnucle-
ated one like a farmstead, is closed from the income tax in two senses.
The first is that, in principle, all persons are equally subject to the
institution of the income tax, although, by various partial or total
exemptions, some individuals may pay less or not at all. Essentially,
boundaries of nucleations are irrelevant to the institution of the income tax, as such. The second is that many, if not most, federally
financed services which are rendered or transferred to localities, in a
form quite different from the original dollar payments of taxes, are
funded by the income tax. There is not a community, locality, nucleation which does not receive some return transferred from the income
tax, returns which relate directly to possibilities, modes, and modalities of living in localities.

Third, in respect to this last claim, let us examine the income tax
game more closely. Certainly many, if not most, Americans know that
on one's income tax returns one can write off interest payments on
mortgages. That fact governs a great array of strategies in house buying and renting, ultimately with strong effects on differential localization of buyers and renters, along with a marked differentiation of
densities, privacy, and space use. Differential capacity to pay down
payments, ranging from none to very large, together with calculations
on income tax refunds or calculated net-income reductions by paying
more interest, which is deducted from income, has a very powerful
effect on residential and neighborhood class stratification in towns.
This tax aspect is, of course, not mentioned in most anthropological
studies of "communities," towns, and neighborhoods. Much less is
there an anthropology of taxation examining individual, corporate,
locality, state, and national strategies with respect to taxes, local, state,
and national (or whatever the hierarchy is). Still less is there a generalization of the principle involved in the specific case: the *intrinsic*
importance of the external linkages discussed above.

No Towne Is an Islande of Itselfe: Specialization and Differentiation

In 1961, Arensberg generalized the methodological conception of
the community study. In essence, *a* "community" was held to be an
object (and, as such, bounded) and a *sample*. Assertedly, as a sample,
all major institutions of the society criss-crossed the "object" of study.

Implicitly (see Chapter 7), any locality was identified as a "community" a priori (see Lynd and Lynd 1929; Powdermaker 1939 and even 1950:1–10, passim; West 1945), and these localities ostensibly displayed all major institutions of the society.

I consider the proposition itself patently false. Even if one posited an identity between any locality and a community and delimited the community as a much larger socio-territorial entity, it is almost certainly false. Take the university as an institution (especially in those societies where most universities are national or church-linked). Clearly, most localities not only do not have them, but have very hazy ideas of their structures, characteristics, access routes, and even functions, though it would be very difficult to deny that the university is a societal institution. I do not think a single one of the classical community studies of anthropology (or sociology) mentions a university. Again, there are a number of institutions, both present and past, revolving about the arts (e.g., court painters and composers, royal chapels for music, national endowments of the arts, art museums, symphony orchestras, etc.) with no representation whatsoever in most localities and local communities and even unknown to most of their populations.

On the foregoing argument alone, it is clear that nucleations are differentiated according to whether they have this or that set of institutions and lack this or that array of other institutions. Obviously the differential in terms of presence or absence of exemplars of institutions also means differentiation as to urban infrastructures and apparatuses, such as transport systems, space uses, buildings, storage places, and so on. From the preceding argument, we see that localities, even if communities, are *necessarily* specialized. With this differentiation and specialization of nucleations, qua nucleations, the whole idea of typicality, of *sample*, collapses.

But, to go further, the *fact* of the absence of some institutions in one place and others in another require explanation. Although some case might conceivably be made that instances were accidental, the notion that most such absences are accidental is wholly preposterous. We look, rather, to explanations in terms of various factors: (1) isolation of a locality; (2) function of a locality with respect to its surrounding territory; (3) policy of a community (e.g., closing down public schools in order to keep blacks in their places—a way of resisting the externally originated intervention of the central State) or of a state with respect to a community (such as legislating the rights of a village

[83]

community of "peasants"); and possibly other explanans. I turn to the first two of these in what follows, setting the discussion in an ecological context.

The specialty paradigm I have been setting forth is not only one of differentiated technical, economic, social, and ideological structure of society, based on specialization, but also of differentiated ecological structure. Ecological variables are necessarily built into the concepts 'space-extensive' and 'space-linking specialties,' and to some extent into that of 'space-intensive specialties.' Together, these are compatible with location theory in geography and economics.

Space-extensive specialties *entail* differentiated localities since the aggregates of specialties constituting such localities are, in part, related to geographical production givens of the territories in which they are located. This is particularly true of localities that originated in a "natural," that is, as an immediate practical response (without major formal planning and preparation) to immediate operational needs as in the relatively recent cases of the initial settlement of Brazil, Canada, and the United States. The character of these settlements was largely governed by the interaction of local geographical conditions and the kind of production system introduced. Clearly, such localities must account to those geographical features and, in longer runs, as the local economies expand, serve in the local ecosystems created as points of exchange, transfer, and transmission.[7]

The preceding discussion leads to asserting the inherent ecological specialization of localities. This assertion can be presented as a general theorem: the more restricted the array of specialties in a locality, the more ecologically specialized it is. The converse is also true. Whether it is because the localities are distant from facilities for transportation or exchange (i.e., because they are isolated) or whether for reasons of marked geographical limitations (as in desert regions), these places are unable to support large superstructures of space-intensive specialties. What space-intensive specialties are present are those adapted chiefly to linking the specialized space-extensive specialty sets of their surrounding territories with more variegated space-intensive specialties in higher-order localities. With only very small arrays of specialties,

[7] As an aside, it is interesting to note that the direction of population movement or of expansion of a societal hegemony, for example, Russia, often governs localization of nucleations; e.g., on the north banks of rivers as one goes south from Recife in Brazil and on the western banks as one goes east in Russia.

arrays which are strongly adapted to the geographical and productive conditions of the territories surrounding them, these sorts of locality are quite small—"villages" in common parlance. They may, in themselves, be conceived of as specialized *nodes* linking to each other the space-extensive specialty sets of their specific areas and the larger, societal system of specialties. In everyday language, we are talking about farming hamlets, mining villages, lumbering settlements, oil emplacements, complex plantation or feed-lot headquarters, fishing villages, and the like—all low-level nodal points in the total hierarchic social system of space-extensive specialties and of hierarchies of nodal points of aggregated specialties—linked by transportation, communication, and coordination systems (space-linking and coordinative specialties, respectively).

The same principle of differentiation and specialization also holds for nucleations at higher levels in the societal system, levels that permit exchanges and transactions among an indefinite number of lower-level nodes, on one hand, and, on the other, an indefinite number of higher-level nodes, as well as among the intermediate-level nodes themselves since each is specialized in some degree (see Strassmann 1958). Not only do such secondary-level nucleations ("towns" in common speech) have specialty sets that function to serve the lower-level nodes (e.g., banks, licensing bureaus, county courts, notaries, machinery agencies, parts supply houses, etc.), but many or most of them are *themselves* adapted to the regional ecological characteristics; that is, they are differentiated ecologically from other nodes of equivalent level in other ecological zones (e.g., by having agencies in, say, Wichita Falls, Texas, that supply oil-drilling machinery and cattle-care equipment and materials). Some specialties may also be adapted to local features of the town, such as specialties involved in transshipment and reloading or packaging in towns which are rail heads or ports. In addition, of course, as part of the increasing aggregation, there are the specialties involved in supplying the transshippers and the suppliers of goods and services with goods and services, including entertainment, food wholesaling and retailing, and the like.

The ecological components just discussed give us a considerable power of prediction as to the characteristics of localities we might study and may even permit us to hypothesize as to modalities of social interaction (as in cattle or mining towns). In any case, the ecological components inevitably *differentiate* nucleations; at the same time, they necessarily connect them into larger systems of interaction, transfer, and exchange.[8]

No Towne Is an Islande of Itselfe: Exchange

The connections of any locality into the larger system (the societal system of specialties) are predominantly those of exchange and inter-action. If one conceives of 'exchange' in a Lévi-Straussian or even a Blauian way (Blau 1964), then perhaps practically all connection is via exchange (or transfers conceived as a subcategory of exchange).

Several major categories of things are exchanged or transferred: (1) products of specialties (including raw materials); (2) personnel, includ-ing specialists (although they may change specialties as a result of the transaction); (3) specialized knowledge and information; (4) property either as objects or rights; and (5) money and other forms of symbolic value, if present in the society. I refer to aggregate movements of such exchanges and transfers through space-time as 'flows.'

Clearly, given the inherent specialization of localities qua localities as argued above, locality exchange is a *necessary* aspect of all societies, or at least of all societies with even moderate ecological variation in their territories, although trade is practically universally reported, even for societies more or less atomized into autonomous villages scattered in a virtually homogeneous geographical area (e.g., the Yaru-ro of Venezuela in whose territory clays for pottery are differentially distributed leading to exchange).

Let me put this another way: for *any* locality, external connections are entailed. Theoretically, *never* should one *expect* to find autonomy, closure, or boundedness. On theoretical grounds, one should *always* expect flows of goods, services, personnel, property, knowledge, infor-mation, or possibly other values going in and out of any locality. The heart of this in and out is exchange—and the heart of human exchange is human strategizing, to which I return below.

From the point of view of the locality or of its component groups, aggregates, or individuals, one can treat the externalities as parame-

[8] 'Exchange' is used here in its ordinary economic meaning, broadly understood. 'Interac-tion' is intended to include such processes and events as political interchanges and swap-pings, bureaucratic transactions, possibly various forms of social behavior (visits, sports competitions, etc.). 'Transfers' refers to oneway movements of goods or services, for exam-ple, grants made by the federal government to a community.

ters, constraints, and expectations, which in most instances are probably measurable. There are equivalent, although not necessarily identical or isomorphic, internal parameters, constraints, and expectations which meet the external ones in the exchange or transfer function. The interactions of these two sets of parameters and expectations govern enormous arrays of behavior, many of which remain either altogether untouched or unsystematically described if one predicts one's description on the bounded, closed, "community" model.

By way of an example, as a youth I lived on a farm in a dispersed neighborhood articulated primarily with two more or less equivalent "villages" in New York state. Jurally, we paid taxes to one of these villages. The other was our post office address. We preferred the latter socially and also for my first school experience in the country (a one-room, six-grade school). The former was better for services such as car repair, meat supply, and lumber; this village also had a junior high school to which I went for a year. The general stores of the two villages, however, were almost equivalent, although the one in the tax village was usually somewhat better supplied and had somewhat lower prices.

We raised chickens to sell eggs and had enough cows to sell some butter. We sold the eggs both in the county seat and, by mail, to New York City; the butter we sold in the county seat only. Thus, money came from New York and the county seat. Part of it flowed to the mechanic, the tax offices (village, county, state, and federal), the general stores, the post office, the meat store, the lumber yard, and so on, in the villages where, of course, we *expected* to find canned goods (for example, Campbell's soups that one stored up against possible days of being snowed in), grains, cereals, dry goods, produce, et cetera, which all came from other parts of the country, as did the car, the truck, the tractor (and parts for all of them), the tools, the lumber for chicken coops, and so on. Most of the rest of the money was spent in the county seat or in New York City for clothes, recreation, and the like.

The "community study" orientation and its latter-day version of urban and urban neighborhood studies simply take all of this for granted. The studies fail to ask endless questions about, let us say, the strategies of general store keepers in buying from outside, in working with different suppliers, in dealing with transport, and so forth. These strategies, in fact, differentiated Robinson's general store from Elmer Devine's sufficiently so that we, equidistant from both, preferred to buy in the latter. The studies failed to deal with differentiated strategies of residents of the localities for purchasing—for example, when and why we did *not* buy in the local general stores but rather in the county seat (which, of course, also had services lacking in the localities such as the ice plant where one could freeze pork, chickens, and ducks at slaughter time for later use). Rather, the studies focused on aspects of the life of the populations delimited by peoples' defining themselves as "belonging" to this or that place. That is, the studies selected and emphasized only those aspects which reinforced boundedness and inwardness.

Note, however, that the highly complex exchange relations described in this almost prototypic and much simplified case led to a whole array of behaviors not restricted to the locality: correspondence and trips to New York City, telephone calls, correspondence (especially bills) and at least weekly trips to the county seat twenty miles to the south for selling eggs and butter, frequent trips to both villages and very occasional ones to another smaller village, as well as trips to one of the county subcenters ten miles to the north which had a bank, a movie house, a drug store, a dentist, and even a small newspaper, along with a couple of real estate offices, and the high school for that entire part of the county. (Of course, I went to the latter during school years for four years; my former history teacher, there, now commutes daily to the high school in the county seat thirty miles away, while some of my former classmates commute daily 15–20 miles from there to the IBM plant across the Hudson River in Kingston).

In sum, I am arguing that the larger system of exchange, in its more inclusive and wide-ranging sense, in which communities were in fact embedded as nodal points, was largely left unconsidered in traditional anthropological studies, so that the nodality and the effects of nodality on behavior were also omitted. "Communities" were largely treated as isolates, congruent with the (German) idealist conception of Gemeinschaft from which the whole paradigm was derived. The contradiction of seeing them as isolates while they were obviously implanted in far more inclusive networks led to theoretical attempts such as Arensberg's, which asserted that the community was a prototype of the larger system and hence a "sample," and also led to the claim that all national institutions could be observed in them. Both propositions, in my opinion, are demonstrably false. It is even questionable (see Chapter 7) whether every locality is a "community," whether used in Arensberg's, Murdock's (1949), Tillich's, Tönnies's, or colloquial senses.

In any case, it is not something to be taken as an a priori, but something to be demonstrated (on the basis of some explicit definition of 'community').

No Towne Is an Islande of Itself:
Externalities as Causes

I wish to go beyond what I have said above to take a still stronger position: namely, that externalities can be regarded as *causes* in shaping internal characteristics of localities (villages, towns, cities). The type of causality is not a strict deterministic, but a loosely coupled, causation, allowing some degree of freedom, of accident, of reshaping by localities of their relationships with externalities. Nevertheless, the *weight* that such causation has in shaping internalities should, or better, *must,* be taken into account when focusing study on any particular internal aspects that have generally been treated as *merely* internal, if not as actually autonomous. Let us look briefly at some examples.

Take, for instance, that domain most beloved of the anthropologist —kinship; here, specifically kin networks in urban settings. As in various now classical studies (e.g., Bott 1957), I start with a genealogy, asking all sorts of questions about descent, affiliation, marriage, household groups, occupations, geographical moves, ages, and so on. Perhaps I extend the genealogical chart to network ties with nonkin. I have then described a variegated, interlocking web of social connections and exchanges, often even involving exchanges of goods and services. But most of the classical studies stopped at this point, without examining the boundary relationships of the networks to understand the parameters governing the shape and size of the webs and what affects these parameters *structurally,* either presently or historically (see also Mitchell ed. 1969, which tends to concern itself more with the properties of the networks as such than with the problem posed here). Let us look at this problem of boundaries in a Portuguese case.

From time immemorial and certainly through the Salazar-Caetano era, one can safely say that almost all Portuguese agrarian laborers (wage workers, sharecroppers, tenants, "peasants") led devastating lives economically and demographically. Income, health, and vital statistics are appalling and conditions of labor almost inconceivable.

The chief response (other than dying) was emigration: to anywhere one could go to get away from "slavery," as informants sometimes called it.

Many of these people survived by a depressed and exploitative subsistence agriculture. Their agricultural condition was governed, in part, by the presence of a system of intermediaries between them and the market, which reduced their take if they sold and increased their costs for what they bought (especially, e.g., fertilizers). Under the Salazar regime, some of this structure of intermediacy was directly fostered or jurally established by the State; some of it was encouraged by a policy encouraging monopoly and oligopoly (by the Lei de Condicionamento Industrial, the Industrial Regulation Law), including control over what crops could *not* be raised in Portugal—cotton, sugar beets, and tobacco—(although soils and climatic conditions were quite suitable) because they were raised by still cheaper labor in the colonies.

Without a major revolution, agrarian labor had no way to cope with such a system directly, much less get rid of it. The emigrational solution, of course, did not make it go away for those who remained, for those who returned from abroad, or for those who moved to the cities.

It is precisely under these conditions (parameters), however, that the genealogical ties and the nongenealogical networks of friendship were *spatially* (as well as socially) extended by the moves to towns and cities of great numbers of people from the villages. In the cities (I shall speak here of Lisbon[9]), many of these people—literally tens of thousands—reconstructed subsistence activities in limited ways (see n.2), while finding, as their main source of income, city occupations, especially in civil construction, but also in commercial establishments, domestic work, and so on. In Portugal, pay scales (governed by Salazar's *modelo económico* of controlled low wages) have always been low in the cities, too, but life, on the whole, was somewhat more secure, social welfare more accessible, health facilities more available, et cetera; nevertheless, conditions still remained very constrained.

In doing our fieldwork, we discovered innovative adaptations to this situation, to the external control of the major marketing and supply

---

[9] Today about 28–30 percent of the national population resident in Portugal lives in the Lisbon metropolitan area, about 2.3–2.5 million people. Of this population, perhaps 10–15 percent (the exact figures are not known, at least officially) or 2.8–4.5 percent of the national population lives in *barrios de lata* and another, perhaps equally large number in areas of *casas clandestinas*, described later in the text.

system, low wages, and relatively high costs of goods and services. Specifically, we observed incredible extensions of kin-friend networks, sometimes stretching over the entire national territory and beyond. These networks were used especially to transfer goods, but also to deliver services (including, e.g., regular and emergency child care), money, and sometimes property in an almost entirely informal economic web. Such webs often made available cheaper food supplies, goods for resale, purchased at a discount, and so on, in return for which payments were made in money, goods, or services (usually, I think, the first).

One such network included, first (from the point of view of our genealogy), a central group of sisters who worked the open fairs in a large area of northern Lisbon selling cloth and other goods. These women had friends, possibly relatives, or other contacts in Porto from, or through whom, they bought cloth in an informal way, that is, *not* through the regular distributors, but in small lots, in exchange for money payments. The cloth was regularly delivered (sometimes in response to telephoned orders) from Porto, the center of Portuguese textile industries, 225 miles away, by small van.

Another branch of the network went back to the sisters' village of origin, which we visited. One villager (a nonrelative) described taking van-top loads of potatoes and vegetables[10] to Lisbon at night (so the road police could not see that he was exceeding the load-size limits of his van) to deliver to the emigrant families—in exchange for what, I do not know (probably money or possibly gifts later on when the families visited their home villages in vacation time). Certainly the potatoes were far cheaper than if bought in formal produce markets in town.

Further, savings were achieved by choosing shacktown (*bairro de*

[10] Especially during late spring, summer, and most fall months, in the relatively mild climate of Portugal, at least the central and southern parts, if is striking to watch the automotive exodus of cars and vans, small trucks and motorcycles, early in the weekend, and their return late in the weekend variously laden with produce. The ties with rural areas for members of all social classes and occupational sophistications are remarkably close and almost everyone has relatives in the country. We ourselves repeatedly had this experience: we took a small gift from our cleaning woman near Lisbon to her relatives near the city of Beja in south-central Portugal and came back with *sacks* of vegetables and heads of unsacked cabbages and other leafy produce that was shared by the cleaning lady and us. We repeatedly visited the mother of a close friend/informant of ours, the latter living in a Lisbon *bairro de lata*. She sent back bags of potatoes with us from very near the northern edge of Portugal. I was upbraided by friends of mine in the same *bairro* for not telling them I was going to visit a collective farm in the Alentejo because I could have taken there and brought back stuff of interest to both (see the case history of network exchanges).

lata) areas to live in, although a large part of the population living in
such places may, at least at present, be partly or wholly constrained to
do so by the general lack and expense of regular housing. The evidence is not clear on this because the alternatives might only be small
hole-in-the-wall apartments (e.g., in *pátios*, the equivalents of *callejones* and *conventillos* in Peru and Chile, respectively; see Leeds
1974b), while living in the shacktowns, in fact (despite endless and
justified complaints) gives the people more space for minimal money
outlays than in the *pátios*. Generally, what is paid is a miniscule
ground rent (see Leeds 1981a).

From the point of view of the individual households and of the
family network, savings, under these conditions, can be and indeed
are accumulated, often for later reinvestment. In this case, for example, two of the households (one of the three sisters, her husband, and
her sons and daughters-in-law) proposed to modernize the house in
the village of origin of the former while getting enough land to make
farming feasible as a means of earning a livelihood. (It is noteworthy
that the daughter-in-law is a city-born woman from Coimbra, who,
with her husband, has recently bought a lot in Lisbon for building a
regular house later on, using savings taken from his remittances from
Switzerland.) Another of the sisters has helped her daughter and son-
in-law to build a house in a suburb on a lot they bought on which they
have built without a building permit. This sort of house (called a *casa
clandestina*) is of solid construction and is, in fact, owned by the
builder; but because it starts effectively illegally, the owner-builders
are regularly fined at various stages of building, a set of costs they
figure into the total cost of construction. Obviously, this implies considerable savings effected, which is where the mother's help came in.

Some of the savings of both sisters and their respective children's
families, or more strictly speaking, here, households, have also been
used to help finance the emigration of the two young men of the four
households in this segment of the larger network to Switzerland where
their earnings are far higher and their relative costs lower than in
Lisbon, so that they can make large savings, which are deposited in
the household accounts in Lisbon.[11] The wives and children left at

[11] These remittances, cumulated from up to two or more millions of emigrants from
Portugal, are crucial in maintaining a positive balance of payments, which, but for these
transfers, would be a disaster. In the gap between being received and paying off foreign
debts, a very large part of the remittances is used by banks and investment companies
(FIDES, Torralta, and others), which have actively solicited emigrants to deposit funds with
them for major investment activities. The banks, of course, use the funds both for intrana-

home are helped, at times, both by family financing and especially by family child care services carried out by sisters, female cousins, and affines of the emigrants. They are also helped by the second of the original three sisters who does considerable child care with her own daughter's child while the daughter works in the neighborhood Social Center as a cook. The mother's relatively flexible schedule as a market woman helps make this feasible. These child care services allow the other young wife also to work at a full-time equivalent job for most of the sustenance of her household while her husband is away and putting his earnings in the bank.

From the point of view of the argument of this essay, several points are to be noted. First, the shacktown in which the largest network segment of these people resides is in no conceivable way a closed community; there are several overlapping "communities," all of which must be taken into account in order to understand the behavior of our informants.

Second, the presence of the shacktown itself is a precipitate arising from a widely shared strategy of thousands of immigrants from all parts of the country, each with its very different particular conditions and problems. However, in the places of origin (and in Lisbon), all of them faced roughly similar external conditions of control, of depressed incomes, of incapacity to overturn the system actively standing against them, that is, the *parameters* of their situation. All undertook the similar solution of immigrating to Lisbon and settling in shacktowns. The shacktown, then, is an urban form structurally generated by the larger system in a complex way (including, of course, the very reduced production of low-income housing by that same government which created the Lei de Condicionamento Industrial and the *modelo económico*).

Third, shacktown residence is, in many cases, part of a structure of strategies dealing with both household and locality externalities and directly responsive to them.

tional and international financial activities including a great part of their credit operations for industry, civil construction, and commerce. The investment corporations were primarily involved in construction of all sorts, Torralta being especially involved in tourist facilities. The civil construction and industrial investments of both sets of investors, of course, changes the landscape of cities, towns, and tourist areas outside of either, as well as of the industrial areas, which, in the north in particular, are dispersed throughout the landscape in a pattern unfamiliar in the United States. Obviously such changes, in the long run, also change the economic strategies and residential ploys of the sort of people we have been examining in the text.

Fourth, the structure of *national* resources flows, the *national* structure of specialty distributions, the *national* structure of nucleational specialization, and the *national* networks, both formal and informal, linking all, these must be understood if one is to understand the structure and localization points of the personal network of migrants I have given as an example. One must know that the textile industry is centered around Porto; one must know where the various agricultural crop areas are localized and where the major labor absorptions in civil construction and other demand domains both inside and outside Portugal are located. One must know the long-term effects of the Lei de Condicionamento Industrial and the *modelo económico* and the more or less deliberate absence of an agrarian development policy for continental Portugal until today. One must know national policies on housing construction and resource allocation for housing (see Leeds 1981a). One must also know an array of jural norms respecting tenure in places like the shacktowns, norms enforced by the Câmara Municipal (in this case, of Lisbon) in the interest of that same elite class which has for decades benefited from the series of institutions and policies which I have just listed. In short, one cannot seek to understand the shacktown as an internality, as an isolate—even, as I have pointed out, from the point of view of individuals, households, families, or aggregates living there.

In conclusion, without studying and understanding the externalities of the microphenomena or microlocalities, one is certain either to miss some of the phenomena altogether or to misunderstand or distort them by cutting off a part of their significance and their causation. The case described is only one instance but illustrates the *principle* involved—a principle for all cases—that of "external" causalities, "external" shaping, of the "internal" forms we choose to study. Further, the case also illustrates the principle of a hierarchy of causes ranging here from the national, indeed, the international, to household orders and individual behaviors. (Note, in this regard, the implications for dispersed localities of the case reported in Appendix B.)

Appendix A

In anthropology, we have traditionally looked at a specialty as a kind of irreducible monad. We could, in principle, list *all* specialties of a society exhaustively and thereby describe the ultimate elements com-

Specialization as a Flow Diagram

Inputs	Output Set (one or more outputs)	Inputs	Output Set (one or more outputs)

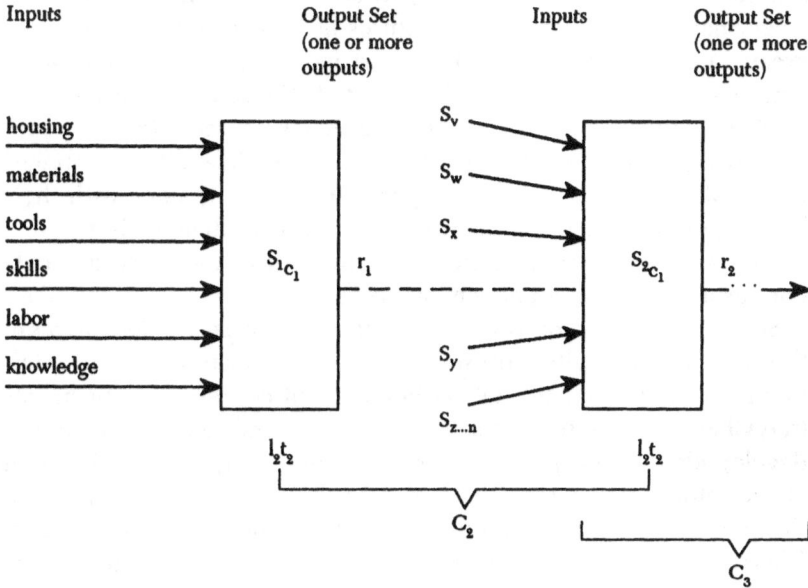

housing
materials
tools
skills
labor
knowledge

S_{1c_1} r_1

S_v
S_w
S_x

S_{2c_1} r_2

S_y
$S_{z...n}$

l_2t_2 l_2t_2

C_2

C_3

S = specialty
c = coordination activity
 c_1 = input coordination to make product, specialists' level or
        first level of coordination
 c_2 = second level of coordination
 c_3 = third level of coordination
t = time
l = location
r = rate

Note: $S_1 \longrightarrow S_2$ as diagrammed is a specialty set to be coordinated
(at c_1 level) with other specialty sets.

posing the societal order (cf. Childe from his earliest works on and the entire line of thought derivative from him, including works, e.g., by R. McC. Adams and others). I have, however, found it useful and theoretically of great interest to disaggregate specialties into component sets in a flow chart. I give in the accompanying chart a mapping of a minimum set of two specialties (one cannot, of course, have a *single*, isolated specialty, just as one cannot have a single, isolated role; see Chapter 3).

[95]

The chart indicates the *necessary* complexity of a system with any specialization whatsoever. It is readily apparent that, if the specialty is a very narrow one, the input structures must involve proportionately greater networks of linkage. The chart indicates time/location problems of coordination and therefore suggests the adaptive advantage of localizing (nucleating, aggregating) as many "space-intensive" specialties as possible in order to reduce the unpredictability of spatial or temporal separation. Localizing specialties together, along with their housing (buildings, physical space, even crania), their tools and machines, and their personnel means creating nucleations or settlements both as a logical and a phenomenal consequence.

Some of the theorems presented in the text are clearly derivatives of the model of specialties presented here. An expansion of the minimum two-set to an n-set, taking into account clustering of specialties (see Chart B in the text) or sets of specialties and sets of sets, we can develop ideas about specialty subsystems of the larger societal system of specialties. Taking the notion of specialty subsystem together with the hierarchic aspects presented in the accompanying chart and in Chart B we can derive theorems about social stratification and the distribution of power as well.

Appendix B

The following item, reproduced in its totality from the *Boston Globe*, February 19, 1979 (by permission of Peter Ward), poignantly illustrates the principle of hierarchic causality—from international, to intranational, to regional, to local. The reader need merely think of local labor in local labor markets generated by the small plants concerned in specific localities, along with ancillary specialties of a service kind, to grasp the entire point of the essay.

U.S. AND CANADA EXPECTED TO TALK TOUGH
By Peter Ward
Special to the Globe

OTTAWA—The heart of Canada's program to upgrade her small and medium industry has been hit by a U.S. Treasury Department decision which is certain to mean tough trade talks between the two capitals this week and may signal the start of a trade war.

If allowed to stand, the precedent set by the U.S. decision could put many smaller Canadian businesses out of operation, and may mean higher prices for Americans for the products involved.

The predicament involves Washington's judgment that Canada has been subsidizing exports by aiding Honeywell Ltd. of Toronto in the production and marketing of a gadget which optically measures the filling of petroleum tank trucks and containers to prevent overfilling.

Canada has a myriad of programs to aid industry, ranging from special deals for companies which locate in high unemployment areas of the country to schemes which pay part of the cost of research and development and market surveys.

The Canadian government helps finance private industrial efforts which are likely to improve foreign sales, creating new jobs.

In the Honeywell case, the U.S. Treasury has ruled that aid from Ottawa has resulted in an unfairly low selling price for the device when it is exported to the United States and the U.S. has imposed a 9 percent "countervailing" duty.

International trade agreements allow individual nations to take such action when courts find that government subsidies unfairly lower the price of exported products.

Literally thousands of Canadian companies are aided by Ottawa under a scheme called the Enterprise Development Program. The U.S. move against Honeywell would be disastrous for Canada if extended to those other companies.

In Canada, the issue is seen as a question of whether or not the United States, with its huge market and tremendous technological resources, will be allowed to take over virtually all the North American market for sophisticated products.

The F.M.I. Helps Portugal [1978]
(A Paean Celebrating the Agreement between
Portugal and the International Monetary Fund, May 1978)

How do you write a poem
about the F.M.I.?

There they sit
in the featureless neons
for eons and eons
ties knotted at their throats
and at the gargantuan throat of the world,
robots of decision-making
looking at our land
with the one dead leaden
and the one live golden
eye
     of the F.M.I.
and start from "purely technical,"
"impartial,"
First Truths
of the First Church of Finance—
Deusdata
for omnes generationes
—there was only
the First Judgement—
for all eons,
featureless,
with or without neons
Robots of the One Way

But how do you write a poem
about the F.M.I.?

Mania for scale,
economies of which
they celebrate
with enterprise efficiency,
while committing
the fallacial sin
of composition:
what is good for the economy
is good for any Charlie Wilson
and, so, even better
for Hungry Everyman.
Enterprise efficiency:
cut the fat
off the lean meat of labor;
cut the lean meat of labor
to the bone, down
to the merest marrow,
till the bone collapse
to be ground
into fertilizer
for enterprise efficiency
(may its drive increase)
to save the nation
while the workless leftovers
beg for a bone
in the city barrens

But how do you write a poem
    about the F.M.I.?

Cut the wormy appendices
from the budget,
slice out the waste
that builds
a decent house
for the poor,
extract the funds
that kept the workless
(lopped off for enterprise efficiency)
from a crawling death
from a metastasis
of sickness
never cured,

built on a skeleton
of malnutrition,
where, in our land,
a fifth of the work force,
hiving in the cabinets
drones on, drones on,
while the cronied clones,
grow portly
on the cut fat
of the meat and the bone,
while licking
the driblets of honey
from the F.M.I.

Can one write a poem
about the F.M.I.?

In the neons
they write reports
about Shylock the Shark
and the rates he writes
for his loans
in the hamlets and towns.
"Usury!" goes up the cry
in the F.M.I.
But now
with twenty-five per cent
readjusted
for the cash-pinched lender
—trimestrally!—
they are merely speaking
(clinically, of course!)
of the package treatment
—purely "technical"
—no options, no alternatives
so drily prescribed
by the good doctors
of the F.M.I.
who look at our land
with deadened eye.

Ought one to write a poem
about the F.M.I.?

No other routes
to spread the goodies:
To whom as has,
it shall be given;
and to whom as hasn't
it shall be driven,
austerely,
from the First to the Last,
in the Judgement
    of the F.M.I.
Glories for pater,
Glories for filius,
    lambs of the F.M.I.,
in the families' firms
where enterprise efficiencies
are making strides
while the hollow ghosts
of the rest
beware as they may
of F.M.Ides.

Can one *really* write a poem
    about the F.M.I.?

Where shall the workless go,
how shall the hungry eat,
how shall the sick grow well,
when they are so evilly
    f–m–eyed,
and given the old one-two
(both front and back)
with the slick packaged deal
    of the F.M.I.?

Should one write a poem
    about the F.M.I.?

Why are so many
of my friends here
lame and halt and blind,
shrivelled at 45,
squeezed dry?

The F.M.I. Helps Portugal

So many widows
(sub-species black)?
And I ask
    the F.M.I.
My friends here—
why are they,
as they say,
so "sandpapered"—
raw and bloody
from skin to soul,
from eyes to I?

Can one write a poem
    about the F.M.I.?

The Green Eye of Xerox in the Tropics [1984]

The green eye of xerox
winked at me—
another gringo
bringing the best
to the unruly tropics—
put the lid on again
   and again
flipped out
bits of wisdom
for the hungry
each paying his little
   pieces of the alms
due to the omnivorous
I Bring More
giant to the north.

The black eye
of the hand calculator
winked at me—
a fellow gringo
who added up the bill
   headily
and from my exact payment
get my dues in change
from the waving alms
of the cashier
after the fifth try
on her a.b.m.,
   no, i.t.t.,
   no, i.s.m.,
—how is it now,
in the unruly tropics?

Casal Ventoso, Lisbon, Meeting of the Directoria of the Residents' Association, June 13, 1978

We sat in the barren room
and they talked small talk
about the houses needing repairs
or the guys down there who were trying to take over.
Erasto looked through the lists of new members,
doled them out to be given to the owners by district.
They waited for the others to come,
but they didn't come and didn't come.
My women were there (all except Teresa),
and I—receiving my sócio amigo card
—my stripes, my badge, my medal,
my belonging, my identity as a worthwhile
human being to be trusted,
a homem de confiança
to these brilliant, set upon, exploited men,
and still we waited for the ones who didn't come,
except Bicho who showed up.
Erasto began to talk of his military service in Mafra
story upon story, while we all listened,
—the idiocies, the ironies, the infantrilities,
armed men Portuguese against armed men Portuguese.
Tell us some more stories, Erasto, said someone.
He went on, and then on to Angola—
the black horror of the "independence war,"
the traições of black against black, of
Agostinho Neto against other leaders, and these
against him, of the UPL and the MPLA and
the Unitá, of the splits, of the leaders against
the black people, of the black soldiers (bands)
against the whites, of impoverishing, of stealing, of
banditry, of denunciation, of betrayal, of

violence, of massacre, of dead bodies, all—
in that barren room where we all sat
transfixed, silent, the sights and sounds and
bloods and terrible tragedy of Angola (and Portugal)
in our eyes and ears and noses
—oh so terrible—and Erasto seeing it
all, and understanding so much of the
politics and humanity.
And then finally Paulo came in
and Angola ended suddenly;
we turned to Casal Ventoso business sharply.
Five times last week, Paulo—where were you?
Doing our work is not mere undertaking
but also doing, being there—
how about Wednesday and Thursday and the
meeting Saturday and when these people
of good will (two of my women and me)
were here to help do our work, and
Monday (when Maria and I had finally
gone to Erasto and asked what was happening)
so we'd know what to do? Where were you,
Paulo? he asked (sometimes like a trip-hammer,
sometimes with ironies and quips).
Where were you? said Bicho, that's not
work said Bicho who always says little
but says it very much. And old Joaquim
in between the coughs asked where he'd been too
—and now incomprehensible gigantic Elídio
also asked (but Relvas, Alberto, Moita, Irene,
Carlos Jorge didn't because they never came
that night to the barren room). And they gave
Paulo a going over—a criticism to the young
revolutionary who kept wanting to leave
from his discomfort
but stayed ("put it in your agenda," said old Simões
in between the coughs)
and then they talked about the questionnaire
and got this and my women planned,
and then they talked about the commission elections
—legality and constitution vs. practical politics
—the lousy corrupting of the political system
which created their dilemmas of action:
Paulo trying to preserve a real revolution

at the local practical level
Erasto trying to preserve a real association
and undivided community at the local
level by practical politics
with—against the higher levels.
With Relvas they will do it,
this time, Paulo's way, because
Ernesto can transcend the immediate and
understand an Angola and a Portugal.

Classes in the Social Order

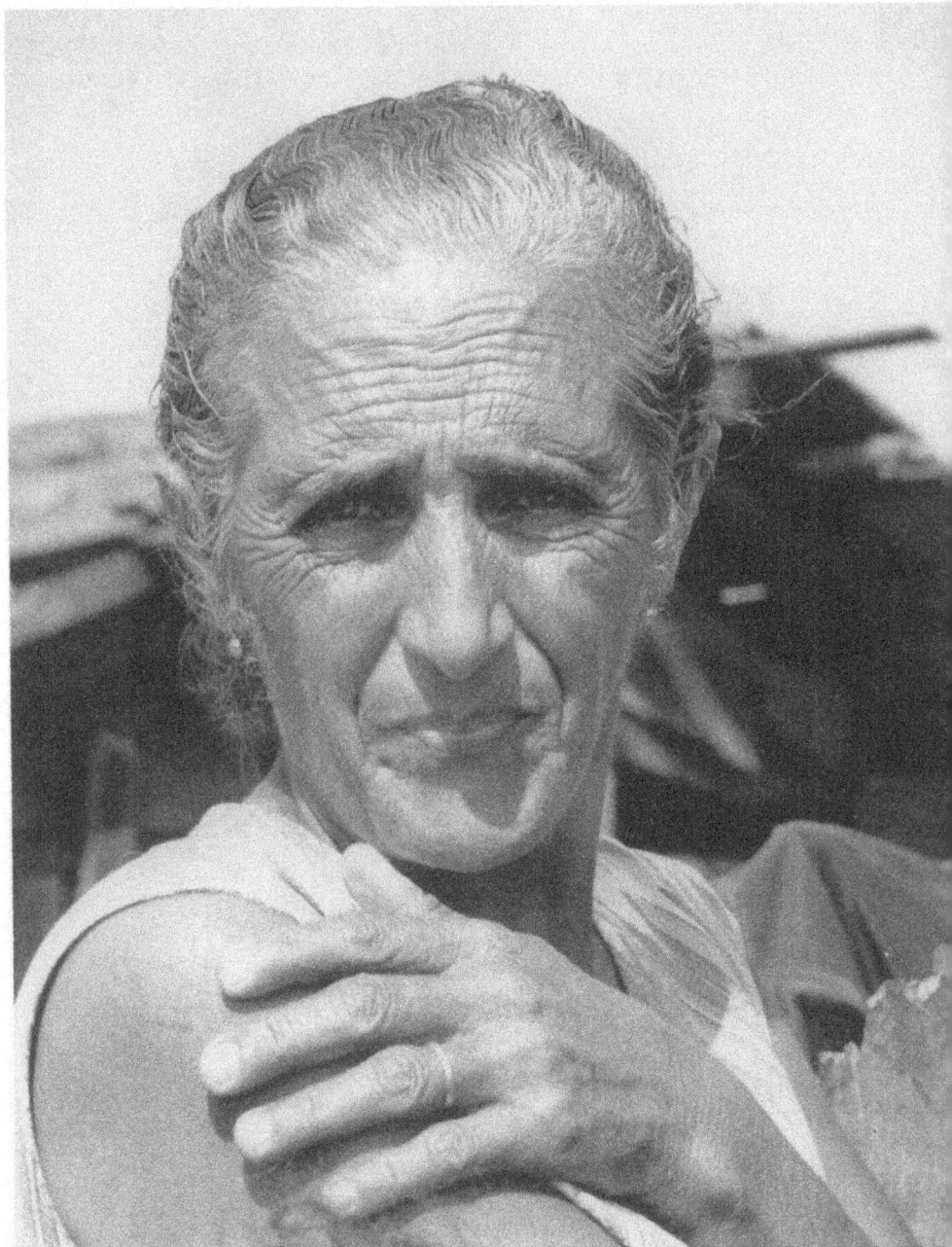

Dona Pantonilha, 1966. A matriarch of Favela Nova Brasília in Rio de Janeiro. (photo by Anthony Leeds)

[3]

Mythos and Pathos:
Some Unpleasantries on Peasantries

It is essential, if one is to arrive at any clarity of view as to the nature of things, to make reasonably precise and theoretically interesting analytical distinctions—categorizations—lest all things be muddled indiscriminately and subtleties of differentiated process or meaning be lost. Further, such distinctions or categories should be theoretically relevant, that is, related to a body of theory in such a way that the distinction made reaches far beyond the mere recognition of two different attributes or two different states of a single attribute to illuminate other distinctions and an ever-broadening series of relationships asserted to exist among the categories. These asserted relationships comprise the body of theory to which the distinctions are relevant.

These tenets seem to me to be especially true when considering the concept "peasantry," with whose multiplicity of referents social scientists in recent years have become enamored. The term has come to shade together under its umbrella everything from "true" peasants, to rural wage workers or "rural proletariat," to "countrymen," "tribals," "primitives," and, more lately still, even fishermen in an etymologically scandalous fashion (Firth 1946; Forman 1970).[1] This last usage

---

[1] Both the *American Heritage Dictionary of the English Language* (1969) and the *Pocket Oxford Dictionary* (1924) give the derivation of "peasant" from medieval Latin *pagensis*, "inhabitant of a district." That the "district" involved is rural is clear from the Oxford's indication of the cognate root, "pagan," from the Latin *pagus*, a "country district." Cassel's *Latin Dictionary* gives *pagus* as a "country district, a canton, village." French *pays, paysan*, Italian *paisano*, etc., from the same root, have always involved a reference to land and/or land use. The equivalent Spanish or Portuguese terms, respectively *campesino* and *campones*, derive from the Latin *campus*, "a field or open land" and, by extension, "crops, produce."

appears to have come about on the basis of the categorical characteristic proposed for peasantries of a small-scale, largely family, enterprise, involving limited but, nevertheless, significant involvement in a money economy. This is, of course, a temporocentric definition since aggregates of people, also usually designated peasants, have existed who were not involved in money economies, nor, properly, were they involved in small-scale enterprise, but rather, sociologically speaking, in corporate enterprises with individual or household responsibility, for example, medieval European and Chinese peasants. Current usage also appears to be like that of the ancient Greeks by which all the "civilized" Greek we are "farmers" (e.g., American and British), and all the rest, the "barbarian" theys, are "peasants" (e.g., French, German, Italian, Austrian, Spanish, Mexican, and even, in shaky persistence, occasionally Soviet agrarian labor). From time to time we soften the ethnocentrism and give recognition to the fact that the term is quite inappropriate by the compromise locution "peasant farmers"—a meaningless rubric applied frequently to the French agriculturalist of today.

On the other hand, some usages are so wide and all-inclusive that they are incapable of differentiating between "small producers" (Shanin's term, 1966:245ff.) who are tribal, prestate, nonurban-oriented groups such as primitive, swidden horticulturalists whom he lumps quite incontinently with "nomadics" ("tribal-nomadic"), displaying a hopeless unawareness of economic, social, political, and ecological differentiation among "levels" of tribal peoples. Again Meillassoux's otherwise brilliant article (1972) is talking essentially about *a single subtype of* hierarchically ordered tribal, nonurban-linked horticulturalists quite different from other subtypes of nonhierarchically ordered horticultural tribals (Leeds 1961c) neither of which, under any common usage of the term, falls within the analytic category of "peasants."

In sum, the concept "peasant" has no precision whatsoever. It is used with different attributes in different situations, and in fact, is more or less uniquely defined in each ethnographic case.[2] It is used to

---

[2] The umbrella use of the term "peasant" to cover endless varieties of situations and social structures can be illustrated interminably. Reading the articles of any two or three issues, or even only one, of *Peasant Studies Newsletter* will demonstrate the point to any careful reader. Or take a single country, like Ireland; here one can find endless references to "the Irish peasant" (note, however, Arensberg's caution in this regard [1937], indicated by use of the neutral term "countryman" which also denotatively translates *campones* and *campesino* referred to in note 1) despite the fact that the vast majority of the agrarian labor personnel were tenants—tenants-at-will, at that, at least in the nineteenth century (Woodham-Smith

cover a multiplicity of forms of production, social organization, jural orders, and ideologies. It is used ethnocentrically and temporocentrically. Clearly the term represents a total muddle and a permeating lack of theoretically useful distinctions. It is essentially a folk term adopted into social science usage without the necessary scientific refinement for appropriate scientific use. Indeed, the term basically has no scientific validity at all.

First, and most important, it is not scientific because it represents a search for essences. Usually implicitly, but also sometimes explicitly, the term postulates essences—or an essence—of peasants, peasantries, or the state of being a peasant (which I shall call "peasancy").[3] A search for essences has no place in science, but is the role of speculative metaphysics. Such a search is also methodologically atomistic since it asserts not only the inherentness, but also, especially, the separateness of some quality or substance of some reified thing—here, "the peasantry." Thus, to my mind, a search for a universal definition of peasantry has no meaning because it flies in the face of experienced structure (the interrelationship of qualities and quantities), process, dynamics, conditioning variables, etc., even though, for purposes of discourse, it is often useful to delineate a sphere of discourse *as a point of departure,* that is, to give a heuristic or delineational definition[4] to be modified during the development of the discourse.

1962). Even to speak of tenants as if they were a homogeneous category is drastically misleading because it hides very different relationships to landlords ranging from collective, cross-generational lease contracts mediated through spokesmen—for example the Irish rundale (Almquist 1975)—to individual, short-term contracts on sufferance, that is, at will. The homogeneous application of the term "peasant" for even a single era such as the first half of the nineteenth century in Ireland thoroughly obscures the dynamics of agrarian operations. Even when an author attempts to restrict usage, the restriction is not of the term "peasant" per se, but of its use for the specific purpose at hand (see, for example, Greenwood 1973), while still allowing the generic use of the term for all sorts of other situations. In other words, such restrictions as Greenwood's do not confront the basic analytic problem at all, but merely bracket a domain for immediate discussion. Such bracketings often turn out to be arbitrary and rather unmanageable because of marginal or borderline cases. Still another illustration of the umbrella use of the term is seen in the title of Firth's book (1946), *Malay Fishermen: Their Peasant Economy!*

[3] "Peasancy" as parallel with such terms as "tenancy," "freeholding," etc., refers to the structure of relationships to land, to other roles, etc., rather than to the persons involved, as in terms such as "peasantry," "tenantry," "freeholders." I shall try to be consistent in distinguishing structure from persons for the reasons given in the text even though it may involve a certain amount of awkwardness, such as neologisms.

[4] Notable exceptions are Marx 1850–52 and Saul and Woods 1971 and, to a lesser extent, Feder 1968 and Thorner 1962, all reproduced in Shanin ed. 1971, which recognize the variation in forms and even in classification under changing historical circumstances.

Second, related to the search for essences is the attempt to find this essence in persons rather than in certain sociocultural orders. I refer specifically to roles as that category of events which is analytically of greatest interest here. All roles consist of culturally delineated clusters of culturally defined norms (rights, duties, prerogatives, obligations). Each cluster, by virtue of its peculiar concatenation of norms, may also be conventionally assigned secondary expectations and attributes. It is of utmost importance to what follows to recognize that the rights are *over* things and persons *external* to the holder of the rights and include the obligatory behavior of the incumbents of the alter roles (see below), that is, *of others;* duties are *to others;* prerogatives are *from others.* This aspect of role has always been implicit in the concept of role but has not been laid out as its theoretically most interesting aspect.[5] What it means is that the very components of roles necessarily delineate sets of relationships between two or more roles in such a way that the irreducible minimum of social organization consists of *two or more* roles—a role and its alter(s). Roles do not exist singly and their separate analysis makes no sense. Any role can only be fully understood in terms of itself and its alter(s) and their *joint* or interactional requirements. In other words, one must describe a set of roles,[6] that is, a social *order,* in order to describe any one role. The implication of this for standard treatments of "peasants" or "peasant society," implying an isolated role called "peasant," will be discussed below. For the present, another implication of the role concept must be pointed out; since roles are clusters of cultural norms, they cannot possibly be identical to persons even though persons may choose, be forced, or be

[5] See the various definitions of role given by Theodorson and Theodorson (1970), all of which focus on the person as occupying a "status position" which has a "role" attached to it (defined by rights and duties)—and go on to discuss the integration of self (a person) rather than the social structural implication of role. This is very characteristic of the social psychological bent of American sociology and its use of role. Note how Southall's sophisticated attempt (1973) to deal with role as a basic concept for urban studies treats roles as single, contained, isolated entities, rather than *necessarily* linked as role sets without a comprehension of which any single role is also, in fact, incomprehensible. Notice his attempt at *counting* roles as some indicator of complexity, rather than looking at the necessarily interlocked network of roles as a key to complexity.

[6] The term "role set" used here as an abbreviation for "set of roles" does not mean the same as it does in post-Mertonian sociology (e.g., Gross, Mason, and McEachern 1958) where it refers to a *set* of norm clusters, closely related in content, each variant cluster of the set being attributed by different individual cognizers, in part because of their differing personal experience, to a specific "status" or "position." The concept is linked to notions of role ambiguity and various social psychological problems of social and individual perception in human interaction.

persuaded to act in terms of these norms for some time in some place. The notions of choice, forcing, or persuasion themselves indicate the key point, here, that of the independence of persons from roles and role structures, a point which has a series of quite fundamental consequences for the entire discussion:

(1) The distinction inherently opens up questions about process, especially about movement into and out of roles ("recruitment" and "extrusion"; see Chapter 5). The question is basic, as I will show in the last section of this essay (see also the articles by Saul and Woods, and by Thorner, in Shanin, ed. 1971). It subsumes others concerning the adaptation of different kinds of agrarian exploitation systems to changing circumstances, the range of options available for persons to move through in coping with their own needs, the sloughing off, by migration, upward mobility, military service, or other means, of certain percentages of those populations designated as "peasantries," etc.

(2) Appropriate definition of any sociological category should always be in terms of its distinctiveness *in relationship* to other distinguishable entities (roles, role sets, role structures), that is, always, to some extent, in terms of each other and as one of a set.

(3) The *fact* of the independence of role and person, since roles are not genetically but socioculturally determined, makes nonsense of Shanin's "analytically marginal groups" (Shanin ed. 1971, section B, 15ff., 81). Indeed, as Feder's article (1968) clearly shows and my own data below confirm, such groups are analytically central to understanding agrarian labor structures since mobility from and into a peasant role is possible. It also makes nonsensical the concept "peasant society," a term and idea that ought to be dropped forthwith, since it becomes immediately obvious that the peasant roles, role sets, and role structures are simply alters of role sets and structures which, jointly and in interaction, constitute the society and include such role sets and structures as the state, urban economic corporations, and the like.

The fact of the possibility of such mobility in virtually all historical periods and world areas in which peasant roles and role structures—peasancies—are said to have existed raises interesting research questions as to the relative fixity of persons in roles; the constraints—a relational aspect set by the role definitions—preventing mobility out of peasant roles; pressures leading to shift in roles (Saul and Woods 1971), and so on. It also permits one to deal simply with the concurrent occupation of diverse roles by the same person in differentiated role structures (e.g., "peasant-worker" or "farmer–urban job holder") or by the same domestic unit of production (e.g., the "peasant household" producing "subsistence" and selling on the market at the same time). In the latter case, the economic and social unit persists, but the sources of subsistence or income may be quite differentiated, for example, noncapitalist and capitalist at the same time.

In short, the distinction between persons and roles and the intellectual consequences which flow from it not only lead one away from a search for essences, but lead one toward a more complex and subtle analysis of dynamics, on one hand, and a concurrent treatment of society and its transformations in analytic *and* synthetic terms, a holistic principle which, philosophically and methodologically, I consider central to social science.

Third, the concept "peasant" is also unscientific since, in all the conceptions of peasancy discussed above and even among those usages which explicitly eschew the value commitments discussed below, it is built on a fundamental underlying cosmology, a teleological, unilinear progressivism which is a secularized version of Christian eschatology. This is especially marked in Shanin's exhumation of a notion of stages (1966:245ff.; see, in this connection, Leeds 1974a, especially 445ff., 453–55, 457–59, 462–66, 471, and appendix B, 480–83) and speaking in terms of grand—and impossible—"stable" periods of history.[7] The unilinearism stands out strongly. It is purely a priori and axiomatic, that is, speculatively metaphysical, and contradicts historical experience. It is closely related to, if not identical with, the developmentalism which pervades the social sciences today.

Finally, the scientific usefulness of the concept "peasant" is frequently further enfeebled because underlying its use are a series of policy questions and commitments, governed by highly local and time-restricted interests, which guide the inquiry more than do scientific questions and scientific commitments. These policy commitments are ones devoted to the ideas of "development" (almost always considered as a Good), of the inherent betterness of capitalism or of socialism

---

[7] His first period, according to now current dating of earlier forms of "tribal-nomadics," would roughly encompass from 2,000,000 to 1,000,000 years ago, his second of "small producers," roughly 10,000 years ago, and his third, "industrializing," perhaps 350 years ago. Rather different kinds of "stability" appear to be involved and one suspects that rather great changes in society, economy, and history may have occurred in the first million or two years as they did in the next ten thousand. One may also wonder if undue weight is not being given, in world perspective, to industrialization—perhaps a bit of ethno- and temporocentrism is involved.

over various other forms of societal integration, or of the right, nay duty, of the "advanced" countries to give aid and comfort to the "backward" countries.

What is needed, if one is to preserve the concept "peasant" at all, is a merely heuristic delineation of types of roles, structures, or situations to which, and only to which, the term is to apply, these classes of events to be distinguished from others of a similar order by criteria which are of theoretical (not political) interest. As a rule, what I should consider to be theoretically interesting are criteria which facilitate explanation of social structures consisting of many "parts" and the dynamics of their changes and which also permit prediction of various states of the systems described (Saul and Woods 1971).

Without here entering upon a disquisition concerning societal theory, I think it true to say that the criteria which consistently appear to be most interesting with respect to the general class of roles under discussion (a class encompassing the physical producers of primary wealth other than extractive products, outside cities) include (a) organization of technology, (b) form and scale of capital, (c) linkage with other delimitable social groups or aggregates (other role sets or structures), (d) internal organization of the social units constituted by the roles, (e) jural relations to the source of the raw materials, the land, (f) jural relations to the raw materials produced, (g) control over the surplus labor value, and (h) relationship to the institutions and form of the city or city hierarchies, especially the state (which I conceive to be the political aspect of urban societies and their urban hierarchies).

It is clear from the above that, ideally, a theoretically interesting typology of the roles under discussion, in fact, involves fairly exhaustive holistic descriptions of societies as such. Likewise it must involve a sophisticated typology of whole-societal forms, also informed by interesting theory (e.g., evolutionary theory or ecological theory of large-scale societies). This entailment of exhaustive societal descriptions of whole-societal typologies runs counter to the part-oriented tendency to search for an essentialist definition of peasantries and counter to the conception of "peasant societies."[8]

[8] There is a related problem here: the contradiction between structuralist and culturalist approaches. Most of the significant discussion of peasantries has been structuralist, including, in a very particular way, Kroeber's (1923, 1948). The main proponent of a culturalist approach has been the unfortunate Redfield (e.g., 1955, 1956), whose thought is always so hard to pin down to observational reality or any kind of rules of correspondence. Anthropological approaches to peasantries, especially since Redfield, though they have implicitly

Barring the achievement of so sophisticated a state of organization of knowledge, preliminary meaningful classification can be done with some of the criteria listed above, as long as one does it systematically and consistently while trying to eliminate the unstated value biases mentioned before. Discussions of peasantries have suffered from the fact that, though classification has indeed often been done with some of the criteria listed, once in a while, even with a larger typology of societies in mind, they have been muddled by the value biases, the search for essences, the unilinearism, and especially the confusion between roles and persons.

Forms of Agrarian Labor and Labor Organization

For purposes of the discussion which follows I offer the following definitions of forms of agrarian labor and labor organization. The definitions are in terms of roles rather than in terms of persons. I do *not* claim (a) that the definitions are adequately precise, (b) that they distinguish a sufficient array of types, (c) that they are sufficiently universal, or (d) that the criteria are sufficiently justified theoretically; some seem almost entirely empirical or even intuitive. I do claim, however, that they help sharply to clarify the issues discussed above and, in each case, to delineate a societal structure and the differential

tended to be structuralist, have explicitly, at least in part, been phrased in Redfieldian, culturalist terms, thus creating an enormous confusion of frames of reference and analysis. The argument of the structuralists is that like conditions produce like symptoms—hence peasantries—whether these conditions be historical, evolutionary, or structural ones (and regardless of cultural content, which can be quite diverse). The culturalist tradition fails to deal with dynamics, process, cause, and structure. It is based on an essentialist metaphysics. Kroeber's analysis of peasants as part-societies stemmed not at all from a Durkheimian tradition as Shanin (1966:254–55; ed. 1971:13) states. Kroeber was virtually uninfluenced by French sociological or British social anthropological thought. Rather the derivation—clear from the whole body of his work—is from the metaphysics of seeing the world as constituted of elements (traits) that enter into different patterns, combinations, or configurations, a tradition arising in German historiography and anthropogeography of which Kroeber was a direct descendant. Redfield may have given credit to Kroeber, but his work on peasants (1955, 1956), like his earlier works on ideal types, organic and mechanical solidarities, moral orders, great and little traditions (1941, 1953), etc., came out of the Durkheimian tradition with a considerable influence from the British social anthropologist Radcliffe-Brown, who taught at the University of Chicago about 1937, a crucial period in Redfield's development. See Leeds 1971 for a fuller discussion of structuralist versus culturalist approaches and Leeds 1974a for contrasts between German historicism and structural idealism. Redfield was also influenced by the German idealist communitarian tradition, especially Simmel and Tönnies (particularly through Robert Park and Louis Wirth, under whom he studied).

dynamics in it, to describe both small- and large-scale process, and to remove many of the scales of mythos and pathos about peasants from our eyes.

"Peasantry" shall refer to persons whose occupancy of a set of roles, to be called "peasancy," is unascribed and not specifically restricted.[9] The roles must be so specified in technological, ecological, power, and jural terms such that incumbents of the roles, "peasants," are strongly attached to localities through possession of freeholds.[10] The product of these freeholds must be allocated by the producing and landholding unit, the family-household (a role set whose membership and composition vary in time and place), to itself for its own subsistence and in some degree for exchange, especially in some form of market, except for more or less set quantities in money, kind, or labor. These latter quantities are specified in the role definitions as the incumbents' obligations in the de facto contract with parties external to their number, that is, with occupants of complementary roles in the inclusive role structure. These latter are generally agents or representatives of the state, though they may also, and frequently do, occupy concurrent

[9] The phrase "unascribed and not specifically restricted" refers to an incumbent's entry into a given role neither by birth, by race, nor by some other definitive marker which either permits no occupancy of any alternative role or only of occupancy of a restricted set of roles. Though, in fact, children of peasants tend to be peasants, nevertheless, the crucial thing— mentioned in most discussions of peasants—is the possibility of moving out of the role, e.g., by migration, by day laboring, by upward mobility, by escape to the city. A peasant is, as a person, not fixed by an ascriptive marker to the role, like a slave, a lord, etc.

[10] Note that in societies where different kinds of tenure are distributed, *all* the forms of land tenure require either voluntary or forced compliance of assent of the major sectors of society if endemic civil conflict is to be avoided. The coexistence of different types of tenure *necessarily* implies a historical process of some sort by which interclass, intersitus, or intercorporative conventions about the location and social distribution of such tenure are established. Where a social system is "disturbed" or is evolving quickly under conditions of significant change of major variables—for example, technology—the conventions are also disturbed and changes in the distribution or even in the kinds of tenure occur, as, for example, disappearance of some (e.g., kin corporations) and appearance of others (e.g., limited liability stock companies). Some degree of coercion, explicit or implicit undoubtedly appears in all, or all "more evolved," forms of the state, but degree and locus vary greatly, and the circumstances of the variation are of greatest interest to us. The key point is, however, that a full understanding of any tenure situation always involves a delineation of a relationship between two or more categories of people, and often two (or more) classes, because tenure specifies who is included, who is excluded, who is restricted, and rights are differentiated among members of the two or more categories. In passing, it is well to note that, because of its jural character, land tenure is a function of the state in its public and community aspect, not in its private and class aspect (see passim in text). The implication of this last point for "peasant studies" is far-reaching because it asserts that peasancy cannot be understood without attention to the state and its maintenance and enforcement of the jural and coercive parameters of peasant (or tenant, or serf, etc.) existence.

[117]

roles in private sector role structures, for example, the medieval European case. The distinction here is between quantities paid as taxes in various forms and jural contractual quantities paid as rents (see "tenancy" below) in various forms; accompanying this distinction there are usually also found distinctions in other jural rights and duties. These obligatorily transferred quantities provide resources of a double sort for the other mutually exclusive set of role incumbents not involved in the physical production process, namely, the personnel of the state or one or more of its agencies. First, they provide the resources of subsistence for that personnel; second, they supply the resources with which the state extracts the resources for its own subsistence. Together these are the surplus labor value appropriations of the state which are allocated to its military, administrative, and, in the frequent circumstances where the church is interlocked with the polity, ecclesiastical sectors. Transfers from the state in addition to exchange transfers from the peasantry, determined by its role definitions, specifically movements of produce into some kind of market, provide most of the means of subsistence for urban nucleations of all sorts.

Furthermore, largely as a function of the basic role attributes listed above, secondary attributes follow as extensions (see Meillassoux's argument 1972, about the *necessity* for larger units, where the basic one is a family-household unit). For the aggregate of the role incumbents of the peasancy, there must be an internal organization of great complexity in which are interwoven most of the important societal role structures and their institutions. These include both the affiliational and alliance aspects of kin and juridical, distributional, exchange (as of labor), community, and other institutions, in circumstances where incumbents of peasant roles, "peasants," are *ceded* the right to maintain internal organizations *by convention* with the state (the other "class[es]").[11] This right is exercised until such time as the peasantry is seen as stepping out of bounds; then the right is abrogated and the peasants are crushed.

[11] The role attributes discussed here are those usually referred to in the literature on peasants as their "autonomy" or "self-containedness." Defining this in role terms, however, reinterprets this alleged "autonomy" in terms of special forms of power relations among classes in the society as a whole. What is involved is a very widespread and characteristic form of integration which our ethnocentrism—over-absorption in a particular form of societal integration—prevents us from seeing as structured, as "valid" a form of integration as our own, and one which is possibly quantitatively as integrated, had we measured.

Such internal organizations are observed in *mirs, panchayats,* village communes, *cargo* systems, peasant courts and villages, *communidades,* and so forth,[12] recorded from around the world, all under structurally similar conditions of state and, grossly speaking, in rather similar sorts of society which I have elsewhere called "static agrarian" (Leeds 1964b:1321ff.).

It should be noted, mythos aside, that peasantries in this definition are ineluctably and intricately linked with, responsive to, and causative of a response in the rest of society. They are *not* isolated, they do *not* constitute a "peasant society,"[13] they are *not* inherently out of touch, they are not necessarily stupid and brutish or cunning by nature, they are not necessarily idiots of rural life, nor are they per se, pathetic, subhuman, marginal wretches. If any of these attributes obtains, the reasons must be sought in the interrelationship of the peasancy as a role structure with the external role structures (see Scott 1975, especially 491–93, 530–32).

"Rural proletariat" refers to a category of agricultural roles to which are attached no jural rights to land at all. Duties of the role render incumbents simple mechanical tools in the production machinery whose capital, organization, administration, product, and surplus value are controlled by incumbents of a mutually exclusive category of roles—"landowners," who in aggregate, or collectively, constitute a class. The rural proletariat are wage workers in an organization whose form is the prototype of all mass production organization and, eventually, even of industrial organization, with interchangeable parts, hier-

---

[12] As corporate kin groups, ayllus in Incaic Peru and calpulli in Aztec Mexico redistributed land internally according to demographic and productive changes of the membership of the landholding group. Their internal organization and external relationships were quite different from those of peasantries and characteristic of proto- and archaic states with respect to whose polities the notion of peasantry may be unilluminating or irrelevant—contra Meillassoux 1972, Shanin, and others.

[13] The West has been dominated by two-value logic. One of its major forms is negation of a positive (note Hegel's special version and Freud's use of this logic), or, if A, then $\bar{A}$. Both A and $\bar{A}$ are seen as homogeneous, and by logic of negation are therefore opposites (see Lévi-Strauss's use in the form of "binary opposites"). In fact, however, generally it is not valid logically to read $\bar{A}$ as "including Z and only Z," which is a rephrasing of the logic above. In empirical situations, $\bar{A}$ may be B, C, . . . N. This point applies to the alters of peasants (P), whom we may designate, for some purposes, $\bar{P}$, but may *not* assume that $\bar{P}$ is homogeneous. Further, the negation of $\bar{P}$, that is $\bar{\bar{P}}$, does *not* necessarily mean a homogeneous class, P, but only a given attribute which is not $\bar{\bar{P}}$, but may be $P, A, B, C, . . . N$. Thus, confronting the $\bar{P}$, say lords or landowners or stewards, may be $\bar{\bar{P}}$ consisting of peasants, serfs, migrant workers, etc. (Homans 1942).

[119]

archies of command, and only segmental delegation of authority.[14] Where the rural proletariat have internal organization as a category, it is almost exclusively with respect to the work situation in the form of unions or syndicates, *not* in some pervasive societal organization interweaving all the major institutions of society for their category (maybe "class") as is the case of peasants. The role is *not* assigned, but indeed, is specifically disallowed, and jural rights over the product is appropriated to the exclusive use of the landholders (who may include personnel of the state acting in its private capacity). The rural proletariat are inherently mobile, not being attached by role definition either to any location or person. They generally do not produce their own subsistence (although they may supplement it with a few garden crops and domestic animals in societies or sectors of societies where this is permitted as a role attribute). They do not own any major tools of production. As a consequence of the structure of these basic role attributes, rights, and obligations, they are only segmentally linked with the rest of society through the relationship to the landowner in one role structure, through syndical links in another, through the market relationship (in sale of labor as a commodity) in a third, through purchase of commodities for consumption in a fourth, and so forth, that is, they operate *in* societies and can only be understood in terms of a society with differentiated, segmented, and semiautonomous role structures.

"Farmers" refers to a category of agricultural roles which include jural rights of ownership of land as freeholds, which the role incumbents use for production. At the same time, the role definition specifies that the role incumbents are to be the physical producers of the agrarian materials, the administrative authority over production and marketing, and the capital investment agent. Farmers correspond more closely than any other form of agrarian labor to the notion of a firm or enterprise making allocational decisions for profit. The enterprise, located in the farmer role and role set, has jural rights to its own

[14] Some form of mass, machinelike labor—whether rural proletariats, slaves, or serfs—appears to have existed for at least 2,300 years since the great latifundia of Alexandrian Egypt, described in Westermann's studies (1929, 1955) of estate management of that era. Such a mass of interchangeable parts was one element in a major, characteristic form of organization for production, occurring around the Mediterranean from southern Portugal to the Levant. The latifundium organization as developed in Alexandrian Egypt, Rome, and later in southern Iberia was transferred to the New World where it became the dominant form of agricultural exploitation, at least in Latin America. See in this connection Mumford's treatment of the organization of men-in-the-mass as machines from early dynastic (pyramid-building) Egypt on (Mumford 1967).

product and to the profits from its alienation. The firm in question is basically a family-household unit (a role set), sometimes with secondary additions, which serves as the central unit of production (as in peasancy) but may, as an allocating firm exchanging in a money market, also buy labor as a commodity or buy capital goods to replace labor.

Internal organization of the farmer category is not inherently a part of the definition of the role, but rather is incidental and situational, varies with external conditions, and functions to serve specific domains of interest to the farmer taken in respect to different attributes of the farmer role: as producer, as marketer, as landowner, and so forth, but not as a class as such, (e.g., in the United States, the Grange, the Farmers' Union, the Farm Bureau, etc.). Farmers are thus segmentally integrated with the society through their concurrent occupancy of producer's, administrator's, capitalist's, consumer's, and citizen's roles separately attached to societal role structures, although in their roles as residents of localities they integrate with community role structures somewhat as peasants do. Formally, their organizational relationship to the society as a whole is more like that of a rural proletariat than that of a peasantry, except in the sphere of community connections. The products of the farmers' operations are their own private alienable property (an attribute of the role) as are the means of producing it, the land, and most of the tools. Their subsistence is partly or largely obtained in indirect exchange for their product though not necessarily so (even not in the United States today, much myth to the contrary notwithstanding). They tend to be geographically fixed for indefinite periods, usually, but not by role definition, except insofar as land is heritable in kin lines cross-generationally.

"Tenancy" refers to any of a variety of agrarian labor roles in which producers pay rents (cash, various sorts of crop-sharings, or labor) in contractual exchange for some sort of right to use the land to produce for their own subsistence or possibly to sell in a market. At best, the tenant has only a partial jural control over his own product. An immense array of empirical variation is subsumed under the key complementary exchange of rents for rights. Rights may be jural or customary, heritable or not so; tools, seed, or other supplies may be provided by the landholder in return for added rent compensation, or the tenant may have his own; percentages of shares to be paid as rent vary greatly; amounts of labor to be "given" vary widely; the tenant may be, and very often is, an individual incumbent of the role, but he may also

[121]

be a corporate body or a representative of a corporation, such as a village community, as in the West Irish rundale tenancy by lease; and tenants may have long-term security or may be almost totally insecure like the Irish tenants-at-will. [15] In all cases the tenancy role is unintelligible without describing its alter, the landowners' complementary role. It is of utmost importance to recognize in this connection that from the landowner's point of view there may be *several* alters, only one of which involves tenants; others may involve peasants, the rural proletariat, serfs, and so forth, and sometimes several concurrently (see n. 13 and, for example, n. 14 and the last section of this essay). This situation again indicates the mythic character of the concept "peasant society." [16]

The producing unit is generally, as with peasants and farmers, a family-household, individual members of which may enter coterminously into other types of role, for example, as laborers, or rural proletariats, urban laborers, and so on. Again as with farmers, organization is not an inherent part of the role definition, but, rather, situational.

The role relation of tenants to the total society is, thus, highly segmentary, mediated partly through landlords, partly and separately through informal ties, and partly, though relatively infrequently and almost always against strong opposition, through organizations of "class" interest such as tenants' associations. These role relations are determined by the nature of tenancy itself. Tenants tend to be less mobile than rural proletariats but more so than peasants.

"Squatting" refers to a role by which agrarian laborers, with no jural

[15] For a classic case of tenancy and rural proletarian labor and combinations of both, see Ireland under English rule, especially before the famine of 1845–48 (Woodham-Smith 1962; Almquist 1975). The insecurity, short-termness, segmentariness of relationship, only partial jural control over the laborer's product by the laborer, etc., are all dismally clear, except perhaps in the case of rundale tenure.

[16] Note, for example, the variety of roles, of forms of labor, standing over against the central controllers of the agrarian production units in question (royal properties) reported in the "Capitulaire de Villis" (from *Monumenta Germaine Historica: Leges II*, 1, 1883, selected excerpts by Contemporary Civilization Staff, 1946). The roles include tenants, serfs, freemen, and other forms. See quite as complex an array of labor forms standing over against the central administration of the ninth-century monastery of Saint Germain des Prés. The long-range tendency was to transform almost all of these into serfs, but the range still existed centuries later, for example, as reported in Homans 1942. One wonders about attempts like Thorner's to classify any society or economy as "peasant" if it has more than 50 percent peasants (1962). Surely, such efforts are statistically meaningless and even more meaningless socially while they obscure varieties of role-links and institutional relationships of great significance.

rights to the land they occupy and use with their own tools, produce their own subsistence and often some minor exchangeable crop. The producing unit is the family-household, living on the land without paying rent to the jural owner(s). Squatters tend to locate in a transitory manner, sometimes by tacit convention with the jural holder of the land, for shorter or longer periods, except under frontier conditions. They are without internal organization as a category and are poorly linked with the total society, even with the landowner; that is, they are marginal and isolated. Squatters too have been referred to, in the same pathetic strain as is so often used for "peasants" in general, as "poor peasants" or the like, although, as conceived here, they should not be conceived as peasants at all.

"Job contract" refers to a role relationship involving agricultural workers who contract with an owner of, or other person with access to, land to do a certain job of production in a certain period of time. In return they receive either pay or the use of a piece of the land for their subsistence or both. As a category they are not characterized by internal organization. The producing unit is the contractor and perhaps incidentally his family-household. His linkage with the society in his role as contractor is highly segmental and partial, as well as rather spasmodic. Generally contractors own their own tools, at least the minor ones.[17] The job contractor is not tied to any particular piece of land nor even necessarily to a given area, although the latter is frequently the case, depending on the kind of contract, its technology, and its ecological aspects, for example, the owner of a combine in wheat areas of the United States.

"Serf" refers to those roles by which persons and their descendants who provide agricultural labor are to be attached to given pieces of land, even when the ownership or stewardship of the land may change hands. Incumbents of such roles are to reproduce themselves, that is, provide new role incumbents. What this role relationship does is to guarantee relatively predictable amounts of labor adjusted to relatively well-known productivities and areas of land for the incumbents of roles external to the category of agrarian laborers, that is, either to the state landholder, the private landholder, some fusion of both, or

---

[17] In the Midwest of the United States and elsewhere, persons who have accumulated substantial capital have been able to purchase very expensive machines such as threshers and combines. During the harvest season, they service farms throughout the area. The farmers pay for the service but do not have to (or cannot) buy the huge equipment. The contractors are obviously tied to the area by the relationship of their machines to the crops.

their representatives. In return the role definition cedes the right of self-maintenance to the serf as part of a de facto contract. Serfs, thereby, also act as subsistence agriculturalists and, indeed, are guaranteed land use for this purpose. Other obligations may be extracted from serfs in payment for this beneficence (e.g., *jus primae noctis*), but the serf, in contrast to, say, the tenant or the rural laborer, has a certain jural minimum of security or protection including the use of the land,[18] which in contrast with peasancy is not his to alienate. The unit of physical production is the family-household or its extensions.

The serf does not have direct jural rights over the land, his labor, or his produce, all of which are appropriated by an exclusive class of role incumbents who also provide the major linkages with the larger society. The internal organization of the serf category appears to vary with the intensity and directness of control and supervision by the administrative class, such control ranging from a relatively autonomous internal community governance through a high degree of segmentation and reduction to individual isolation. I would suspect that the degree of control and supervision is itself connected with the nature of the linkage of the administrative production unit (the manor, the latifundio, etc.) with markets, urban nucleations, even other polities, and monetarized systems of exchange (Smith 1975); the greater the linkage with any or all of these, the more intense the control and the greater the internal segmentation of the serfs and the isolation of individual units of physical agrarian production.

"Slave" refers to a set of roles by which persons who are to provide the physical agricultural labor and their descendants are to be attached to an owner of land or capital and are to move with that owner if he changes localities or capital uses. Unlike serfs slaves are also commodities with no jural rights that fix them to a given owner or place; that is, they can be sold or exchanged. As commodities it is not intrinsically part of their role definition that they reproduce themselves, although in some conditions this may be a desired state of affairs in the long run.[19] It is not part of the role definition as such, because if it were, it would involve capital investment in "human resources," that

[18] It is interesting to note that where the state (almost inevitably bourgeois) has undertaken to "free" serfs or persons tied to communally held lands, the position of the serf or "emancipated" "peasant" has deteriorated—as in Mexico in the latter half of the nineteenth century and in Russia.

[19] Slave labor is adaptive to a system of production involving cycles and other kinds of unsteady states over long runs because one can divest oneself of, or take on, extra unit-workers (assuming the capital is available). The ecology of slavery seems to me different from that of serfdom, involving, typically, for the former, monocropping, subject to long-term

is, maintenance of women and children largely by the owner, in a de facto contractual exchange for labor, much of the subsistence coming from outside the administrative production unit. Here is a cost accounting quite unlike the situation with serfs or possibly tenants, that is, measurement of the cost of raising a slave against the long-term labor profits, the stability of the market, and the possible gain from selling the slave, raised as a commodity, on the market for labor. In any formal definition of the slave role, internal organization of the category is absent—if slaves organize it is essentially by operating outside the role definition, under great constraint, or escaping from the localities of their enslavement (as in Palmares in Brazil). Definition of the slave role has to do with their labor power, not inherently with their persons; thus in some slave systems slaves may have jural rights as persons even where they have none as labor, that is, they may have redress for ills visited on their persons. In extreme cases of slavery even the personal jural rights are denied by incumbents of the role structures external to, and owning, them.

Variability of Agrarian Labor Forms in Society

In the preceding discussion, a number of points are interwoven which would be made explicit although only cursory treatment is possible here.

First is the more or less obvious distinction between the physical producing unit and the administrative production unit. The two units are more or less coterminous for peasants, farmers, and squatters, but are quite distinct for slaves, serfs, the rural proletariat, job contractors, and tenants of many types. Forms of labor,[20] then, and the various ways they are organized into a production system are not

---

ecosystemic effects such as soil depletion, erosion, etc., as well as cyclical market rises and falls in price; while for the latter, there is multicropping with fallowing and rotational systems tending, generally, to regenerate land, and a minimal subjugation to price vagaries. This is especially so as the unit of labor is the slave individual, most characteristically in gang-labor form (even when both sexes may be used), rather than any household unit. The household division of labor is not advantageous for this sort of labor organization closely linked with large-scale monoculture.

[20] I shall use the term "forms of labor" as more familiar and simpler than some unwieldy phrase such as "agrarian productive labor role and role set with their respective definitions" which I used in the preceding technical exposition, addressed to the theoretical perspectives which underlie my thinking about case materials. Such perspectives are usually not detailed in a case study but assumed as understood—usually with much resulting ambiguity. The technical exposition will be presupposed in, and subsumed under, "forms of labor."

[125]

identical. More fundamental than the forms of labor for the study of history, societal dynamics, social relations, and the like, is the distribution of these forms in a society; the study of the various choices made among conceivable alternatives in the organization of labor in production, rather than the self-contained study of one of the forms such as, say, peasancy. Such arbitrary singling out of the one has as a consequence the mythos of "peasant societies," "peasant economies" (see Thorner 1962), and so forth. Further, emphasis has been on the productive aspects of agrarian organization rather than on its administrative or distributional aspects. Attention to these latter would inevitably have led into role structures which include not only such role sets as peasantries, but also large landowners, merchants, state distribution systems, and so on, and into several possible alters for each of them comprising other role sets such as tenancy.

Second, though the scale of the enterprise has played a considerable role in discussing peasancy, it has not been directly mentioned in the role definitions above. It is not clear what the significance of scale is if it is used as a measure without comparison, as in the sentence, "peasant production units are small scale." The problem is twofold. On one hand, without a comparison for a standard one cannot establish what the scale is, and, with the comparison, one has immediately indicated an agrarian structure which is multiplex and not comprehensible only in terms of those personnel that can be designated as peasants alone. In the latter case, the significance of scale lies minimally in the producing unit per se, but much more basically in the social institutions of land allocation to various role sets. The range of scales does not inhere in the producers but in the societal system of the distribution of the means of production. On the other hand, even if one can establish what the scale is, what it signifies is still unclear. Scale, per se, seems to generate no propositions. Significant propositions only derive from connecting scale to something else, for example, competition in a market, but the effect here, again, is to link the scale to much more significant features of the situation.

The issue of scale has been even more clouded by the failure to concentrate attention on the administrative aspect of production units discussed above, especially of peasant units; different forms of administration require different scales, even though means and tools of production are alike. The scale of production may be a function of the forms of administration, and the distribution of the forms of administration are almost certainly functions of societal institutions. Further, scale as a measure is not restricted, of course, to peasant units but applies also to farmers, squatters, and even plantation owners and tenants. What appears to be significant is not the scale of peasant enterprises per se, but the range of the scale in comparison to the ranges of scale of the forms of agrarian enterprise occurring either independently or in some hierarchic arrangements (e.g., serfs and peasants, both administering their own units, and agrarian laborers, all subsumed under a centralized manorial administration). The contrasting ranges indicate differential access to means of production and wealth. They may also be indexes of the relative rates at which surplus value is appropriated—the greater the appropriation by incumbents of role sets external to the physical agrarian producers, the smaller the scale.

Put another way, the treatment of agrarian labor in terms of role definitions throws a different light on the problem of scale. Scale becomes interpretable as a result of constraints exercised on the behaviors entailed by the roles or role sets in question, that is, by *external* role structures, the state, a landowning class, and so forth, rather than as an inherent aspect of the "peasant economy," based on technology, access to capital, and the labor group. In fact, each of these, especially technology and access to capital, are largely *externally* constrained, either directly by the role definition and its formal or de facto contracts or indirectly as a function of the role relationships between the agrarian labor roles and the external roles. The technological and capital access aspects seem to me to be two major variables determining the nature of the labor group. If they develop radically, the labor group will change accordingly; for example, family-household peasant production units will begin to hire hands and become "large peasants" such as *kulaks*. Other major variables include the forms of articulation between agrarian production and surplus value appropriation. In this view, scale is a rather minor measure of limited value in examining the types in which we are interested; more interesting are the stimuli to, and constraints against, change in scale in the perspective of role incumbents in the society, complementing those in agrarian productive roles.

Third are the differential relations in, and effects on, the society and its infrastructure of the various role sets defined above. These relations and effects can only be suggested here but seem important for further exploration. In the first instance, each of the role structures of agrarian labor appears to involve quite different degrees of control over, or facility for exploitation of, the laboring population involved. These differences are functions of the role definitions, that is, necessarily of the *relations of different categories of persons* in the role organization of the inclusive society. What permits such variation in degree of exploitation to be built into role definitions seems to me a central problem of inquiry, though beyond the scope of this essay. What, for example, are the constraints which prevent a dominant exploiting class not only from maximizing exploitation but from reducing all forms of labor within the society to that form which most maximizes exploitation? The fact that this apparently never happens requires explanation.

In the second instance, each of these societal role structures of labor seems to produce different ecological effects, as I have suggested elsewhere (see n. 19). One observes the contrast between, on one hand, the devastating ecosystemic effects of slavery, as in the southern United States and in the Brazilian Northeast where gully and sheet erosion, leaching, and laterization have gone on for hundreds of years reducing fertility and even the regenerational capacity of the soil, and, on the other, the relatively soil-maintaining socio-technological systems in serf and peasant agricultural production. Tenancy, especially in its extreme forms such as in Ireland in the century before the great famine of 1845–48, tends to be equally devastating because it minimizes improvements, investments, and any long-term interest on the part of the tenant and fosters a kind of monocropism (Woodham-Smith 1962:15ff., 26ff., 31). Mass rural proletarian labor also tends to be destructive because it is unconcerned with the regeneration, or even maintenance, of the agrarian bases since it has no interests in the land or the productive matériel (Leeds 1957, chap. 3).

In the third instance, each labor type has a different relationship to the urban system and the urbanization process both in terms of how agrarian produce is channeled to support the towns and in terms of the channeling of personnel from the countryside to the urban nucleations. Also the various types involve differential effectiveness of the towns in dealing with the countryside. Note, for example, that one of the functions of serfdom, whether purposefully originated or not, was to prevent the movement of persons from countryside to towns, a situation not jurally true of slavery although largely so, de facto. With overwhelming city dominance in society, serfdom is no longer viable and virtually disappears. Each labor form—that is, each production system—involves different relations to investment in cities (Marx 1850–52).

Fourth, the exercise of looking at the forms of agricultural labor in terms of role definitions instead of in terms of persons has several interesting results. It becomes quite clear at once that from the point of view of any given *individual* the roles or forms I have defined here are not mutually exclusive unless the role definition itself is so phrased as to make it impossible for an individual to hold two of the roles concurrently. From the point of view of the physical producing unit, especially the family-household, this nonexclusiveness is even more the case, since the role held by one member of that unit does not necessarily determine the role of the others unless the roles so specify (e.g., a child of a serf shall be a serf). The exception—its occurrence requires explanation—is where the roles involve descent and/or affinality as part of their definition, as is usually the case with slaves and serfs. In most of the other cases persons can shift from one role to another, do so cross-generationally, move out of the entire congeries of roles, or, sometimes, hold two or more of the roles concurrently, or, perhaps still more frequently, shift back and forth. The questions of the frequency of these patterns and the conditions under which they occurs thus become major ones. They lead one promptly to an analysis of the larger societal system and its role structures and dynamics. Put inversely, fixity in role needs to be explained as much as mobility, although in most of the literature on peasantries, as part of the mythos, fixity is simply taken as an axiomatic consequence of a prior Peasant State of Being in which persons exist by nature rather than by social process.

Finally, a comment concerning the degree to which the various agricultural labor forms are alternatives. This seems to me to be a question absolutely crucial to all discussions of peasantries and agrarian systems in general, especially as it involves the stances one is to take regarding causality and determinism, or in my view the overdeterminism that appears in much of the literature. Impressionistically, at this point, it appears to me that there is some degree of freedom with respect to the forms of labor which may exist in a given society; the forms are not somehow inherently determined for any given array of technological, ecological, and social inputs. Put another way, there are options or at least degrees of option. The observed forms of labor and their incidences are *tendencies* rather than absolutes, even where the incidences approach one hundred percent. As tendencies, the forms can shift direction, be changed, or vary their own internal structuring (see Saul and Woods 1971 for a clear example). These tendencies and their changes are governed by considerations as, say, relative economic cost, control problems, administrative problems, coercive force available, humanitarian ideologies, the political pressures of humanitarian social groups like the church or abolitionists, and so on.

The question of degree of freedom relates directly to the question of the *linearity* of the evolution of forms. I suspect that the degree of freedom is limited by the scale, complexity, and intellectual difficulty of the technology and by the degree to which any producing unit is attached to external sources for inputs. But even with such constraints varying organizations generally seem possible. That the literature so often speaks as if only one kind of organization were possible is another symptom of the essentialism, the Platonism, which underlies so much of the thinking on peasants, from definitions through typologies to characterizations.

The Brazilian Cocoa Region: Complexities of an Agrarian Labor System

In what follows I turn to the cocoa-producing region of the States of Bahia, mainly, and Espíritu Santo, Brazil, in order to look at the productive and administrative systems in terms of the preceding considerations.[21] The focal idea to be illustrated is that the total agrarian labor system is quite complex, composed of a number of interdependent categories of labor with a considerable amount of shifting among forms at any given time and a drastic shift of forms historically. Any single categorization of the labor of the region as consisting of "rural proletarian production units" in "latifundist administrative units" is misleading because it hides both the historical and present dynamics of production, labor absorption (or extrusion), and administration and would completely obscure both the present social order and insight into future trends.

---

[21] The following account is based on Leeds 1957 and on my visit to the cocoa zone in December 1969.

The following forms of labor are found today in the cocoa zone: a preponderant rural proletariat, a minuscule peasantry, a small number of squatters, and a small number of job contractors. Tenants are absent or negligible, although it is a form very prevalent elsewhere in Brazil. Serfdom never existed in the cocoa zone and slavery was formally abolished throughout Brazil in 1888. This subject is revisited below.

For a year or two near the turn of the century the Brazilian cocoa zone was the world's leading producer of cocoa. By the 1940s and 1950s it had dropped to second place, and today it wavers between third and fourth place, having been surpassed by Ghana, Nigeria, and the Ivory Coast. Brazil's present production ranges between 150,000 and 170,000 tons a year, whereas Ghana's has gone as high as 600,000 to 700,000. Bahia's cocoa output is grown on land with approximately 1,000 trees per hectare, each tree, excepting those in a very few modern orchards today, yielding on the average less than half a pound. It can readily be seen that planting, upkeep, and harvesting of roughly half a billion trees requires an immense mass labor force, especially at crop time, as no cocoa-producing area has yet developed really effective machinery for any phase of production. The crop is bimodal, the peaks occurring approximately in May–June (*temporão*) and August–October (*safra*), although March, April, July, and November also involve substantial collecting of the fruit. The slack months are from December through February, the southern hemisphere's summer, when the trees flower and set new fruit. This season is used for weeding orchards, pruning trees, repairing mule trails, equipment, and buildings, preparing new areas for planting, planting trees, and so forth. But even with all these activities, labor needs—hence absorption—tend to be considerably less than in the harvest season.

The entire area is dominated by cocoa. Only the river flats and the coastal strip are not suited to cocoa. The former are used for pastures for mules and for some cattle. The latter has considerable numbers of coconut trees. The usual Brazilian tropical crops—manioc, beans, yams, corn—all will grow there, but the great preponderance of these staples, as well as wheat or wheat-manioc flour for bread, is imported from elsewhere. Rubber trees will also grow successfully.

Cattle, subsistence crops, and rubber provide alternatives to cocoa's dominance, but because of cocoa's historical economic preeminence, due to its relatively greater profitability in the area, these alternatives are still peripheral. Cattle are also geographically peripheral in that they increase in number as one goes west and upward to altitudes, temperatures, rainfalls, and soil types less and less suited to cocoa, and which thus ring the cocoa producing zone.

At the time of my fieldwork in 1952, rubber was of commercial value in only one area, where it was planted in lands appropriate also to cocoa, although another very large tract had been started a year or two earlier in another area to the south. By 1969 when I returned, the area planted in rubber had grown considerably, and apparently continues to do so, but still amounts to only a few tens of thousands of acres at most, partly because planters had encountered technical difficulties, such as rubber tree diseases, in the intervening years.

Subsistence crops are internally highly peripheral and are restricted mostly to small plots of land interstitially scattered among great latifundia, at the edges of the ever-decreasing virgin jungle, on the inland edge of the coastal strip, on the lower-lying lands near lakes and rivers, and in transportationally more remote areas. They are ever fewer, existing largely as residuals of an earlier era (see below). Subsistence crops are also grown in tiny patches by landless laborers on those latifundia whose owners or managers permit them to do so. Many owners will not permit them, on the grounds that such crop growing absorbs cocoa-growing lands or that it lessens the dependency of the worker on the administration or the company store.

Aside from the tiny garden patches that an individual rural proletarian may make, what subsistence crops are grown are grown largely by peasants, that is, freeholders operating with family labor and administering their own enterprises. In the cocoa zone, these people are called *burareiros* and their titled freeholds *buraras*. As indicated, they are scattered here and there and almost always are not contiguous to each other but "autonomous" and "self-contained" as production and social units. Buraras are relatively few in number, at most a few thousand all told. I would guess their total population, including all household members, at maximum to be on the order of 30,000 to 40,000 (4.6%–6.1% of the area's population), although no census built around this category exists. The burareiro has his animals—mules, pigs, and chickens—and raises manioc, other edibles, and usually also some cocoa. He sells some manioc either as root or in the form of flour which he has made with his own equipment, and he sells the cocoa. With the proceeds he buys what he needs: cloth, clothing, machetes, supplies, some foods. Often the purchasing is done at a neighboring *fazenda* (latifundium or plantation) store at jacked-up prices, with the result that he gets less in return for his produce than if he bought in the towns. Money may actually never be used in the exchange since the store may simply barter goods for his manioc or cocoa. Because of the peripheral location of buraras, they tend to be dependent on, and exploited by, the fazendas, more especially so because the burareiros are generally illiterate.[22] Sometimes members of the burara family will work seasonally or otherwise on the fazendas. Thus the buraras function as a reserve labor pool, as secondary suppliers of food material (mostly imported from other parts of Brazil) for workers on the plantations, and as very minor producers of cocoa, often funneled out through the fazendeiros to the latter's advantage.

Thus, in sum, there are peasants but not properly a peasantry. There are no peasant communities; replenishment of peasant personnel may be from workers on fazendas, from squatters, from town lower-class people, but not necessarily from other peasants, of whom they are unlikely to know more than a very few. The buraras are largely semiautonomous appendages of the fazendas, with labor functions which can only be fully understood in terms of them, since, concurrently or at different times, various members of the family-household can occupy roles as rural proletarians, peasant dependents, job contractors, and so forth. It is to be noted that classifying these family-households as "peasant" is likely to be both erroneous and misleading, even though the title holder may be more or less consistently a "peasant."

Squatters (*posseiros, roceiros*) may be as numerous as peasants, but again it is not a census category. Squatters find areas of land which are essentially unused and, either with or without permission of the owner, set up householding and subsistence production there. If without the owner's permission, it is probably the case that the squatter has inquired around the neighborhood as to the degree of supervision, that is, the regularity of absence of the owner or his administrator if he has one. Finding the area essentially free of surveillance he buries himself in it, cuts his plot out of the forest, and behaves much like a burareiro, although probably even less commercially since he is less well established, has no official tenure, and in the course of events

[22] The peripherality is, of course, in no sense absolute, but relative to the particular historical situation in which all the role structures that are central to the economy and their territorial localizations in land tenure marginalize, and, therefore, isolate the peasants and their holdings. In other historical conditions, such role incumbents and their holdings might comprise the central role structures of the economy.

probably will have to move. Thus he makes less of a permanent capital investment than the burareiro.

If the owner gives his permission, a kind of contract may be established whereby the squatter uses the plot for a relatively prolonged period, say five to seven years, for his subsistence needs, plants cocoa, and moves on, perhaps, to another plot on the same fazenda when the cocoa has come in to production so that the regular gang work of harvesting and orchard care can go on without impediment from the squatter's family's use of land and labor for subsistence.

In both cases the squatter brings land under cultivation by tearing down jungle. The squatter with permission also converts that reclaimed area into orchards. Thus the fazendeiro, by means of an informal long-term contract, gets one basic task of the fazenda done, planting, although he rarely relies on the squatter alone for this; he also uses his laborers and may also use a job contractor (see below). The advantage to the fazendeiro is that it costs him nothing; he loses nothing, he thinks,[23] during the five to seven years the cocoa trees take to come into production, and he may even feel that he has done a humanitarian act by his patronage, by giving a family a place to set up house and household for a long period.

It is impossible to estimate the number of job contractors (*empreiteiros*), which varies by season, year, and area and which is sensitive, I suspect, to the price conditions of the cocoa market. When or where prices are low and economic activity relatively stagnant, laborers look for fixed, regularly paid positions, not for casual but better-paid contracts; if the market is expanding, the reverse takes place. A contractor offers his services to do a piece of work in a given time—he is essentially a piece worker—in return for a certain payment. A typical contract is to plant or clean an orchard, a matter of one or two month's work perhaps. If the land situation is propitious and the duration of the contract sufficient, he may also be able to plant subsistence crops, but this activity is extremely marginal. Job contract labor tends not to be family labor, but that of a single man. If he has a family, it

---

[23] Actually, unless, as is infrequently the case, he both specifies how he wants the cocoa planted and supervises the planting, he is likely to end up with more of the ad hoc orchards in disarray, essentially unselected, and more difficult to administer than those he inherited from his predecessors. The squatter tends to plant on a purely "empirical" (*empírico*) basis and where convenient to him, rather than to do organized plantation work. Squatters tend to be associated with less rigorously run large plantations rather than with the efficient agribusiness plantations.

may be located on a fazenda, a squatter plot, a burara, in two or more of these, or even in town, and he eventually returns to one of them.

The final category of labor is the rural proletariat, constituting by far the preponderant form of labor and a major part of the cocoa zone population, perhaps, in 1951-52, on the order of 200,000 to 250,000 persons including family members, or about one-third of the total population, towns included. Although women and even children occasionally participate as paid labor at reduced pay scales, mostly at the peak of the harvest, the rural proletariat consists essentially of adult males (sixteen or seventeen and upward), owning their own machetes but no other tools. All major tools and installations, of course, belong to the landowner as part of his capital investment. The rural proletarians work under a de facto contract from the plantation owner or his representative, the administrator (*administrador*) or manager (*gerente*), the latter being a higher position restricted to large and internally complexly organized agribusiness plantations. Each worker is part of a larger aggregate, the *operários*, who are the bottom level of a more or less graded hierarchy of command and supervision.

Officially, the workers—unlike job contractors, burareiros, posseiros, roceiros—are under national labor law, receiving national minimum salary, paid holidays, social welfare benefits, and the like. The actual situation of workers ranges from actual fulfillment of these conditions—a rarity existent only on the best-run, most businesslike plantations, usually with records of high productivity—to debt bondage with nonobservance of any holidays and total absence of fulfillment of social welfare benefits. The latter situation was quite frequent in 1951–52, though it has somewhat improved in the intervening quarter century because of action taken by the national government.[24] The most frequent situation was payment well below minimum salary, occasional observance of holidays, and some help, patronally handled, in cases of sickness or death. It should be noted that national law allowed fazendeiros to subtract rent for the housing ("hovels" generally is an appropriate term although some had decent housing of two to four rooms for families) provided for workers, a right the fazendeiros

---

[24] The government created a number of markets and research organizations, encouraged the labor courts to function again, and pushed for minimum salary enforcement. All of these governmental acts are examples of actions on the part of an array of role sets, linked into a complex role structure, external to the one(s) under consideration. The results of such actions are such as to affect the internal conditions of the latter—in this case with the results on labor distribution discussed in the text.

sometimes extended to the patches of ground they allowed workers for planting gardens.

Many fazendeiros did not allow families on the plantation for various reasons. Their chief reason was that it cost them money because families absorbed living space without any useful return in labor; by not having families, one could pack in four times as many laborers in the same space. I would guess that this situation obtained for perhaps half or more of the rural proletariat. The men, then, were at a great disadvantage in terms of family living, child rearing, sexual gratification, and so on. They were forced into characteristic patterns of living involving enormously high use of prostitutes (who comprised 10 percent of the adult women in the town where I lived), a vast drain on scarce funds, abandonment of wives (some of whom then turned to prostitution to make a living), living separately from wives and children who were located in shacks on the edges of town, or simply suffering a bachelor existence far away from the village or town among a group of *companheiros* on the fazenda.

In passing, the peculiar double role of a large percentage of these workers should be underlined. It is a double role jurally established by the incumbents of one of the major external role sets, the government, as a double exploitation: by law they are grossly underpaid as rural workers, with a legal status as such; and legally they are tenants in the houses and garden patches they use on the plantation, though not tenants on the cocoa- or crop-producing land of the same plantation.

In sum, in a *system* of labor roles in which the rural proletariat preponderate, other forms are manipulated by fazendeiros on criteria of cost, land use, tasks to be performed, and occasionally a bit of humanitarianism. The different labor roles—job contractor, squatter, peasant, rural proletarian—are viable only insofar as they are role alters useful to the owners of plantations of varying scale, especially the medium-sized and larger ones. Each individual labor form cannot be adequately understood without reference to all the forms and to the structures of administration of production into which they fit, on one hand, and the state and regional-national economy, on the other. In the system the peasants have a minor role as suppliers of subsistence goods and minor quantities of cocoa and of a reserve of manpower for the other labor roles.

It is important to note that, from the point of view of peasants, first, role alters exist—contra the usual isolational treatment of peasants.

Second, the role alters fall into two major categories: (a) those alter roles into which peasants cannot enter or transform themselves, in essence, "external" or other-class roles—the "ruling classes"; (b) those alter roles into which peasants *can* move, that is, "internal" or like-class roles—the "working class(es)" or some such locution. Third, a peasant's other-class alter roles are not simply reciprocals of his, but also involve an array of alters in their own right; the fazendeiro has not only *all* the forms of agrarian labor as his several other-class role alters, but often also urban labor roles, incumbents of which may frequently be recruited from the rural labor personnel. The general theoretical point is an attack on the simplifying one-to-one reciprocal model of peasant/lord (or equivalent) which has been perpetuated as mythos in those peasant studies which do not isolate the peasants entirely.

The foregoing paragraphs bring us back to the discussion of the independence of role and person. It is quite patent that no *person* in the cocoa zone is ascribed or formally restricted to any of the labor roles; there is no legal or even customary bar to his moving among the roles. This seems to me of the essence in understanding not only the production system of the cocoa zone but also people's coping with the exigencies of life there.

Coping with the structure of society which agrarian laborers confront as persons involves strategies in the manipulation of roles—those directly accessible to them, and, hopefully, those that might become so, for example, by upward or outward mobility. Instead, then, of seeing a person as inherently a social type, as existing in a State of Being—a peasant, say—we are led to ask about his strategies as he sees them, the constraints he faces in putting his strategies to work, and the consequences both for the individual and the aggregate.

The principles of any of the strategies, as a rule, involve maximizing income, maximizing the possibility of family living, maximizing upward mobility possibilities, maximizing security, and maintaining flexibility. Some of these involve contradictions—for example, the larger the family, the less flexible the options. A strategy dedicated to acquiring a piece of land in freehold means maximizing security and family living, generally at the expense of income, upward mobility (except in the rarest cases), and flexibility. At the same time, it provides a base for forays back into the other labor roles for additional cash, particularly for younger members of the family. Working as a wage laborer is generally not so favored unless one can get work on those plantations which (a) allow family living, (b) pay regularly and do not try to exploit

[137]

debt bondage or to charge rents, (c) allow for occasional promotion, (d) do not fire during slack season—that is, guarantee a degree of tenure in the job. But such situations are much more the exception than the rule, so that the very unsatisfactory conditions of most wage employment lead to a constant search for better ones and for alternative labor roles: a vast internal circulation of labor both geographically and through the roles.

A little thought will make clear the sorts of constraints operating. One cannot easily become a peasant for lack of capital to buy a piece of land or to pay to get it titled. Even if one had such capital, one would be constrained by the unavailability of lands under the present distribution of holdings (see history, below); the landholding system as it evolved peripheralized the smallholders.

Constraints on job contracts were discussed above. Probably job contracting is the most desirable form of labor from the point of view of the worker—if he can be guaranteed a regular flow of contracts. But contracts are chancy, depending on the state of the market, the geographic distribution of tasks to be done, competitors looking for contracts, and the informal and accidental nature of information flows. From an income and self-governance point of view, the job contract is desirable, but it is an unreliable system tending to close off in bad times and generate too much competition in good ones.

The constraints on maximization within the wage labor market have been detailed above; there are very few jobs which get remotely near maximizing most of the interests of the workers and the rest tend to do nothing for them or actually to cause their situation to deteriorate.

Evolution of the Cocoa Zone Agrarian Labor System

This system has been in relative equilibrium for some decades now, more or less from the late 1920s till the present. But even in the seventeen years between my fieldwork in 1951–52 and my visit in 1969, slow change has taken place in the same direction that characterized the very rapid changes of landholding and labor organization from the beginnings of the cocoa zone about 1880 to the 1930s and 1940s. The general rule has been the elimination of most smallholders, the peripheralization of the residual ones, and the partial conversion of the several agrarian labor roles into the single one of wage laborer.

Although cocoa, imported from the Amazon, existed in the area at least as early as the mid-1700s, it led a marginal existence in a few plantations near the coast where the old lands push up out of the coastal tertiary deposits near the ancient city of Ilheus (founded 1535?) Cocoa markets began to expand rapidly in the last decades of the nineteenth century and cocoa plantings in Bahia correspondingly increased hastily. What is now the cocoa area was then unsettled jungle, beyond the frontier, so planting meant conquest of the jungle, pushing forward and in (Amado 1942).

It must be recalled, also, that slavery was abolished in Brazil in 1888. Though, by the time of the census of 1872, the slave population of the area had already decreased to about 10 percent of the total population, nevertheless abolition released a significant number of people, many of whom wished to strike out for themselves in the hopes of real independence, possibly even of acquiring wealth by producing for the rapidly expanding cocoa markets—of which they were aware!

Early conquest of the jungle and plantings of cocoa in the interior, then, were closely associated with an infiltration of ex- and possibly escaped slaves and also of freemen from the coastal areas in a pattern of squatting, subsistence agriculture, and cocoa planting under the most difficult circumstances of transportation and communications. Concurrently, but more markedly from the turn of the century on, or even a little later, persons with substantial capital, sufficient to employ numbers of men and open up large tracts all at once, began to move in. The model for occupation was essentially that of the latifundium, which was to employ large numbers of wage workers—a model known from sugar, coffee, cotton, rubber, and other crops which had been the major foci of the Brazilian economy for four hundred years, using slaves and, later, free labor (Leeds 1957, chap. 9).

Thus by 1910 there existed a situation of sharpening competition for the land between what were largely smallholder squatters and the emerging latifundists. Some of the latter came from outside the region; some grew from smallholders. The solution to the competition was expressed in three major forms: (a) land wars, (b) *caxixis*, and (c) purchases (Silva Campos 1947, chaps. 37–41).

The peak of the land wars occurred between about 1912 and 1920. Smallholders were murdered by hired thugs (*jagunços*), or in kinder moments simply driven off, leaving the better lands for the men with the capital to buy arms and hire henchmen. Large owners with jagun-

[139]

ços also fought with other large landowners with *their* jagunço gangs. Some former smallholders became jagunços or paid laborers for the men (or their enemies) who had driven them out. The dispersion of family units of production, indeed sometimes of the families themselves, began at this time.

Caxixí, a local term, means "swindle." These were varied and inventive. The great majority were to the advantage of the large landholders and the literate; many made use of pseudolegalisms as devices for cheating; others involved promises of commissions ("colonelships!") in the military for which the smallholder signed with his X (actually signing a promise to sell his land in exchange for the office); and many other devices. A few *caxixí* involved smallholders' pulling fast ones on large landholders. One case involved a smallholder known to be illiterate who had, as part of his planned cozenage, learned in secret to read and write and used that fact in tricking the large owner's land away.

Purchase requires no comment.

By the late 1920s the present basic arrangement of landholding and labor had been established: most independent smallhold squatters eliminated; some of them converted into peasants, the predominant form being latifundia with the forms of labor already described. It is to be noted that a peasantry, as defined above, never properly existed at all in this region; what there is now is negligible.

Since the 1930s, some further consolidation has occurred. Squatters have become fewer; wage labor more marked. At the same time, some of the smallholdings have slowly tended to convert more and more to cocoa. One way this has become possible is by the expansion of work opportunities in the city so that some burareiros are able to earn money regularly in the city, even living in the town as absentee microlandlords, while accumulating sufficient small capital to permit them to convert their subsistence buraras into cocoa-producing tracts. They thereby enter at the bottom rank in the range of scale of cocoa plantations—as small-scale and relatively inefficient producers, but not peasants. These would correspond more to the category of farmers—family-household, commercially oriented producers, operating as (petty) capitalists, making decisions, allocations, and profits. If successful, they may even hire one or more hands from the proletarian labor pool.

Thus, in sum, the entire structure of labor has become more and more market-oriented, more and more monetarized, while all forms of family-household producing units served a major function only in the phases of opening the region—as a transitional labor device not viable in the long run, given the dominant forms of Brazilian production, capital control, coercion, and governmental policy exercised by incumbents of role structures mutually exclusive with the agrarian labor roles.

The Cocoa Zone as Model for Brazil, Latin America, and Beyond

Without here entering into minutiae, I assert that the pattern described for the cocoa zone has been the dominant one for most of Brazil through most of its history (Leeds 1957, chap. 9). In an economy and society dominated by commercial monoculture, the smallholder and peasant, though he has existed, has always been peripheral, a refuge group, a reserve labor force, and a marginal supplier of foods and produce (Antonil 1711).

In the Brazilian context, where there were or are areas of fairly extensive peasant holdings, they have been economically marginal and of little interest to the state or the larger economy and its personnel.

What has been much more important in certain parts of Brazil, mostly in nonmonocultural areas, has been a variety of forms of tenancy (*parceiros, meieiros*, etc.), which, as I argued above, are quite different in a number of major ways from peasants, particularly in their extreme exploitation in the role relationship with the landowner, in the deteriorative effect on the ecosystem—observed all over Brazil in tenancy areas—and in their sense of class interest reflected in the development of the Ligas Camponesas in the late 1950s and early 1960s—consisting mainly of tenants (Leeds 1964a; Julião 1972).

In general, then, I would urge strongly that Brazil has never had a significant peasantry; what peasants it has had have been increasingly scattered and marginal and numerically reduced. From the point of view of societal process, social conflicts, power relationships, the great categories of agricultural labor of interest have been slaves and their latter-day translation into rural proletariat and tenants. To interpret Brazilian economic and social history in terms of conceptions of peasantries is to distort Brazilian history, social structure, and dynamics—in short, to create a mythic picture.

I believe this principle holds widely for Latin America. Most of the countries, with the exception of some of the densely populated indigenous areas of the highlands, have never been peasant but rather rural proletarian, tenant, or serf-like production systems. Subsistence production has been assigned more to tenants and peasantries, but even then not always, as, for example, on the large self-sufficient haciendas and fazendas all through Latin America, operated with slave or serf-like labor. Where subsistence production has been in the hands of smallholders, fairly elaborate systems of rent, taxation, labor payments (Julião 1972), and other forms of appropriation or even extortion (including looting) have siphoned off surplus value to provide the subsistence of nonagrarian classes and their means of coercively maintaining the system. At the same time, these same classes generated a progression of legal devices to complement their coercive strength which consistently eroded whatever independence the smallholders ever had, converted the more independent ones into greater dependency (e.g., by making tenants out of peasants) or pushing them altogether out of landholding into rural proletariats.

What, in conclusion, I would then urge is that Latin America not be examined in terms of the notion of peasant at all, but rather that one look at it as a dynamic interaction of all forms of agrarian—and even urban—labor as part of a societal power system. From this perspective, one should then ask why a peasantry occurred at all in Latin America—when and where it did. I think the answer to this is that peasantries always had transitional roles to play, as in the opening of new areas, as in providing labor reserves, as in being temporary holders of land while the major institutions of landholding were undergoing pervasive change (as in Mexico in the second half of the nineteenth century). Peasantries, rather than constituting more or less "naturally" evolved populations as in Europe, India, or China, tended rather to be, at crucial times and places, instrumentally created aggregates of people serving rather specific ends of state or emerging indirectly as a function of actions taken by the state or the private sector. In short, the concept of peasantry seems to me one of the less useful categories for understanding the history of Latin American (or, say, African) societal structure and process. Its usefulness for the analysis of other world areas where it has been overwhelmingly applied may also be questioned on the basis of the considerations raised in this essay.

Its use appears to have created interpretations of state societies, structured fundamentally around agrarian resources, which are substantially mythopoeic. At worst, the mythos is pathetic in its simplifications, obscuring social and societal dynamics, distorting actual historical sequences, and eliciting wild overgeneralizations such as Shanin's three stages of human history cited early in the essay.

Where's Boston? 1976. Exterior of building housing the "Where's Boston?" multi-plex slide show during the Bicentennial. Leeds's concern was with ambiguity of image and of viewer's point of reference. (photo by Anthony Leeds)

[4]

Economic-Social Changes and
the Future of the Middle Class

The argument presented in my comments below runs counter to many contemporary views on the middle class in Latin America or, at least, reanalyzes them in such a way as to cast doubt on their usefulness[1] and suggest new descriptive approaches relevant, as well, to the analysis of ethnic groups such as the Jews. Two major sorts of assumptions which I find increasingly either untenable or unuseful inform views concerning the middle classes in Latin America (and other parts of the so-called Third World).

First, there is an often unspoken assumption that, if not all societies, at least the societies under discussion must develop along specific lines in a specific direction—that is, an assumption concerning their unilinear evolution. With respect to the question of middle classes, this implies that, since "advanced" "Western" societies, in the course of their evolution, developed a middle class or middle classes, this development is inherent in societal "advance" and therefore must occur in other societies as they "develop." Thus, all "modernizing" or "developing" societies should, with time and "maturity," look more and more like what is sometimes, ethnocentrically, called "Western Society." This assumption denies the possibility of alternative modes of societal organization, of alternative evolutions under differing conditions of history and structure.[2]

---

[1] Views expressed here are necessarily rather more purely theoretical than might be desirable, but this is not to be helped (a) in the virtual absence of reasonable social science materials on "middle classes"; (b) in the absence of any significant material at all on Jews in Latin America.

[2] Evolutionism of this sort seems to me ethnocentrically metaphysical, rather than based

The second assumption, almost universally made, is that the language of middle class analysis, developed largely in England, France, Germany, and the United States, and fuzzy enough in those places, can be transferred to quite different situations.

More and more, I believe that neither of these assumptions holds, but rather that the evolution of Latin America and other Third World societies can move in several directions, different from each other and different from that of Western Europe, and that this differential evolution involves the production of alternative forms of societal organization, such that the conceptions of middle class development in the analysis of Northwestern European and perhaps North American society cannot be transferred readily or at all. I believe there is a great deal of evidence for this in virtually all aspects of the existence of these societies, whether economic, political, or social.[3] Some of the best evidence comes from Latin America in terms of what has actually been observed happening there, poorly interpreted as it has often been.

The premise (or half-conclusion) of my argument, then, is that such observations ought to lead us to quite different models of these societies as a whole and of "middleness" in particular; models which, with some methodological considerations, I discuss in the passages which follow. This premise is central to the whole question I raise as to whether we can talk in any intelligible sense about a middle class in Latin America. If we cannot, then as a consequence, it is inappropriate to talk about Jews in Latin America being middle class or in a middle class. If it is inappropriate, then we must reconsider the structural position of Jews in Latin American society—or better, societies, since the different countries are quite distinct from each other and seemingly not uniform with respect to the status of Jews or of supposed middle classes.

The difficulty in dealing with the empirical referent of the term "middle class" in Latin American societies has been obliquely recog-

---

on inductive inferences from observation of real world objects, relationships, and process. It is an article of faith, and hence has no place in science. Note a strong unilineal evolutionism in Leeds 1964b, which I tend, now, in large part to reject (see Chapter 8, n.10).

[3] Economists, for example, constantly find they have to modify fairly standard "classical" economic notions in order to cope with the political conditions of the economy in societies such as those here concerning us in which the separation between the polity and the economy is much less sharply marked than it is in the rather rare type of society which evolved in Northwestern Europe—the private enterprise, price-making market society. Likewise, political scientists (e.g., Payne 1965:vii–ix) have had drastically to modify their views of what constitutes a "normal" political system to recognize that there are alternative "normal" systems even when the economies are basically similar.

nized in various ways, sometimes explicitly, sometimes implicitly, in great part by evasions of the term, as, for example, by writing about the "middle sectors." Other phrases serving this evasion include "middle statuses," "middle levels," "middle elements," "middle groups," "middle segments," "middle components," "middle mass." These phrases are evasive because the writers are essentially saying, "Well, I don't want to talk about the 'middle class,' because I'm not convinced there is one; I find I cannot deal with it with conventional conceptions, therefore I'll talk about 'sectors'." This procedure solves no problems, dodges analysis, and evades rigor in specifying empirical content to the conceptual terminology. It is interesting that the collection of terms, including the original "middle class(es)," is not properly analytic at all. None of the terms refers to a unit structurally or functionally delineated, that is, to some delimitable part of some specified whole in Latin America. At best, the terms are scalar (e.g., clearly, in the conception of "middle levels"), designating no *sociologically* interesting sets of relationships; at worst, they are sophisticate translations of essentially Western folk idioms and have no place in social science.

What is at fault is the poverty or absence of analysis regarding the dimensions, variables, or elements that are to be used to specify what is to be meant by "middle"—and, more still, the seeming unawareness that this *is* the problem. This poverty of the literature seems to me quite obvious whether one starts with a collection such as the Pan American Union (PAU) put out on the middle classes in Latin America in the 1950s (Crevanna, ed. 1950–51) or looks at such works as Johnson's (1958, see especially pp. vii–x, 1–3) or Adam's (1967, see pp. 47ff. et passim) and many others. The PAU documents, like the later works, are useful to have as compendia of impressions relevant to more basic analysis, but otherwise are quite useless. They are the more useless as rather far-reaching assertions are based on the suppositious existence of middle classes, sectors, levels, or statuses, for example, that military personnel are of "middle class" origins. The meaning or content of this assertion is never made clear or, worse, is vacuous.

I propose, then, to talk about "middleness" in a particular way. I assert that the concept must have structural (hence functional) meaning if it is to be useful for the analysis of societal dynamics, of action and interaction, or for the prognosis of future conditions, as of, for example, Jews in Latin America. In this instance, by "structure," I mean that those people who, or roles which, are to be designated as "middle" must be divided off as some distinctive subsystem from the

[147]

rest of society (itself divided into other equivalent subsystems such as "proletariats," "elites") by various mechanisms, by definitions of positions (statuses, roles, status and role sets; their rights, duties, prerogatives, and obligations), by social linkages of one sort or another.[4] The dividing off is such that there must be a clearly delimitable group or category of people in society, recognizable by appropriate characteristics and relationships and by systemic action.

In societies classically supposed to have middle classes, a part of this setting of boundaries is organizational in character. For instance, in the case of the United States, one finds an enormous array of associations. One can, I believe, on one hand, quite easily delineate middle-classness by designating a certain range of associations and by specifying the people who are members of them. Further, one can show that members of such associations tend to be linked with persons who hold like positions in similar kinds of associations by other kinds of ties such as kinship as well. On the other hand, by contrast, one can delineate elites by a quite different range of associations and the specifications of their members who occupy quite different positions—say, as example, the central positions of State—and whose members are *not* linked genealogically or by marriage to members of the first set of associations. In short, between the two sets of persons exists a boundary fabricated by associational, genealogical, marital, and, indeed, informal network inclusions and exclusions.

Let me express this differently, using myself as an example,—I think a fairly typical one of middle class America or the intellectual-academic subsegment of it. I belong to a series of professional associations as do most of the members of my kin group. Most of the members of my social networks who are *not* kin also belong to professional and/or business associations[5] such as wholesaler and retailer associa-

---

[4] This definition has certain rather strict methodological implications for empirical research, as will become plainer in the text passages which follow. Basically it sets forth the requirement that one must empirically *map out* the roles and statuses; their set relationships; the associational memberships; the social linkages, networks, genealogies, or nexi; and the mechanism of inclusion and exclusion, of recruitment and extrusion; the boundaries thus established between persons, as well as the inventories of persons involved (for purposes of proof of the existence of the asserted boundaries). See Leeds 1964b, Chapter 5.

[5] These exclude corner candy stores, small household concerns, self-employed agents like artisans but rather are associated with wholesale and retail networks and businesses of a certain minimal scale upward, linked into significant distribution functions in localities. The scale of the business and the significance to local distribution operate as boundary designators to exclude small operators, leaving the latter unprotected and at a competitive disadvantage with respect to the businesses of a certain minimal scale upward—a *class* difference.

tions and semicommunity businessmen's clubs like the Lions and the Rotary which also influence the business policies of local communities. Still another category of associations comprises the cultural ones (such as museums, choral groups, movie clubs, theater groups, etc.), whose *memberships* (as opposed, often, to boards of directors) overlap with those in the professional and/or business associations.[6] Scarcely any members of my genealogical or nongenealogical networks, or, to my knowledge, of those of my associates have any significant or lasting linkages[7] whatsoever with the powers that be in the United States (even if, occasionally, we have met individual powers). We are fairly systematically excluded from such power networks either by our own memberships, our own self-exclusions, our own ideologies or by their controls over resources and their associational recruitment controls (e.g., the Social Register). At the same time, we have virtually no significant or lasting links with the proletariat or the "working class," or whatever the current American phraseology is.

Two points are worth noting respecting the above. First is the phe-nomenon, repeatedly experienced, which we express by the phrase, "What a small world it is!" This always refers to the surprise we feel when, meeting someone new, we find a series of connecting friends, acquaintances, or even kin; when, meeting someone we know in unex-pected contexts, we discover the connection between the usual and unusual contexts through intermediary personal or associational links; when various circles of connections, circumstances, and positions

[6] The matter of membership vs. board stratification requires the formulation of both more generalized and precise models, as well as further empirical research and structural analysis, with special reference, in description of the internal organization of associations, to the power and role relationships which are manipulated by boards to maintain boundaries between themselves and the membership (see, in this connection, Burnham 1942).

[7] "Significant" and "lasting" can be given quantifiable or semiquantifiable empirical con-tent. Significance can be measured in terms of the types of major transactions and the numbers of each which take place between two positions. The significance of my relationship with, say, David Rockefeller could be measured by whether we exchanged political, finan-cial, administrative, marital, critical informational, and other substantial resources and by the frequency with which we did so. "Lasting" refers to the length of time over which such transactions continue. Thus, though I may have met Rockefeller, without some significant transaction of the types listed, no breaching of the class boundary has occurred or, more significantly, the strength of that boundary is emphasized. One-shot transactions, even if of considerable scale, tend also to emphasize distance and the control exercised by the more resource-laden party. Lasting relationships without significant transactions, e.g., purely social contact, also emphasize the class barrier. To these two criteria, one might add "direc-tion" of the major flow of resources in the transactions. If they are consistently in one direction, as, say, from Rockefeller to me, the class boundary is again emphasized. See Mitchell, ed. 1969; Chapter 5.

illuminate the "astonishing" closedness of the networks we move in, even in societies of scores of millions of people. What is interesting about all the people involved in these cases is the likeness of their positions, their associational memberships, their ranges of activities, and the degree to which they stand over against other aggregates of people, such as "the working class" or "the ruling class," if one happens to be "middle class."

Second is the question of the mobility of persons from one such organized category (or "class") of people to another. The *fact* of organization does not preclude a degree of mobility of individuals among the "classes." It is only requisite, to be able to speak of "classes," that there be a relatively reduced (if widely varying) degree of such mobility. Mobility cannot be total because then one could not, logically or empirically, distinguish any category from any other; it could, however, be completely absent, though factually this has never been the case, even in the instance of castes or estates. What is, perhaps, more important than this variable degree of mobility is the tendency of the mobile person (or group which moves with him or of itself) to unhook the old links as he (or they) hook into the new links of the associations and networks of the category of people into which he moves. The last of the old links to yield are the kinship ties and even these ties tend to disappear in a progression from, first, distant collaterals through close collaterals, to, last, primary relatives. As the latter die off, the mobile person tends to be totally dissociated from his old ties, totally hooked into his new class. Sometimes, this occurs only in the generation of the children of the mobile person or group.

Related to both of these points, as a kind of corollary, is the fact that the networks turn back on themselves (that is, lead back to coordinate positions and associations filled with persons who could, in principle, be replaced by those persons from whom one starts tracing the networks), rather than lead to the other sets of aggregates, the other classes. The *experiential* aspect of this in the United States is the extremely limited range of knowledge among members of the middle class, say, as to whom the members of the elite, other than a few publicly known national giants or local moguls, are, and an even more limited knowledge as to links along which one should move to make significant contact with them. This corollary is of the utmost importance for understanding the situation in Latin America because the network relations, there, are in such sharp contrast to those in the United States, a point I shall elaborate later. Briefly, the import is that there is no boundary between a "middle class" and an "elite" to be traced in the Latin American countries.

In sum, what appears to have happened in the cases of Northwest Europe[8] and the United States is the evolutionary emergence of bounded aggregates of people divided off from, and standing over against, each other by virtue of organization, position occupancy, and network interaction, as well as by cultural mechanisms (such as speech pattern, area of origin, and other discriminants as in England). The bounded aggregates appear, in their broadest and most simply understood forms, to be a "proletariat" (including agricultural labor, a structurally defined and segregated "middle class," and an "elite," although each of these probably has major significant, bounded subdivisions set off, for certain ends and interests, against each other (e.g., academics vs. businessmen in the American middle class).

What does "middle" in these kinds of society mean? The term has a dual meaning, a dual referrent. One is that referring to an intermediating or linking societal function attached to a socially delimitable aggregate of persons; the other is to positions on scales neither at the bottom or the top of the continua used for measuring.

First, then, the term refers to a large, loosely internally organized bounded aggregate of people—a class—which has certain kinds of functions, most of which are what one might call "lubricatory": the making effective of transactions involving the strategic resources of society; the implementation of the exchanges of resources, including money; collection of information; transmission of knowledge; the processing of information for ultimate users—all of which I have elsewhere called functionary activities (Leeds 1957). These lubricatory or functionary activities are the operational aspects of the kinds of positions and organizations to which the people designated as "middle class" are attached. The *function* of these activities is the linkage of the positions, networks, and organizations structuring the proletariats with those structuring the elites in such a way that the necessarily interdependent societal functions of *these* two aggregates can be made to operate more or less predictably.

Second, the term refers to abstracted but relatively minor attributes usually (but neither always nor necessarily) attached to and only loose-

---

[8] After half a year of trying analytically to understand British class structure "on the ground" in Oxford and London, I am no longer so certain that this happened completely in England; the English class system strikes me as perhaps, in some respects, nearer the Latin American, or specifically the Brazilian, than that of the United States.

ly correlated with that function. I refer to the scalar attributes of intermediate levels of income, types of housing, kinds of occupation (seen as subjectively ranked entities on a scalar hierarchy), styles of living, and so forth. Particular measures on any of these scales may be associated with *any* of the structural classes, even though the distributions of such measures tend to concentrate medium levels of measures with the middle class, low ones with the proletariats, and high ones with the elites. It is interesting that it was these abstracted attributes that got elevated to primary or exclusive importance in the American positivistic treatment of "class" (e.g., Warner and Lunt 1942; Kahl 1957, etc.)—at the expense of any structural view. The positivistic empiricist approach matched and reinforced popular ideology of a "classless" society with ever-spreading "upward" mobility (see, however, Lynd and Lynd 1929, 1937; Mills 1951, 1956, to the contrary)—even though the question from *what* this "upward mobility" took place remained unanswered. It is also interesting to note that the typical American models of "class" analysis—the "continua models" of class based on the reified scalar abstractions approached by means of the positivistic operationalism of questionnaires often applied without basic prior ethnography—were widely borrowed in Latin America in the late 1950s and early 1960s (e.g., the Four Cities study; see Hutchinson 1962). There were transferred to Latin American social science two deeply inappropriate conceptions of "middle class" (also transferred to postwar German sociology which in turn had a secondary influence on both American and Latin American stratification studies; see Mayntz 1967)–that of a structured, bounded, specialized aggregate and that of intermediate ranks on a series of disarticulated "dimensions" measured by scales or continua. These were then imposed on the Latin American realities, which I assert, are quite different. Observers have always felt the difference but, rather than cope with it directly in terms of observations and reconceptualization of the models, dealt with it only verbally by creating terms such as "middle sectors."

Turning to Latin America in general, I see *no sets* of functions separately attached to *structurally* differentiated corporate social bodies of the kind discussed above. That is, as in all state societies, the functions exist, but they are not systematically carried out separately from other functions (e.g., decision-making, allocation) carried out by the elites in European societies and they are not carried out by a systemically segregated body of specialists: a functionary or lubricatory, that is, a middle class. At most, such a class is rudimentary in localized pockets of the larger countries with very great resources which began their developments already in the last century. They would be Argentina, Brazil, Chile, Colombia, Mexico, Perú, Uruguay, and Venezuela, and then only in the great metropolitan centers (e.g., in Brazil, in Rio and especially São Paulo, but not in Belo Horizonte, Recife, Salvador, etc.).[9]

Despite these rudimentary structural classes, what essentially exists in all the Latin American countries are two-class societies, within the classes of which various kinds, means, and degrees of ranking exist. To shed light on this situation I wish to turn again to the corollary above.

To the mechanisms for the maintenance of boundaries between two classes may be added that of blockage of access, not only to resources and associations, which are obvious, but most especially to and along the various informal networks that move persons from one vantage point to another through the agency of one or more key intermediating parties, the contact links.

Thus, for example, A, with an inferior vantage point, x—believes that he can accomplish his aims by gaining access to a vantage point, y—say, a capital source. At this juncture several conditions may obtain. (1) A does not know who controls y and finds great difficulty in finding out because C, who in fact controls y, and his networks make every effort to keep that information secret and within their own group. (2) A *does* know who controls y, but finds that he cannot get through to C, cannot find a contact person, is not presented to C, since B, the contact (one person or a chain of persons), is instructed by C not to facilitate contact or is, in some other type of relation with C such that he maintains the blockage of access perhaps even in his own interest. (3) A, having actually made contact with C, finds that nothing can be done or nothing happens, even if he meets C repeatedly. A finds that whatever he has to offer in exchange is of no, or too negligible, interest to C. In general, A represents the American middle class and C represents, say, one of the more remote members of the elite, like Howard Hughes or, at a regional level, the Texan wheeler-dealer, stock-fraud king, Frank Sharp.[10]

[9] The great primate centers are also the areas of earliest industrial development. What appears to have happened for a nation in the case of Argentina (see n. 14 below) appears to have happened, *partially*, in these national urban centers and then equilibrated into the more general pattern of class I have described for Latin America.

[10] But for higher interplays of power involving President Nixon's attempt, starting about 1970, to capture the Texas electoral vote in the presidential election of 1972, Frank Sharp's incredible speculations and fraudulent bank and stock dealings would probably not have

This sort of blockage—essentially, ultimately, a blockage of access to resources—seems to me very characteristic of the United States. It is very much a part of the boundary maintaining mechanism (even where boundary-crossing acquaintances have been struck up). It is reinforced by the self-identifying, almost self-laudatory ideology of the middle class. Although empirical data are highly anecdotal at best, mobility over the boundary seems extremely reduced and to a large extent controlled, in rate and personnel, by the elite's recruitment mechanisms.

Blockage of this kind contrasts radically with the situation in Latin America when one considers other than proletarian functions (mainly labor in production and distribution), that is, when one considers all the functions carried out in Northwestern Europe and the United States by the segregated two classes, the "middle" and the elite. Visualize, rather than two such bodies with mutually exclusive functions, *partially* stratified, as ordered bodies, by differential control over the resources of power, a single body delineated by its mutual exclusiveness with the proletarian (including rural) masses and its inclusion of everyone else in the society whom I have elsewhere (1964b) called "the classes." The aggregate of "the classes" is virtually infinitely ranked *internally*, but has no significant, enduring, internal boundaries demarcating one group as over against another, although small grouplets—cliques and "circles" (e.g., *panelinhas, roscas, pínas, argollas*, etc; see Leeds 1964b)—form and reform as small nodes within the total aggregate. The ranking of persons is based doubly on functions performed and on differential access to resources in a system where everyone is conceived to have some minimum resource(s) at his disposal for exchange—a key to the whole situation.

---

been exposed; the agent of exposure is alleged to have been John Connally, by that time former *Democratic* governor of Texas elevated to the *Republican* Nixon's cabinet as Secretary of the Treasury. The stock scandal involved the then governor of Texas, Preston Smith, the lieutenant governor, Ben Barnes, the speaker of the Texas House, Gus Mutscher, and a variety of other unsavory high office holders of the Democratic party. Victims of the manipulation were large numbers of depositors and investors including a Jesuit college in Houston. The point of the example is that the networks within the governing subelite of Texas were all aware of the opportunities and the manipulations, while all the rest of the population knew absolutely nothing about the situation until interest in destroying Smith's power base, Barnes's control of the Democratic party machinery, and Mutscher's control of the House and all its committees led to the defection of one of their number in his own interest at a still higher level of elite control. The effort was highly successful; all are out of office now, and Texas went for Nixon. The stock operations were inaccessible to virtually everyone else including substantial businessmen and bankers (all this an example of case 1) above.

The greater the number of functions one performs, the higher up the ranking system; the greater the number of functions one performs, the denser one's linkages with others of like rank; the greater the number of functions and the denser one's linkages, the greater the control over certain types of resources, but not over all resources. The resources not controlled directly as one goes higher up the ranking include masses of people (as in electorates, mobilized mobs, strikes, military followings, large personal networks), services and the skills attached to them, production efficacy, mobilized sums of money from large aggregates of people (such as the millions saved by proletarian housing co-operatives or by elite mutual savings associations in Perú), certain kinds of political information, and so on.

We have, then, a situation which can be characterized as follows. First, there is an aggregate of people, all distinguished from a functionally segregated body we can call the proletariats. All members of the aggregate have access to at least one of the functions characteristic of the aggregate as a whole which include the "lubricating" and decision-making and allocational ones. Increasing rank is associated, not with sloughed off or delegated functions associated with a differentiated class as in the United States, but with the accumulation of more and more functions in specific individuals (the multiple job holding phenomenon; see Leeds 1964b for extensive discussion of this point).

Second, as the distribution of functions becomes denser, the number of persons involved decreases. In other words, there are quite few highly ranked people who perform multiple functions, but do not perform these exclusively. As performers of multiple functions, they also become complex nodes through which linkages to resources and other such nodes are to be made. Third, at the same time, *they must also keep open their own access to the much greater number of individuals who perform fewer functions*, since these directly provide certain resources (e.g., frequently what are the effective electorates or union supporters, etc.) and services and indirectly may provide others as links to resources holding persons or bodies to which the top ranking men cannot have access.[11]

The picture, then, is of ramifying linkages toward the lower end of the system and concentrating linkages at the top—an inverted tree composed of patron-client relationships, *clientelas*, and hierarchically

[11] See in this connection, Chapter 7; also E. Leed's discussion, 1972, of the *cabo eleitoral* and the *puleiro;* see also Skidmore 1967:40, on *pelegos* in the labor unions.

linked cliques (such as *panelinhas*). The operation and continuity of the system *depend* precisely on the maintenance of linkages, making the contact points known, flows of information about vantage points, the eternal possibilities of accumulating functions for persons at all ranks. All this, in turn, depends on the exchangeability of resources or of products (such as a vote) which the resources can generate if used by the right persons (such exchanges are known as *trocas de interesse* in Brazil). The whole *structure* is one of positions, hierarchically ranked, but laterally only partially specialized, with all kinds of criss-crossing linkages—horizontal, vertical, and diagonal—among which rewards are exchanged in the interest of each participant. The rewards circulate only among members in this structure and are *not* exchanged with members of the proletariat. The system permits rapid reallocation of all sorts of resources *outside* formal channels—including electorates (*currais eleitorais*, see E. Leeds, 1972:26) service personnel, rewards to be passed from the politico-administrative sphere down the hierarchy for redistribution, and so forth. The ramaged system also provides the routes for upward (and downward!) mobility. Each route has its appropriate markers such as the performance of appropriate exchanges, the contracting of appropriate commitments, and the attaching of appropriate new networks to the network along which mobility is taking place, the establishing of appropriate contacts.

In general, it is my impression for Latin America as a whole[12] that there is, first, no convincing evidence anywhere, with the *partial* exception of the primate urban centers mentioned above, of a bounded, segregated middle class exclusively exercising a set of societal functions and, second, no evidence that such constructions of boundaries of a middle class, as over against other classes, or of middle level statuses away from, especially, the decision-making bodies or institutions of the two-class societies is increasing or even taking place.

---

[12] I use the word "impression" advisedly. Aside from skepticism whether anyone can really know twenty complex countries of a continent well, it is certainly the case that I do not. I know Brazil well and something of Perú and Colombia. I have been for brief visits in Argentina, Chile, Mexico, Uruguay, and Venezuela which have afforded me some sense of the place (I have actually spent several months in Venezuela, but most of it was with an Indian tribe). The others I have never seen. The impressions come from reading, conversations, encounters with the nationals of the respective countries. I think it well to keep in mind the distinctiveness of each country, each with its quite separate history: to know any one or two of the countries well is a major feat. It is my *impression*, then, that most of the countries have the kind of system I am describing, although with some variation in the openness of the system from country to country and from time to time.

Put another way, I do not see any aggregations of people, positions, or small corporate bodies of people becoming large-scale, separate, bounded groups, but rather see that those people, aspects, or functions, which we would ordinarily, in the perspective of a "Western" model of class brought to bear, expect to segregate in this manner, are all tied by a variety of networks—genealogical, personal, patronal, institutional—with the central positions and bodies of the State and the private sector.

That there is no clear indication of such a development seems to me particularly true in those societies which have been both "dependent" (or "secondary" or "third world", etc.) and characterized by a long history of structurally very marked elitist orders—the case of most Latin American countries. On the contrary, there appears to be very considerable evidence, not only for Latin America, but many other countries around the world, that secondary, dependent societies, characterized by an essentially two-class system with elaborate intraclass hierarchies and specialized cross-class links,[13] are extremely viable, functional alternatives to class societies organized on the model of the United States, Germany, Great Britain, and so on. Further, there is no reason to assume that the kind of class society represented by the latter model, so familiar to observers who come from the Northwestern European and American societies represented by the model which they then impose on other realities, need necessarily evolve in Latin America whose own ordering of class is equally viable.

A possible exception to this generalization, in Latin America, appears, again, to be Argentina. Argentina seems to be the only Latin American society with a notable development of a structured middle class. It is also the one society in which the class position of the Jews appears to be systematically different from that of any of the other countries. One suspects that Argentina was heavily influenced by European modes of organization at a critical juncture in its developmental trajectory in such a way that the impacts of that influence on its

---

[13] The intraclass hierarchies have been discussed in the text and illustrated in the charts. The specialized cross-class links that permit limited and specific relations to take place over the edges between the two classes consist of certain formal institutions such as taxation and job contracts (including work-for-pay exchanges, and "social·costs" such as social security benefits), and informal ties, most particularly the patronal relationship (including exchanges of favors, *compadresco* and informal contacts in the secondary labor market, see Machado 1971). All of these cross-class links serve as markers of social distance and maintainers of class discrimination.

[157]

prior structure rendered Argentine society more like that of Western Europe and the United States.[14]

As to the rest of Latin America, especially the larger countries, economic development and economic growth started later and evolved more slowly than in Argentina in quite different demographic and labor contexts. The results, therefore, were quite different. By "economic development," I refer to changes in form and content of the economy; by "economic growth," I refer to additions to, and expansion of, what is already present in the economy. The distinction can be illustrated cogently by the case of Brazil where, although there has been major economic development, certain aspects of the economy have been characterized, rather, by growth; this was indicated in earlier discussion by reference to that salient feature, the income distribution figures. Distribution has not much improved (though, over a half-century or so, it has fluctuated) during the entire period of major development, even though the *range* involved in income has increased substantially, that is, it has grown but it has not changed form, especially as no major social change of wealth distribution has taken place.

This fact, more or less paralleled in other Latin American countries other than Argentina (where the worsening of income distribution appears to have occurred only substantially *after* industrialization, or "economic development"), is of central importance to my argument because it implies that, under the conditions of population, labor, and delayed development holding in the other countries, the class ordering of "predevelopment" phases (probably mythical, historically) can be perpetuated throughout the developmental trajectory, whereas in Argentina it had to change. Changes now necessitated by development are handled, say, in Brazil by *intra*class modifications, expansions of the range of ranks, multiplication of functions, while maintaining the old two-class boundary intact (see Hutchinson 1960, 1962).

The internal modification of class is paralleled in the sphere of the polity—as one would expect from the internal structure of positions and functions of the elite classes. Both economic development and

[14] One may hazard the guess that the variables involved in this situation included relatively high national income from cattle, low population, the absence of a history of mass slavery or a mass Indian work force, an (absolutely and relatively) exceptionally heavy European immigration, early development of extensive transportation networks, and strong British influence on economy and polity, all occurring about the same period and creating a large industrial establishment very early in the developmental sequence.

growth are integrated by members of the elite with changes in administrative structure adapted both to new conditions external to the specific countries and to the organizational networks of the class and its self-maintenance inside the countries. I suspect that much of what Silvert sees as *political* change and possibly even change in participation is really this sort of change without much social significance. It is not really broad, societally based political change at all, but essentially change in the structure of the administrative apparatus of these societies, adapting both development and growth to elite interests and the entire society to external dependency relationships. The seemingly greater participation—in terms of actual control, essentially fraudulent—is a mechanism for redistributing personnel through the ranks of the class system (see below).

To rephrase the considerations above, I argue that the societal systems consisting of two classes so generally prevalent in Latin America throughout the nineteenth and first part of the twentieth centuries have not, except in Argentina, been basically reordered into structural three-class systems, but have remained two-class systems in which the internal composition of class has changed by expansion of ranges of positions, roles, types of organization, rankings, and functions. I think the evidence for this is vast and is to be seen, for examples in studies on work and social mobility such as Hutchinson's cited above. The kind of change of the two-class system described here seems to me to have begun *at least* with the initiation of industrialization (see Johnson 1958: Preface, 1–3) in about the 1870s or 1880s and on, for example in Perú or Brazil and some of the other countries. This is the period which, for instance, in Perú represents the beginnings of the process called *cholificación* and, in Brazil and elsewhere, the emergence of what people have tried to label "middle class" (see for instance, Skidmore 1967, throughout the book, without a single specification of what the reference of the term is).

All these shifts occur concomitantly with a shift to a fully developed, pervasive, price-making market economy organized around the capitalist form of profit-making and reinvestment (see Polanyi 1945) which has affected the internal structure of these classes. Liberal capitalism in a state of expansion requires more open recruitment systems and, at least periodically and for longer or shorter times, more open upward (*or* downward!!) and geographical mobility possibilities in order to redistribute personnel and available skills socially and geographically and stimulate the production of new skills. This can be done in the context

of a two-class system where the creation of a new entrepreneurial-
technocratic class such as appeared in Euramerica is made unneces-
sary because of the absorption of its positions and functions directly
into an extant elite class which shifts major portions of its resources
to the new entrepreneurial-technocratic endeavors added to its old
agrarian-commercial ones at all levels.

A network structure, such as I describe above, is admirably suited
to the maintenance not only of the two-class system but superbly
facilitates the internal expansion of the classes since it provides the
framework for movements of resources and skills, for the redistribution of both as well as of personnel, and for social and geographical
mobility, while, at the same time, it provides the mechanisms for
maintaining class boundaries, for exclusions, for blockages (see Leeds
1964b: 1331–40).

In the perspective of the foregoing, I turn briefly to the question of
Jews in Latin America. Given the almost total lack of literature,[15]
virtually all we know from the point of view of the social sciences is
anecdotal. What I say below, then, has the character of being anecdotal, based simply on either personal experience or what I have indirectly gathered from comment or an occasional question.

As a rule, it appears to me that in almost all the countries, with the
possible *partial* exception of Argentina, the Jewish populations of Latin America are located in types of positions which in Western Europe
and America would be designated grand bourgeois (although, consis-

---

[15] One rather poor book on contemporary Jews in Latin America exists; most of what one
finds on Jews deals with their history—especially the early centuries, e.g., *Nova Cristoes*,
the maranos, etc. More attention ought to be given to this period in terms of the *present*
situation: I sometimes suspect a very broad Jewish influence in Brazilian and some other
Latin American cultures. In any case, there are substantial numbers of persons with Jewish
ancestry, who recognize that ancestry even though they have been Catholic for centuries,
e.g., the Spinolas, the Davís, the Nogueiras, the Pereiras, the Aranhas, etc. (the tree and
animal names paralleling the surnames Jews assumed in other European countries). I know
of no social science field studies of Jews in contemporary Latin America. Most of what is
known about Jews in that area from a social science point of view has been picked up
incidentally to other work or because the social scientists are themselves Jewish or have
close ties with Jewish colleagues. It is worth noting that field studies among Jews in the
United States, aside from those in the larger New York area, are also scarce. Studies of Jews,
say, in Texas, itself deeply influenced by Spanish and Latin American culture, would be most
rewarding since there are extremely interesting Jewish settlement histories both in San
Antonio and Galveston, including fairly early migration in the mid-1850s from the larger
West German Jewish immigration to the United States. Many are in extremely influential
positions in the business and political circles of these cities.

tent with my argument above, not a *grande bourgeoisie*), with relatively few persons in types of positions one might call petit bourgeois and, in my experience, no personnel whatever in the proletariats, working class, lumpenproletariats, or like aggregates. The closest approximation to a proletarian Jew I have met is a Polish refugee who came to Brazil after World War II. He sells notions in squatter settlements, but does not live in one, but rather in a middle class neighborhood.

With the possible exception of this man, the Latin American Jews of a petit bourgeois type whom I have known have links *upward* through a variety of kin or personal networks including the characteristic patronal ties of Latin America. Access to new links is widely fostered by professionalization—that is, the acquiring of skills and information which satisfy a broadened range of functions and open still further upward-reaching networks, as described above. Obviously, the links of the grand bourgeois Jews are all upward, often to the topmost decision-making levels of the society—if they are not within that level themselves. Conversely, there are *no* links downward into the proletariats for the purpose of mobilizing whatever resources they might have—whether by linking into their networks or their corporate organizations—not even for political purposes, as far as I know. This fact bears investigation for the insight it might give as to whether or not and in what ways the political role of Jews in these societies is limited—and why: whether by non-Jewish discrimination, which I strongly doubt, or because of self-defined roles and interests which do not lean toward the political.

In Brazil, Colombia, and, it is my impression, in Mexico, Venezuela, and Perú, numbers of Jews with network links to critical decision-makers of the State and of the private sector exist or they have themselves been such decision-makers or occupiers of key positions. For example, in Brazil, perhaps the most notable case, there have been the Lafers, the Klabins, the Moseses, the Blochs, and the Levys—major ministers of State; heads of the largest-scale industry; owners and directors of the major communications and mass media chains and associations; outstanding bankers; commercial moguls have been and still are Jews. They are also heavily involved in the arts, especially painting and music, and a few are in the sciences. I find it remarkable, however, that among the social scientists, only a very reduced number is Jewish. Finally, there have been and continue to be Jews in high government posts and in significant military positions. There is extremely little evidence whatever of anti-Semitic exclusion from significant positions of the society.

The pattern described for Brazil seems to me the common one in Latin America, with two qualifications. First, it is not clear that Jews have reached equivalent heights of power and influence and probably not as often in the other countries. In general, Jews have been involved at intermediate ranks of the elite classes, often exercising several functions at once, but not moving into holding a greater number of the decision positions and their functions. At the same time, however, they have relatively open access to these through complex network ties and exchange of interests.

Second, Argentina, as in many other respects, seems to have a unique situation. Although it, too, appears to have Jews in the grand bourgeois positions and networks just referred to, it also seems to have a much more clearly delimited middle class in which a large part of the population of Argentine Jews is found. The occupational inventory of Jews in Argentina seems also to be different (at least statistically) from that in other countries, involving occupations more characteristic of those of the middle classes in Western Europe and the United States. For example, there appears to be a relatively high proportion of Jewish social scientists—a situation not characteristic of the other Latin American countries.

Anti-Semitism seems to be quite marked in Argentina.[16] Although I have been told about fairly active anti-Semitism in Mexico, it seems to be less virulent and pervasive in nature. It is slight in Brazil. Most of the countries, with the possible exception of Argentina, seem to have no discriminatory behavior or clear exclusionary activity, like quotas, nor do I see any evidence that Latin American societies are now moving, or will move in any foreseeable future (unless they change drastically from top to bottom), in the direction of increasing anti-Semitism or major discrimination against Jews.

Indeed, it seems to me that the major targets of repression and discrimination are quite different in ways that are inextricably linked with the structure of class as I have analyzed it above and are related to nationalism in the sense of a community of people. The main target of

---

[16] The only place where I have directly observed anti-semitism is in Argentina—partly in the prevalence of Nazi symbols such as swastikas, and more directly in the form of anti-Semitic graffiti. The one that has stayed with me most poignantly is this: *Judio! Comed! Cresced! Haced Gordura!* "Jew, Eat! Grow! Make fat!"

repression and discrimination is the entire body of the lower or proletarian classes, or, if you will, the masses, the lumpen proletariats, and so forth (including all forms of rural labor). These aggregates are to be kept in line by a variety of juridical, social, and other techniques (see Leeds 1964:1331–38) which also serve as class boundary-maintainers with a dual function: (a) keeping the greater mass of the population from access to the major wealth, power, and prestige of the society; (b) maintaining vast, cheap labor forces available to generate the wealth of the society.

The second major collective target of repression and discrimination is the *primarily non-Jewish,* native elite intelligentsia (again with the possible exception of Argentina) who are linked by kin and personal networks, by their professionalization, or by their access to, or possession of, wealth, power, and prestige, often over many generations, to the central, private and public sector decision-making and institutional apparatus of the society. They may also at times have been occupants of positions in this apparatus (e.g., the intellectuals who comprised the Instituto Superior de Estudos Brasileiros (ISEB) or Darcy Ribeiro, the anthropologist who became the Brazilian Minister of Education and Chefe da Casa Civil). Perhaps even more significantly, they may have been, as opponents of that apparatus and the crucial positions of society, heads of major social movements, like Hugo Blanco in Perú and Che Guevara in Cuba, some of the student movement leaders such as Vladimir Palmeira in Brazil, some social scientists, or, in Brazil, the left-wing Church.

These two are objects of repression and discrimination because, though the personnel involved are almost entirely of the elite class, closely interlocked with the rest of its membership, they threaten the established structure and mechanisms of class organization and domination by opening doors to the proletarian aggregates which can thus gain access to the preserves of wealth and power arrogated by the elites to themselves. The continued protection of these preserves, of the barriers against outsiders, has the most urgent priority, and repression of those involved in disturbing the control follows directly. As a rule, the Jewish populations, from the point of view of the dominating elites, have been on the side of the angels—that is, their side— and belong to them. For a long time to come, in any foreseeable future, the targets of repression and discrimination will continue to be the intelligentsia threatening the established orders. In Latin America, these are composed mostly of non-Jewish native elite personnel.

Where Jews have been involved it has been purely *as individuals* in the intelligentsia—and infrequently at that. I do not see that the Jewish population or the "Jewish community," if there is one in any of the societies, figures in the picture of repression and discrimination at all. They are thoroughly integrated into the internally open, elite class structure. I see no threat.

In sum and conclusion, both models of class developed in Euramerican thought are inappropriate for Latin America. Even terms like "middle sectors," "segments," and the like, are misleading because they obscure the structures of networks, exchanges of interest, the peculiar distribution of functions, the mobility possibilities, the community of interest which binds together a large number of people within a social boundary on the other side of which are the ranked proletariats and inside of which are the ranked elites. If this view is correct, it would suggest ways of studying class and class action—relevant to the most general societal dynamics—quite different from those heretofore prevalent.

[5]

Some Problems in the Analysis
of Class and the Social Order

Prevailing Conceptions of Class

This essay has arisen out of a number of efforts both completed
(Leeds 1957, 1964a, 1964b) and in process to understand "class" phenomena in various countries, and out of an increasing dissatisfaction
with the verbal tools and conceptual frameworks available. In review-
ing a multitude of publications on class research and in reflecting on
my own explanation of Brazilian commodity cycles in terms of the
arrangement and values of the class structure, I became disturbed not
only by what appeared to be major unwarranted a priori assumptions
about class, but also by the question of the ontological status of class as
an empirical phenomenon.

This discomfort was enhanced by the many meanings and referents
that have come to be subsumed under the term "class" (Bohannan
1963). I need not review these here beyond pointing to such distinct
usages as those of Marxian class analysis, Warnerian class analysis, and
that contained in such phrases as "caste is complete class" (Hoebel
1958:425). The still more generic term "stratification" covers a welter
of meanings and problems, as Mayntz has shown (1967).

Despite an increasing emphasis on empirical data in reporting on
class, much of the literature, especially recent American work, implicitly assumes an ontological status that needs no epistemological or
methodological justification. In other words, class simply *exists*, or *is* a
thing "out there," and to it certain kinds of data are ascribed by definition. That the concept of class in this a priori sense is relevant to the
data, or that these data prove the social reality of class, is in general

[165]

less than adequately demonstrated according to the canons of empirical social science. Class often seems to be regarded as a kind of vehicle that people enter and exit from in a continuous flow.

To me, such a conception is contrary to all that we know of actual social operations, of interaction, of the dynamics of statuses, roles, actors, their reference groups, and all other more or less easily delimitable social groupings. It also seems contrary to the procedures of either empirical-inductive or logico-deductive science; it is, in fact, a kind of metaphysics—ontological knowledge given by pure reason alone.

What is the social locus of class? What sort of entity is it? What is the ontological status of class or classes? Much of the language surrounding the use of the word "class" simply assumes for class a reality in the great buzzing confusion outside the observer, as in such tropisms as "the ruling class wants . . .", "social classes function to . . .". If "class" indeed exists "out there," then neither the conception of "class as the vehicle-to-be-filled-and-emptied" nor McIver's notion of it (1937:166–67) is an empirically adequate formulation—the former because it is based on post hoc empirical attributions and the latter because it does not demonstrate any existent operating organization at all. At best the former conception, if not entirely metaphysical, is at a more abstract and a higher level of inference than the data ostensibly illustrating the existence of class, which themselves are inferred from various kinds of empirical observations.

It is crucial in any description of an operating social system to make clear which of these levels of inference we are working on, especially with respect to conceptions of class such as the "vehicular" and Marxian notions and their derivatives. The term "class," particularly in these latter conceptions, appears to serve as a kind of metalanguage term referring to lower-level sets of terms in a categorical or shorthand manner. In the way that it is often used, then, it tends to cloak the detailed intricacies of both the organization and the dynamics of the social order. Thus, we are rendered less able or less likely to see the microcosmic processes of variation and selection whose quantitative cumulation ultimately leads to qualitative change.

The Need for a Set of Terms

Critically needed at the present time is a systematized set of terms—one that is based on minimal assumptions and that does away with a priori suppositions regarding the existence of class. It should refer as precisely and unambiguously as possible to objective entities or categories of entities of organization and to kinds or categories of relationship at relatively low levels of inference from empirical data. From the descriptions obtained with such a set of terms we may make higher-level inferences with regard, for example, to class, if we want to and if it is still useful to do so. The empirical status of such constructions will then be much clearer and the justification for their use in discourse, or in some logico-deductive argument with regard to, say, social change, more justifiable.

The social sciences do not, at present, possess such a set of terms or language; one must be created. Here we are faced with the problem of what words to choose: whether to redefine terms in current use or to form neologisms. If currently used words, such as "class," already display acute ambiguity, neologisms seem called for. Unfortunately many of the important social-science terms are in just such an unhappy condition—for example, " status," "role," "group," "relationship," "organization," "power," and even "society" itself.[1] "Organization," for instance, may refer generically to orderings of many kinds including arrangements of persons who are not, properly speaking, organized at all—publics, audiences, and even crowds and mobs (to which the term "group" is sometimes also loosely applied). The ambiguity is intensified by the use of "an organization" or "organizations," which almost invariably refer specifically to associations, thus excluding other forms of organized entities. Each term individually and the three together refer to different levels of generality and specificity and involve varying ranges of inclusion and exclusion in the category. Here, surely, are grounds for creating neologisms.[2]

In this essay I propose a set of terms to deal with entities and relationships of the social order at relatively lower levels of inference than the referents of "class," "organization," and the like. The terms are intended to point to the kinds of units or entities that it is useful to look for, especially in qualitative research on social systems. What I

---

[1] A perusal of the papers by Mayntz, Stavenhagen, and Banton in Leeds, ed. 1967 will illustrate a number of the uses of the word "status": as prestige, as summary social position, as juridically defined sets of rights or duties, and so on. "Group" may refer to organized entities, to categories, to agglomerations. "Relationship" may refer to ties and links, to correlations, and even to analogies, or it may refer to connections seen in the data or to logical connections in a theoretical language.

[2] Note the precedents for the creation of neologisms, arising out of the necessity for new, precise language to deal with old, confused issues, in Harris 1964; Barker and Wright 1954; Nelson 1964; and Parsons 1951 and other works.

have just said implies, of course, that I am making certain assumptions. One is that a qualitative mapping of relationships among forms or entities *must* precede quantitative work, else there is no way of determining the significance of the quantities. This is true even though the quantitative analysis may often be implied in the qualitative. The less that is known about any subject matter, the more must this be so.[3] I am convinced that most of our basic research work on social structures will have to be of this sort until we have a much broader and more fundamental conception of how social systems are actually built. Moreover, I fear that most quantitative work today is woefully inadequate, if not actually irrelevant. The proposed kind of description of entities and their links is an approach that might be called qualitative or "natural-historical."

Another assumption underlying the present scheme is that any socio-cultural system may be exhaustively described by a finite series of categories or types of units and relationships and, further, that exemplars of all these categories must be looked for in the field, even though, in the description of particular cases, some may prove irrelevant. If this is not done, variables significant to the system under study may be omitted. Much of the recent sociological literature on class, and especially that on so-called community power, has been marked by the consistent and drastic omission not only of significant variables but often of the most important ones.[4]

The terms proposed are, in a manner that is clearly only preliminary and exploratory, fitted into a scheme of analysis or, looked at another way, a generic model of social orders. Once the scheme has been set forth, higher levels of inference, such as "class," "society," or "state,"

[3] This assumption appears to be confirmed by the history of such sciences as analytic chemistry, which only relatively recently turned quantitative; biology, whose mathematical approaches developed long after basic classificatory and structural work had been broadly accomplished; geology, which is only now coming to grips with quantitative methods; and anthropology, which as yet cannot really be said to have successfully broached quantitative methods at all. Sociology, especially in the area of stratification research, seems to me to have leaped far beyond what its qualitative, analytic foundations yet justify.

[4] Compare Dahl 1961; D'Antonio and Erickson 1962; D'Antonio et al. 1962; D'Antonio and Ehrlich, eds. 1961; Form 1945; Hunter 1953; Mills 1956; Polsby 1959, 1960, 1962; and Wolfinger 1962. What is omitted in these studies is the relationship between the objects of study—largely elite factions—and the entire rest of the community in which the power decisions are being made. Most of them also omit consideration of the overarching national power structure and of loci. Both of these contexts of elite decision-making are quite critical to an understanding of the society. Much of these authors' controversy and many of the objections to Mills (1956) made by the others would evaporate as spurious if they were to take this approach in their analysis of social systems. In this connection, see Chapter 7.

can be presented more precisely. I intend to examine these briefly here.

In the final section I shall suggest some theoretical uses of the scheme by application of the general principles of equilibrium and evolutionary analysis. The reader should understand, however, that the scheme is in itself no more than that, even though it allows for the description of a system's dynamics, as I shall briefly point out. Its sole justification is its usefulness for a more precise description of social systems—one that makes fewer assumptions as to the nature of the reality being described and is less metaphysical than most of the present approaches. In other words, the entire effort may be looked at as an attempt to come somewhat closer to a behavioral description of situations[5] than has been usual in the literature on class.[6]

As a final note, I should like to point out that the scheme is intended to treat only the variables within the social system. The technology and the ideology are considered external variables whose effects on the system are a subject for the formulation of propositions of a theoretical nature once they themselves have also been adequately described. Improved qualitative descriptions of each of these spheres would permit more insightful theoretical formulations than we are able to make now. We also need good schemes of analysis for ideology and technology.[7]

Node

The term "node" is intended to refer to the loci of social structure that occur "naturally"—in the sense that they are abstracted or in-

[5] By "behavioral" I mean based on those field procedures—participant observation and a number of others—that lead to discovery of the structures in a society with a minimal use of what in the current jargon is called instrumentation (for example, various kinds of questionnaires whose categories are the observers' artifacts rather than known realities in the observed society). "Instruments" consistently tend to introduce frames of reference that are foreign to or at least distort the usual perceptions and reactions of the persons interviewed. The interviewer is then in the ambivalent situation of not knowing whether his results reflect the true situation or are a product of the instrument itself. This problem seems to be especially prevalent in Warnerian and post-Warnerian types of stratification studies, particularly since any verification of the results, independent of the instruments used, is seldom attempted.

[6] Elsewhere I have attempted to use the form of analysis presented in this essay, though without formal use of the terms, and to construct "class" and "society" from lower-level units (Leeds 1964b).

[7] The recent work in anthropology on semantic or componential analysis is bringing us closer to techniques for adequate descriptions of ideology (Leeds 1965b).

ferred directly from sense data rather than being derived from theory or definition.[8] They are, so to say, the specimens that we describe. As such they are connected more or less immediately to the sense data by which they are known. Some nodes may present directly observable characteristics, as in the case of the nuclear family household, a hiking group, or a repertory company; or observable symbols such as men's houses or sumptuary differences. Or the characteristics may be "observable" only by inference from indirect evidence—for instance, events that become intelligible only if certain types of interpersonal connections are assumed, as in the case of elites. I use the term "node" partly because, so far as I know, it has no common-language sociological connotations or denotations and partly because it conveys a notion of point-of-origin, or structural center, from which organization may spread out to similar or different nodes. It is useful, also, because it does not have the ambiguities of the word "organization," or of "elements" (Firth 1951)—which is often used to include action of various kinds—or of "group" (as in "reference group," which may sometimes simply be a category). The meaning of "structure" as it is used in reference to "node" is discussed in the following pages.

For present purposes, the term "node" may refer to the entire congeries of organizational loci that have already been differentially classified in the sociological and anthropological literature as groups and organizations, but it is *not* intended to include "groups" that are defined rather by an arbitrary selection of criteria than by a natural-history approach. I may cite as an example of the former "all persons of income level X" as opposed to, say, Caplow's "ambience" (1955), a particularly interesting node since it is neither association, kin group, nor clique.

As of present knowledge, the following appear to be the main taxonomic categories of nodes: kin groups, voluntary associations, cliques and their special subclass elites, Hindu-type castes, friendships, ambiences, agencies of state.[9]

---

[8] The Marxian analysis of class involves two aspects: a definitional and an empirical. The definitional follows deductively from the definitions of surplus labor value: producers make up one "class" or category, and those who control surplus labor value but who are not also its producers form another. The definitional aspect of class per se does not refer to an empirically observable set of events. If there are empirical characteristics that are attributes of the definitionally derived categories, these must be described with data. These data, for Marx, are the multifold organizations and relationships that may be displayed by the definitionally established categories of people. The description of the organization of these categories corresponds in fact to nodal analysis as formalized here.

[9] Such localized social units as communities and neighborhoods are made up of single or multiple nodes related to a territory through institutions of appropriation, ownership, or

In passing, I may note that such social entities as the ethnic group, the minority (Harris 1959, 1967; Wagley and Harris 1958), the class, the state, the varna, and so forth, are taxonomic categories of a higher level (Simpson 1961:19–20). They involve, as I have said, a greater degree of abstraction and are several inferential steps removed from the total mass of empirical data. They comprise, following Simpson's expression (1961:20), a "set of sets."

Nodes, therefore, belong both to the lower-level taxonomic category and to the higher-level one, whereas class and the like belong to the higher level. As I have argued above, the methodological operations used in describing and defining them must, practically and logically, *follow* the description of the nodes and their relationships (Simpson 1961:23, 108–109).

The significant attributes of nodes, as nearly as possible holomorphically classified (Simpson 1961:71–72; Olson and Miller 1958; Goodenough 1964), may be briefly discussed.

All individual nodes are structural social units that can be found in human populations. Analytically, they are equivalent in level to organisms in the biological world. In this sense, the term "node" refers to a subset of the referents of the term "organization," since the latter may also include reference to (a) relationships among members of the various node categories, (b) the broader ecological relationships of all such nodes, and (c) simpler elements such as statuses, roles, and status and role networks (see below).

The nature of the structuring varies from node to node (thereby barring us from using the term "organizations," which commonly refers to voluntary associations and their special form or forms of structuring). Structuring may revolve around personal or impersonal ties, face-to-face or secondary interactions, continuous or interrupted intercourse, and so on.

The structured units exist as real, functioning entities for which operational tests, such as attempting to achieve membership, can be devised by an observer. Such operational tests are quite different from description operations performed by means of instruments, which are so seldom subjected to any independent test of validity that often one cannot tell whether the data thus collected actually describe or relate to any structural entity in the real world. Much of the literature on

---

usufruct built into the institutional structure of one or more of the component nodes. Here we may speak of "localized nodes." A clan barrio and a deme are examples of localized kinship nodes.

class and on community power based on reputational and evaluational research techniques seems to be in this dilemma. Are "lower upper classes" in any sense structural, functioning entities? Or are they merely sets of attributes coagulated and created by the instrument used? More often the latter seems to be the case. Unless operational tests of the sort mentioned demonstrate the structural reality of the asserted unit, in fact or in principle, it cannot be considered a node. In this sense, the referents of the term "nodes" are more restricted than those subsumed under the term "group," which may also be applied to statistical sets, aggregates, and evaluative categories.

Nodes are characterized by a relative temporal stability; in fact, the personnel of the node generally assume that they are permanent. The term "node" therefore excludes all relatively momentary arrangements of persons—interactions—unless the interactions are demonstrably governed by the existence of a node. Interactions of various sorts are among the "elements of social organization" (Firth 1951) but do not necessarily entail structural units, which are also such elements. The term "elements" therefore cannot be used without ambiguity.

Finally, nodes are minimum units in much the same way that organisms or molecules are minimum units. Though they may be internally differentiated, the differentiated parts cannot exist without the whole unit or cannot retain the same characteristics as in the whole unit. Such dependent internal parts would include elements such as statuses and roles or status and role networks[10]—"father" or "president-bursar-registrar—etc." of a university, for example.

---

[10] "Status" as used here refers to juridically defined sets of rights, duties, characteristics, rewards, privileges, and immunities—for example, President of the United States as defined in the Constitution. "Status network" refers to statuses linked by specific reciprocal rights, duties, and so on, among the sets that define two or more statuses—for example, the organization table of the executive branch of the United States Government. "Role" here refers to sets of rights, duties, and so forth that are informally or customarily, rather than juridically, defined—President of the United States in popular definition: white, until recently Protestant, of Anglo-Saxon or Dutch background, never-divorced, churchgoing, God-believing, and so on. "Role network" refers to roles linked by specific reciprocal rights, duties, and so forth among the sets that define two or more roles—a coterie, for example. "Institution" may be defined as a set of reciprocal relationships between or among the rights, duties, and so on of one or more statuses or roles or status or role networks and one or more other statuses or combinations of statuses, roles, status networks, or role networks—for example, the duty of a citizen (status) to pay a sum of money to the Internal Revenue Service (status network), the government (status network), or the state (set of statuses, roles, and status and role networks) and, in turn, the rights of these latter to collect, which is an institution called "taxation."

Nodal Structure

Let us now turn to the term "nodal structure," which refers to the internal organizational characteristics of the various types of nodes. Internal organization embraces not only arrangements of the component statuses and roles but also the dynamic aspect of nodes—their institutions of temporal and structural self-maintenance, including the acquisition and transmission of resources.

The structurally simple nodes may consist of a number of identical or similar statuses or roles and may have institutions of self-maintenance that tend to coincide with the defining rights, duties, obligations, and so forth of the component statuses and roles, rather than to constitute attributes of the nodes as a whole.

An example is afforded by an informal discussion group. The participants have more or less identical roles and the roles define relationships of the individuals to the group. The group, as such, has no clear modes of operation. For instance, it cannot, as a corporate body, enter into juridical or informal relations with other groups; it can only take in new members in the same way that previous ones were admitted.

More complex nodes involve differentiated systems of diverse statuses or roles, or status or role networks, often in complex arrangements and accompanied by a multitude of self-maintenance institutions. These institutions are attributes of the entities as wholes rather than of any single status, role, or network in the structure. Examples of complex nodes include modern corporations such as United States Steel, the Roman Catholic Church, universities, all large associations, elites, and so on. United States Steel, for instance, executes contracts as a corporation through coordinated, differential operations of its parts; the allocation of corporate proceeds of sales to various parts maintains the entire corporation, and so on.

The self-maintenance institutions are of the greatest importance. Every node has a normative structure, either established by custom or juridically formalized. The term "charter" will be used for these. In the first place, the charter vaguely or clearly defines the rights, duties, obligations, privileges, prerogatives, and rewards of the statuses or roles—undifferentiated or differentiated—that individuals fill as members of the social unit. It also designates, even where not formally codified, the kinds and numbers of positions of which a node is to be composed. Thus, for example, it provides grounds for control over the expansion of any sort of table of organization, over the recruitment and inclusion of new members, and so on. Its best-known forms are such codifications as constitutions, bylaws, articles of incorporation, and letters patent, but it may also consist of a sometimes logically exhaustive series of position-types or categories, such as, ideally, kin types in a kinship system.

The charter also contains norms defining who may appropriately be included or excluded in the node; that is to say, it specifies what kinds of persons, and with what qualifications, may be recruited into or separated from "membership"—the general term that may be used for the rights or obligations acquired by an individual as a result of some recruitment institution to occupy some status or role in a node. The means by which inclusion or exclusion is to be carried out are also normatively specified.

The rules furthermore designate the behaviors for members to follow and also the institutions within the node that are to maintain such behaviors. These would include, for example, negative sanctions such as restraint, shunning, fines, spankings, and assassinations, and positive sanctions such as giving honor, prestige, glory, prizes, birthday parties, and so forth. Socialization and enculturation may also be regarded as maintenance institutions. The institutions for recruitment of personnel to fill the normatively defined positions of the node need not be exhaustively listed here. They may include befriending, filiation, descent, succession, falling in love, and marriage, especially in respect of kinship nodes; the use of examination systems, apprenticeships, and other formal and informal training procedures; invitation to, advertisement for, sale of memberships, and so on. These recruitment procedures fall into a few major categories based on the candidates' attributes by reason of birth, acquisition, or ascription (usually in virtue of other characteristics he may possess; for example, if he has prestige he may then be deemed powerful and hence worthy of recruitment into an elite). The recruitment processes may provide one of the dimensions by which node categories can be distinguished.

Then there are the separation processes—those by which personnel of nodes cease to be such. There are various functions of separation: to control the number of persons in the node, to eliminate personnel undesirable for one reason or another, to maintain a continuous process of internal realignment, and so on. The procedures are legion. They may include estrangement, having a falling out, purging, ostracism, expulsion, suspension, superannuation, graduation, death, lapse, mutually exclusive membership, retirement, abandonment, expiration of term, and so forth. These procedures may also fall into a few major categories revolving around condition of life (for example, age, as in rites of passage or death), voluntary acts of the personnel (abandonment, contraction of mutually exclusive memberships, lapse in the duties of membership, and so on), acts of the nodal group against the member despite the will of the latter (ostracism), and acts of the group deriving from other formal institutions of the node (expiration of term, superannuation). These categories, too, may serve as dimensions for distinguishing the nodes.

A full description of the personnel of a node would then include an account of the roles of inclusion in a node, the institutions of recruitment and of separation, and all instances of irregularities in obedience to the rules and in the operation of the recruitment and separation institutions, since these are subject to "abuses—manipulation of genealogies, falsification of work records, suppression of relevant information, and so on.

Nodes maintain themselves with some form or other of resources, whether these be strategic goods; privileges, rights, or prerogatives; specialized bodies of knowledge and information; titles or names; or like assets. These may be corporately controlled by the node or allocated for ownership, control, or management by the node to its members according to some reward system governed by the arrangement of the constituent nodal statuses or roles. Some resources are extrinsic to any particular node in the sense that there is nothing inherent in the resource that relates it to any given social order; iron ore is an example. Other resources may be considered intrinsic—that is, they are linked to the normative and institutional structure of the node or to its products—for example, patented technical processes developed in industrial laboratories by company engineers, or heritable titles of nobility. Still other resources, like labor, whose physical and technical qualities are extrinsic to nodal organization but whose interactional aspects must be socially ordered, become of interest to nodes in consequence of the aims and ends defined in their ideologies. Such resources become the locus of appropriative action by some nodes at the expense of others and provide arenas of conflict and competition. The matter of resources is dealt with in "Differential Distribution of Controls" below.

Finally, nodes also have sets of norms or rules that specify how the units of the node category may combine with other units of their own category or of others. The world of business provides a multitude of examples of rules stating how one node may or may not enter, as a node, into relationship with another, with what frequency, and for what duration and purposes, and also indicating what other kinds of nodes are eligible for combination and which ones are to be excluded. Conflict-of-interest and nepotism rules are both interesting examples —the latter especially as it refers to two different types of nodes.

Nexus

The next term I should like to introduce is "nexus," which will refer to ties and links between or among nodes. This term is more specific in reference than the word "relationship," since the latter may also refer, for example, to aspects or qualities predictable of two or more things considered together (as in the case of resemblance). The kinds of nexuses permitted for a node will have been defined, in many cases, by the rules of combination of the node; but in other cases the subject may not be recognized normatively at all. For example, in the United States there is normatively no rule of combination regarding the personnel of a kin group and a bureaucratic agency (whereas in Brazil a president's near kin, consanguineal or affinal, may not succeed their incumbent kinsman). In fact, there are intimations that a nexus of this sort is mildly contranormative. Nevertheless, the recent head of state of the United States appointed his immediate kin to prime positions in a number of bureaucratic nodes.

Since the two or more nodes involved in the nexus may have quite different rules of combination, it may, in fact, not correspond closely to the rules of combination of either. Rather, it may entail a reciprocated compromise by all parties or even a link of active opposition, composition, or conflict. For these reasons, the nexus must be described as a phenomenon separate from the nodes it connects.

Several categories of nexuses may be listed. Minimally, though further analysis may distinguish more, there appear to be four major ones: genealogical, personal, customary, and contractual. These four categories may themselves also serve as dimensions for distinguishing nodes. Two nodes may be linked by one or several of these kinds of nexus. Thus the ties between two corporations may be both contractual and, through face-to-face relationships of the presidents, personal. The relationship between two Chinese joint families named Yang, living in the same village, is, putatively at least, genealogical, but may also be contractual in a family mutual-aid society and customary in the observance of Yang surname or clan festivals.

[176]

The connection between two nodes may, significantly, shift from one type of nexus to another under changing external conditions (Leeds 1963:71). Thus, changes may take place in the manner of relating without discontinuity in the interaction between the nodes. The greater the possibility of mobilizing or shifting about among different nexuses in the interrelationship among nodes, the more flexible will be the social system or subsystem. One may note, in this connection, the mobilization and alternation among nexuses practiced in the Brazilian politicoeconomic cliques known as *panelinhas* (Leeds 1964b). A given panelinha not only connects with a variety of other nodes by means of genealogical, personal, customary, and (through the agency of individual members) contractual nexuses, but may even establish various types of nexuses with a single other node. For example, it may be tied to an agency of the state through genealogical, personal, and contractual nexuses all at once or in succession. The multiplicity and variability of nexuses between panelinhas and other nodes in Brazil imparts a great flexibility to the operation of the politico-economic system that is not observed where nexuses between two or more nodes are characteristically more restricted, as in the United States of today, which finds itself, relatively speaking, at an economic and political stalemate.

Particular types of nexuses may not only vary greatly in frequency from one society to another but may indeed even be absent in some. On the basis of such frequencies, we might construct a typology of societies that would prove to have evolutionary significance in terms of the predominance of one or another type in the major institutions of the society.

Nexuses may operate with respect to only one or two of the nodal institutions discussed above, rather than to all at once, and perhaps especially to the operational and recruitment institutions. Thus recruitment into a social club may be largely carried out by genealogical tracing in the families of members, with no further ties between the club and the family. On the other hand, the contractual nexuses between two corporations are likely to obtain with respect to operational rather than recruitment institutions. Both ties occur at once in the cases in which the United States government or one of its bureaucratic agencies has insisted that, in order for an operational institutional nexus to be opened, a private company redefine its recruitment institutions so as not to exclude Negroes.

The significance of nexuses is that they connect loci of structure into

[177]

larger social orderings. Through the linking of nodes, complex systems displaying different degrees of exclusiveness are built up. Ultimately, the totality of links defines the structure of the society as a whole.[11]

Nexuses can link various kinds of assemblages of nodes—sets of like nodes or sets of diverse ones. With respect to a given assemblage of nodes, like or diverse, the nexuses may be variegated. As a result, they create among the nodes a number of possible types of interaction that may be differentially mobilized with respect to different kinds of situations and needs. Again, the nexuses linking two or more nodes may be all of a kind, repeated over and over, like marriage exchanges among corporate kin groups. Here the possible kinds of interaction are limited to a very few kinds of situations. The condition of nexus diversity is more difficult to describe empirically, especially where informal ties are numerous and proportional to the number of diverse nodes and nexuses involved. Furthermore, the boundaries of the constituted larger ordering are likely to be much less clear than in simpler conditions. For diverse nexuses may not parallel each other in the ties they establish; indeed, they may even be contradictory in that a formal nexus may establish one kind of relationship between two nodes and an informal one a different and antagonistic kind. Conflict-of-interest situations are characteristic examples. In passing, it may be suggested that the evolution of society is characterized by development from situations involving like nodes linked by like nexuses (bands, for example), through various combinations of like and unlike nodes and nexuses (complex "primitive" societies like aboriginal Hawaii), to complex interlockings of unlike nodes by diverse nexuses (modern industrial societies).

Finally, it must be explicitly noted that the conception of nexuses is not limited to harmonious or cooperative relationships. Clearly, nexuses may establish antagonistic cooperation (Sumner 1906:16–19, 49, 346) and a number of forms of conflict (for instance, ritualized warfare, single combat). Other forms of conflict (strikes, for example) may be described as abrogations or abuses of existing nexuses. Even in the

[11] In this connection, we may note the vagueness of the term "society" in most current social-science usage. Definitions are notoriously feeble and the empirical content referred to by the term is nebulous. As used here, the term "society" refers to the total inventory of primary structures (nodes), their secondary higher orderings (node networks), and the interrelations among all these within a system whose boundaries can be defined according to some reasonable criterion—for example, the population and its territory to which the decisions of the state with regard to such matters as citizenship apply. The description of society in such terms is structured, concrete, and accessible.

extreme form of conflict, war, certain links are maintained (Leeds 1963:71). In general, the nexus, from the point of view of a single given node, is by definition a cooperative link. But where two or more nodes with distinct ideologies and interests are involved, the nexuses established may be only partially or temporarily cooperative.

Nodal Boundary and Nodal Network

In the discussion of nexuses and of nodal structure, self-maintenance, resources, and personnel, the concept of "nodal boundary"—the demarcation between what belongs to the node and what does not—is useful. Looked at from within the node, boundaries are created by its institutions of organization and self-maintenance, since these define, even if only generically or by implication, what is to be considered extranodal, what kinds of positions and personnel the node is *not* responsible for maintaining or sanctioning, and so on.

At another level, but just as important, two or more nodes, together with their nexuses, form a bounded structure during such time as the nodes are linked. The term "transnodal boundary" may refer to the demarcations among these larger orderings. "Transnodal networks" may also, as I have indicated, have their rules of organization and combination that establish boundaries over and above the delimitations set by the rules of the constituent nodes. The feudal estates were a case in point, since the estates as such were juridically defined bodies in addition to being entities constructed from kin, elite, associational, and other links.

It is very important to note that the dissolution of transnodal networks is by no means a dissolution of organization, whereas the dissolution of a node signifies the breaking down of organization itself. The breaking down of the nexuses between two or more nodes merely means the separation of the component nodes. The context in which this event occurs may give it great functional importance—for example, in a case of conflict between the nodes the separation may permit them to enter directly into organized conflict.

In examining such transnodal networks and their boundaries, several significant attributes may be considered.

The first is duration—the length of time during which the higher ordering of nodes persists. Duration may have important consequences with respect to the *process* of linkage, since the longer the duration, the greater the possibilities of elaborating nexuses and developing autonomous institutions for the transnodal network itself.

The second is the comprehensiveness of the nexuses. As the number and variety of established ties increases, long-term autonomous institutions at the level of the transnodal structure are more likely to develop, and greater resistance to intrusion from conflicting nodes or transnodal structures or other outside antagonistic pressures is inclined to build up. The transnodal networks may also be more resistant to development because this process involves the realignment, changing, or discontinuing not only of the internal structure of the nodes concerned but also of all the nexuses. The more complex the linkages, the more difficult is it for thoroughgoing change to occur without severe disruption of the entire system. The social system in Brazil as it relates to technology, the market, and competing procedures is a case in point (Leeds 1957).

The third attribute is similarity of ideologies. This can be of outstanding importance in providing the rationale of linkage; that is, in exhorting the personnel to maintain boundaries by observance of the institutions of the node and of its transnodal network. Ideologies also provide rationales for the *exclusion* of nodes and personnel from linkage—exclusion carried out by applying the rules of recruitment and separation and of nexus formation.

Various boundary states themselves depending on the internal structures of the nodes or of the transnodal networks can be described. At one pole we may conceive of a boundary approaching complete impermeability. By "permeability of boundary" I shall mean the capacity of a node or transnodal network to absorb new personnel, in particular, and also new statuses or status networks and new resources, sanctions, rules, or ideologies from external sources, especially from other nodes or transnodal networks. In a situation approximating impermeability, a node or node network consistently tends to exclude all the personnel, statuses, norms, and so forth, of any other node or node network in the society.

At the opposite pole we find highly permeable boundaries. Permeability may revolve around liberal rules of recruitment. For example, open examinations or self-training in the context of an expanding opportunity structure (Leeds 1964b) contrast with recruitment achieved by birth. Permeability may involve the gamut of constituent statuses and their arrangement in the node or node network. Or it may be connected, particularly in the case of internodal linkages, with the diversity and dispersion of nexuses among the constituent nodes. This is especially true where both informal and formal nexuses exist in a complex array and sometimes at odds with each other. Possibly the extreme versions of this kind of boundary are found in the American system of social stratification and associational organization.

A high degree of permeability, however, does not mean the absence of boundaries (and hence, for example, an absence of "class," as some have argued for the United States), much less of nodes. It means, rather, a fluidity—especially of recruitment and of nexus—that functions as a boundary-maintaining mechanism for nodes or nodal networks. I think this point has widely failed to be recognized in American sociological literature on the social system of the United States, which often appears to be conceived as having little or no objective social order.

Between the two extremes described there may be diverse kinds of partially permeable boundaries—various combinations of impermeability with respect to some nodal institutions and of permeability with respect to others. Most associations fall within this range. Members may be recruited from, or concurrently be members of, many other kinds of nodes. New rules and sanctions may be incorporated, as in the example of fair employment regulations imposed by the government. The Brazilian transnodal network, made up of ties among panelinhas, associations, government agencies of various sorts, and even families, provides a number of ways to recruit new personnel and new resources (Leeds 1964b).

The concept of partial boundary permeability has perhaps the greatest significance when one is dealing with the structure of the polity itself. The level of the polity, for many effects, is also the highest level of ordering of transnodal networks. No society in which the most comprehensive transnodal networks presented impermeably boundaries to each other would be viable. This is so because of the differential distribution of resources, labor, and so on, across the networks. Though the differential distribution serves the interests of various nodes and networks, it also, on the other hand, requires nexuses with other networks, since labor must be supplied and rewarded and goods and services must be produced and consumed—across nexus boundaries. Thus it occurs that boundaries may be totally impermeable and nexuses absent so far as, for example, personnel is concerned; recruitment and separation procedures do not move personnel from one node network to another, as in the case of the medieval estates or

[181]

between the Balinese aristocracy and the commoners. However, the impermeability of boundaries with respect to personnel is paralleled in these cases by complex relationships between the larger orderings of node networks as regards movements of wealth, use of force, distribution of produce, and so on. Thus with respect to, say, resources, boundaries are at least partially permeable.

In passing, we might hypothesize that the more complex the internal structure of the transnodal networks, the greater the permeability of their boundaries. Increasing permeability would then be characteristic of sociocultural evolution, producing increasingly "open" societies.

In describing the nodes and nexuses of a given society, we would be bound to describe ever more inclusive social alignments, with more and more inclusive boundaries, up to the level of the polity itself and, in some respects, beyond it to interpolity networks such as cartels and intergovernmental bodies. All these alignments are built up from the minimal loci of organization, or nodes, present in the society.

These larger orderings may be relatively stable or they may be given to frequent realignment.[12] Realignment may merely be a constant flux of rearrangement of the same entities within certain parameters (a functional process of reassortment) or it may reflect a change in the nodal and nexus content and pattern of the society (a functional process of transformation or evolution). These two later conditions seem to be well represented by current situations (in the United States in the first instance and Brazil in the second (Leeds 1964a, 1964b), whereas some of the more "traditional" Latin American countries, such as Haiti, or medieval Europe or Japan exemplify great stability. The actual condition of stability or flux would largely be indicated by the description of the nodal structure and institutions.

The structural and institutional attributes of nodes are such that they tend to elicit in the transnodal networks characteristics and operations of their own. These are especially clear when contrasted with those of other networks paralleling or opposing them. To the extent that the component nodes of a network conjointly reinforce the linkage by every conceivable institutional, juridical, and ideological means, the networks they build will be correspondingly bounded and "visible." The opposite necessarily also holds true: to the extent that

[12] A theory concerning the conditions that maintain stability and the classification of types of realignment would be highly desirable, but it cannot be considered here.

the component nodes diversify their nexuses and weaken their ties with any one other node by creating crosscutting nexuses with other categories of nodes or even node networks, the higher orderings will be that much less clearly bounded or "visible" and hence less accessible to observation and verification, though no less structured. Here again, Brazil and the United States may be contrasted.

Of itself, the purely structural description achieved by the approach I have been presenting makes no assumptions as to hierarchy or rank-ordered importance of nodes or node networks—an importance implied in such terms as "high," "upper," "lower," and the like with reference to "class." That this notion has hitherto been axiomatic in our approaches to complex societies is clear, I think, in view of the length of time it has taken to develop an alternative model to vertical stratification represented by the concept of "situs" or "horizontal stratification"[13]—a recognition that not all large-scale orderings are arranged in ranks of a hierarchy. Description in terms of nodal orderings also requires an empirical description of the ranked ordering of the nodes or node networks per se—if, indeed, any such ordering exists. It is an empirical question, not an axiomatic one, and the nature of the hierarchic superposition and subordination must be shown empirically. I shall return to this below.

The term "class" has been applied as a generic term for node networks that are or at least appear to be hierarchically or vertically arranged. Where the networks are sharply delimited and in active opposition to each other as well as hierarchically arranged, a Marxian or Millsian class ordering has been described. Where networks are ambiguously delimited or overlapping and in relatively neutral or varying relationships to each other as well as hierarchically ordered, something like a Warnerian class ordering[14] has been described. In principle, there is no reason why both types of description should not apply to a single society—as they do in the United States.[15]

---

[13] Even the term "horizontal stratification" reflects the axiom of hierarchy, despite its inherent self-contradiction (clearly, strata cannot be horizontally arranged).

[14] Not only Warnerian but also a great variety of subsequent class analyses, especially in the United States and increasingly in Latin America, have been of this kind.

[15] We might inquire why American sociologists have so consistently used one rather than the other type of analysis (see Mayntz 1967). Why have they eschewed the Marxian or Millsian approaches? Do they really wish to assert that large-scale organization of the kind these authors describe does not exist or is unimportant? Is there an ideological set among American sociologists that leads them away from a more structural analysis, especially where it leads them to examine conflict and antagonism in a "democratic" and "open" society?

Where node networks are arranged not in hierarchy but rather in parallel or horizontal relationships, the term "situs" is applicable. No systematic work that I know of has been done with regard to distinguishing different kinds of situs by relationships of opposition, neutrality, or cooperation, nor has the question of sharpness or ambiguity of delimitation been pursued.[16] It seems likely that some highly interesting classifications of sociopolitical systems might emerge from such distinctions and that considerable light might be shed on the development process. With respect to the notion of parallelism, an external criterion for establishing parallelness is as necessary as is one for demonstrating hierarchy. Parallelism cannot be assumed axiomatically; it requires an empirical referent.

A third possible relationship of a set of node networks to appropriate external criteria is that in which each network relates to the criteria uniquely—in other words, no parallel or hierarchic ordering can be established and a completely asymmetrical system results. This situation, though a logical possibility, is unlikely to have much empirical significance.

Differential Distribution of Controls

Up to this point I have presented a purely structural approach to society. The introduction of external criteria for the establishment of hierarchy, parallelism, or some other ordering begins to give us, however, the basis for dealing with the internal and external dynamics of a society both synchronically and diachronically—with such critical descriptive problems as societal articulation with the natural environment and with environments provided by internal and external sociocultural entities. In this essay, it is possible only to adumbrate these dynamics and to suggest the utility of nodal analysis in describing and understanding them as well as in resolving certain empirical problems of the description of hierarchy.

Of central importance here is the differential distribution—whether through ownership or by managerial, political, or other means—of controls over the basic sociocultural values: strategic resources, wealth, power, and productive labor. What characterizes strategic re-

---

[16] For a discussion of the overlap of situs at the level of the Brazilian national cupola, see Leeds 1964b.

sources, such as the sources of food and matériel wrested from the environment, is, first, their critical importance in the maintenance of society itself, and, second, the fact that because of their very origin in natural environments, they are not intrinsic resources (like patents or copyrights) of any given node or node network: they are either appropriated or held by right of some prior appropriation. Thus we can define a variety of relationships—conflicting, antagonistically cooperative, cooperative, and so on; in short, the internal dynamics of the society. In addition, where the relationships involve nodes or node networks of other societies, we can define the external dynamics as well. In other words, a society may be regarded as a dynamic system of node networks differentially appropriating strategic resources. The differential "success" in appropriation depends on (a) the internal attributes of the nodes or networks concerned such as their intrinsic resources, aims, rules of combination, and so forth; (b) quantitative differences in other attributes, such as control of force, between two (or more) networks competing for the control of the same strategic resources; and (c) the nature of the relationships between two (or more) node networks—for example, partial dependence of one on the other.

The descriptive delimitation of nodes and node networks is, of course, also a description of the distribution of the control of strategic resources, wealth, power, prestige, and productive labor, and of the relationship of the nodal personnel or of the nodes or node networks per se to these basic social values. However obscure and difficult the task of delimiting transnodal networks may be, the relationships between the nodal organization and the distribution of the basic social values and between any two nodes with their respective assemblages of appropriated values are more accessible to nodal analysis than to analysis in terms of "class." We are thus in a position to give empirical meaning to the concepts of hierarchy and parallelism.

Where the basic socioeconomic values are differentially distributed among nodes and node networks in such a manner that one set of nodes or networks makes decisions for or exerts social, economic, or political controls over the other set(s) of nodes, node networks, or their personnel, the situation may be described as hierarchic and the groupings may be termed "classes." On the other hand, where the basic socioeconomic values are differentially distributed among nodes and networks in such a manner that each set makes similar, though obviously not identical, decisions or possesses similar social, economic, or political controls, the situation may be described as parallel and the groupings may be termed "situs." The elements of such a distribution within a situs may be termed "factions" and, within the class that has the broadest decision-making power or the greatest control, "elites."

It appears, then, largely a matter of convenience whether, on the basis of a differential distribution of resources, power, and so forth, with respect to nodes and transnodal networks, we wish to speak of "class." Doing so can serve as a kind of shorthand, so long as we have already described the underlying structure of the system and so long as we know that class is not an entity existing merely by definition or by postulation. In modern literature it often appears to be thought of as an ontological phenomenon in its own right, treated as if it were a fleet of societal first-, second-, and nth-class buses created by Providence to be continually filled with appropriate persons and running along in time and space in self-generated perpetual motion. Not infrequently has it been regarded as a phenomenon separate from its own components—a kind of Platonic ideal or a verbal hypostatization.[17] When treated this way, the membership of the classes is often extremely difficult to identify, not to mention their internal construction. Moreover, the classes themselves take on the attributes of acting organisms, as is reflected in such phrases as "the ruling class creates a mystifying ideology." Such an approach to the treatment of social phenomena seems to me unsound in empirical science.

The word and concept "class" might perhaps be entirely dispensed with in sociological discourse by establishing a more systematic cross-societally valid set of terms referring to those components that have been associated with at least one approach to class—one that may be called "extra-subjective" or "analytic."[18] Doing without the word and concept "class" forces one not only to take a closer look at situations,

---

[17] For example, *The Monthly Review*, a journal known for its insight, often fails to clearly understand sociopolitical situations and dynamics, especially in Latin America, because it thinks in omnibus terms of a "ruling class." It fails to see the diversity of elite groups, their conflicts, their different cooperative and antagonistic ties with other "classes." (*Monthly Review*, 13(11):505ff; 14(7):370–88; 14(9):487ff; 15(2):111–12; 15(5):252–57; for a practical departure and considerable improvement, 14(11):593–612; for a lapse from that improvement, 15(2):111–12; and for a critique of many of the positions taken on Latin America, 15(11); see also Leeds 1964a, for a criticism of such positions and a description of the complexities of organization within a ruling class.)

[18] "Extra-subjective" because the class exists or is seen as existing independently of subjective individual views. The class analyses of Marx and, to a great extent, of Sombart, Weber, and Schumpeter are of this type.

like the Polynesian, for example (Sahlins 1958), that may vary quite considerably from classical conceptions of class, but also to examine in a much more refined way the varieties of organization, the subtleties of realignment and reorganization, and the phenomena of conflict and schism within what have conventionally been called classes. Furthermore, we may avoid the hopeless semantic entanglement of attempting to distinguish between class and stratification or among types of stratification.

The Advantages of Nodal Analysis

In this section I should like to discuss some advantages of the type of analysis I have been outlining. First, it seems to me that many of the problems in the analysis of so-called social mobility, and especially mobility between classes or strata, evaporate. It has long been a problem to define social mobility, particularly in contemporary U.S. society. Many of the definitions are inherently vague because they have omitted definitions of the entities within or among which, or the boundaries over which, mobility is said to have taken place. Often, indeed, there is no specification of these entities; mobility is defined, rather, in terms of evaluated positions whose structural place in the society remains undescribed.[19]

Nodal analysis intrinsically defines social entities, their internal structures, their intra- and transmodal boundaries. Consequently it defines several types of mobility: intranodal mobility, as in an individual's life history, particularly with respect to shifts of status or role within a node; internodal mobility, where the nodes are not connected by nexuses in larger social orderings; transnodal mobility, where the nodes are components of larger orderings; and, finally, mobility from one transnodal order to another. Insofar as nodes are spatially dispersed and shifts take place from node to node, we also observe geographical mobility. Thus, social mobility, far from being a single phenomenon, may be seen as a number of types of movement of persons or even, as in caste mobility, of whole nodes.

---

[19] Occupational mobility is quite easy to demonstrate because occupations are delimitable by job descriptions. Demonstration of occupational mobility, however, does not carry us very far unless we can define boundaries of occupational sets or systems—in short, nodal orderings. Change in evaluated position may also be relatively easy to show, but we still have virtually no good theory to take care of the relationship between scales of evaluated position and social structure (see Mayntz 1967 and Stavenhagen 1967).

[187]

Social mobilities might perhaps best be seen as attributes of nodal and transnodal structures, built into these structures by the structures' own social and cultural definitions both of the internal organization of the boundaries and of their relations to other node structures. Putting this argument more forcefully, I would say that social mobility is, in fact, not a subject for independent examination at all; its study is merely ancillary to structural analysis. I must emphasize, however, that I see this as a problem quite separate from the question of the temporal change of social structure—that is, the dynamics of social evolution—which may have relatively little or nothing to do with questions of mobility as such. The latter may be, and apparently often is, simply an equilibrium mechanism operating in certain types of society as a device for personnel selection.[20]

Second, this approach seems to lead more directly to the answering of empirical questions and to the construction of research designs. For example, I believe that it helps us to see more clearly the actual social structure of power—economic, political, or other—and how it operates. It also provides better grounds for establishing the existence of larger social orderings, since the scheme itself refers us to the relevant empirical data, whereas terms like "class" or "ruling class" do not. We must observe the actual personnel of nodes; we must observe the processes of recruitment and exclusion; we must observe the internal institutional structure; we must observe external relationships of the nodes. Put another way, in terms of actual field experiences—the daily observations of events and situations—we are provided with a scheme that orders and interprets our observations more immediately than the "class" concept does (Leeds 1964b).

An example of the scheme's usefulness in pointing to relevant data is the case of overlapping personnels of nodes. In the field, one of the first questions asked about the organization of the social life of the unit of study may be the degree to which this occurs. It can easily be answered by a mapping, much like a genealogical table, of the members of all possible nodes and of the nexuses among the nodes.[21] This almost at once gives a picture of boundaries of social orderings, of the exclusions, of the probable lines of conflict, of group antagonisms, and so on.

[20] See Davis and Moore 1945, which I consider not to be a model of social mobility or stratification at all but rather, essentially, a model of the process by which occupational equilibrium is maintained.

[21] Note the use of this technique by Leeds (1964b) with regard to the personnels of the various oligarchies, cliques, and so on.

Third, the scheme also seems useful in describing action and inter-action among persons and nodes. A great part of the actions and interactions of individuals in the society will be defined by the de-scription of the nodal norms themselves. For example, a full descrip-tion of the nodes involves the mapping out of the normative division of labor within or among nodes, together with the related reciprocal or complementary relationships. Similarly, in describing the nexuses among nodes we are mapping such interactions as contracts, agree-ments, "deals," and the like. And in describing situations of node or transnodal antagonism or conflict we are mapping out constraints, litigations, force, and other sanctions.

Fourth, the scheme seems to me extremely useful in the construc-tion of research designs concerning the spatial arrangements of the social order. For example, we may make a cross-sectional study of a society at a given moment in time, selecting major types of commu-nities in the body politic as loci for study. We might choose a national capital, a state capital, a county seat, a village, and possibly a farm neighborhood. We could then map the distributions of node types and their spatial nexuses, the spatial distribution of the recruitment pro-cesses, and so on. From the mapping we would get a picture of the nodal-spatial exclusions and how they operate. This would perhaps be particularly evident in political nodes and in large economic associa-tions, which are generally spatially centered in big cities to the exclu-sion and often to the expense of smaller ones—a competitive or con-flict situation. Put another way, this procedure would produce a map of hierarchic layers of access to strategic resources of power, showing how they are nodally and spatially organized.

Fifth, the scheme also seems to be useful in dealing with the tempo-ral aspects of organization. To begin with, it provides a set of catego-ries, including the names and descriptions of nodes and their person-nel, that are eminently suitable for use with historical documents. We can therefore work out the history of a given field area with a satisfac-tory degree of detail and probable accuracy, again by a variety of mapping techniques. The historical and field research can be done within the same analytic framework, with parallel and equivalent ar-rangements of data rather than with entirely different frames of refer-ence as in the historical and field aspects of the four-cities stratification study.[22] There is no problem in coordinating the two areas of the

---

[22] The field aspects of these four studies are reported on in Leeds, ed. 1967: Introduction. The historical aspects of class and stratification were, for the most part, treated in the historians' framework rather than in that of the sociologists.

research, as seems often to have been the case in anthropological and sociological studies.

Sixth, on a broader historical scale, even at an evolutionary level of analysis, the scheme is useful for tracing changing emphases among the nodes in the total social structure. In Brazil, for example, there has been a marked shift, especially in recent decades, from the preeminence of kinship nodes to that of associational and bureaucratic nodes. Such shifts are not merely symptoms of change in the social structure; they constitute the evolutionary change itself. I believe it might be possible to develop mathematical treatments for dealing with the quantitative relationships among the node types in a society and the shifts in their relative weights in the social system. In still longer evolutionary perspective, we might arrange a typology of societies on the basis of the presence or absence of node categories.

Seventh, in addition to the intracultural comparisons emphasized in the two preceding points, the scheme is useful for cross-cultural comparisons as well. For example, heretofore it has been difficult to make any fruitful or meaningful comparative statement in a single set of terms about medieval estates and, say, the social structure of the United States today, since as class phenomena the two appear to be entirely different (see Mayntz 1967). With the terminology and concepts of nodal analysis, however, they both can be viewed in terms of different kinds of alignments of structures of the same categories or different kinds of definitions of institutions of like categories (such as recruitment institutions). Both become intelligible in a single conceptual framework and possibly, ultimately, in a single theoretical framework.

Eighth, the understanding of societal structure in terms of nodes, their structures, and their arrangements seems to me to have interesting extensions that cannot be worked out in detail here, though a brief indication may be of interest. To begin with, node-nexus organization arranges the occupational inventory of society into more or less exclusive groupings. In my opinion, whatever validity occupation has as an index to social stratification derives from this fact; however, to *start* the study of social stratification with occupations is to put the cart before the horse and is guaranteed to produce considerable ambiguity in the delineation of the stratification system, if, in fact, anything at all can be determined about stratification from occupation. Moreover, node-nexus organization, with its associated wealth and power distribution, also governs the distribution of money rewards in a general way. It therefore accounts for the scalar assessments of wealth as "class" or "rank" or "prestige" markers corresponding more or less to occupational rankings, which in turn also serve as markers. Since node-nexus organization accounts for both occupational and wealth distribution, it also in a general way accounts for differences in standards of living such as housing and neighborhood. Finally, as a result, it also accounts for the kinds of ranks that Warner has described, since these are built into the structure of node and nexus organization. It does *not*, however, account for the choice of the particular values that underlie the ranking scales. To account for such choices is still a major problem of theoretical social science.

In conclusion, the approach presented here avoids some of the sterility that has fallen on much of contemporary stratification research because of its emphasis on the psychological and on the individual, its social atomization, its concern with the subjective rather than the objective loci of social stratification, and its inability to know or deal with actual structural realities regardless of the personal evaluative views of individuals participating in it. The present scheme focuses on the systems of organization in which people are actually enmeshed and toward which they may display a variety of views that, though worth recording, do not validly represent a social reality unless they are shown empirically to do so. The present approach provides ready access to such validation and also to the dynamics of stability, change, and evolution. Finally, it avoids some of the epistemological problems involved in the verbal realism that infects so much of the discussion about class and stratification today.

Desafio, Brasília, 1976. Group of singers in one of Brasília's satellite cities performing a "desafio," an improvisational musical form common to northeast Brazil. (photo by Anthony Leeds)

[6]

Marx, Class, and Power

All my professional life has revolved around several main problems
—some originally related, some not. I have tried to bring them together, over the years, into a single theoretical framework. My earliest
approach, perhaps, but one that persists still, is that of giving substance to the concept of class—chiefly in a Marxian sense. Marx or
Marx and Engels together (I shall refer to either, hereafter, simply as
"Marx"), neither invented the concept of class nor defined all the basic
understandings that form their view. The concept of class is already set
forth in its economistic and structural meanings in, for a highly significant example, Adam Smith (1776)—significant because Smith is, in
the same work, also ancestor to classical, formalist economics, which
Marx repeatedly attacked, though Marx's own economics is intimately
derived from it and Smith's assumptions play a very important role in
the structure of Marxian understandings about the economy. However, Marx integrated the discussion of class into a systematic attempt
to create a theory of class and presented substantive analyses of class
derived from that theory. In essence, these analyses constitute special
theories of particular, postcapitalist societies.

Marx's effort, as we know today, was only partly successful. It left us
with many unresolved problems that every major theorist of the twentieth century—Weber, Tawney, Lenin, Luxemburg, Lukács, Mallet,
Bottomore, Mills, Dahrendorf, Althusser, Poulantzas, to mention only
a few—have struggled with. Why the persistent effort to resolve these
problems? The answer is not immediately self-evident, and one might
respond to them by asking, "Is it not possible that these are not

problems at all, but simply conundrums created by the theory itself?" Judging by their productions, American stratification theorists, like Kingsley Davis and W. L. Warner essentially took this view.

The answer resides in the *sense* human beings have that human populations seem to act as if supra-individual entities exist as actors in society. Individual wills, cognitions, actions, and actors are widely, if not universally, seen as relatively secondary or even insignificant before these entities, for which a huge array of terms exists—"us" and "them," the State, classes, groups, estates, associations, agencies, corporations, institutions. The entities as actors are *sensed* as operating in the standardized patterns and structured ways we call "institutions" and, indeed, supra-individual patterns can be directly discerned, as in ceremonies and seating plans. Further, in our apprehensions of how life and experience are shaped, of conflict, of change, we *sense* the centrality of these entities.

I emphasize *sense* to indicate that the epistemological foundations of all such concepts and their supposed ontological referents are ambiguous, not because *sensing*—our only direct route to knowledge—is ambiguous, but because most of our scientific translations from direct sensing to empirically testable propositions, linked by standard forms of verbal logic, remain to be made methodologically explicit. Specifically, this means we need to develop a theory of the nature of supra-individual orders that specifies characteristics unique to these orders, per se—that is, characteristics not reducible to individuals (see Samuelson 1955, on the reductionist fallacy; Koestler and Smythies 1969)—a theory that also explains what the processes of generating and maintaining supra-individual orders are, since these must *necessarily* be carried by congeries of individuals. Such a theory must also explain how individuals articulate with the order.

Further, such a theory must make explicit its epistemological foundations, especially the rules of correspondence linking the original sensing with its subsequent concepts and constructs and the latter with methodologically refined observation. Put another way, I accept as axiomatic the almost universally *sensed* apprehension of the world, but, accepting it, I then, as a scientist, am required to clarify the metaphysics of such a sensed apprehension. I must root out its purely speculative or philosophical aspects and replace them with strong empirical foundations, method, and an appropriate logic. I accept that the problems Marx dealt with are indeed proper problems, since both our Western and virtually all human experience seems to display a common sensing of the nature of the human world.

Marx's achievement in clarifying what was at issue in the analysis of class was stupendous. His clarification eradicated much speculative metaphysics in the social science he developed, and he elaborated many aspects of an empirically oriented methodology, including concepts whose rules of observation are implied in their definitions. He was, nevertheless, caught—as he needs must have been at his time in the evolution of the history of ideas—in certain metaphysical difficulties which he, in part, did not see and, in part, seeing, could not resolve.

One of these difficulties is a rampant dualism reflected in his choice of a logic—the Hegelian form of dialectic (even etymologically implying dualism)—a logic whose borrowing from Hegel was not compelled by any necessity, not even by the character of the ideologies present at the time. Why did Marx opt for a logic so intimately tied to Western, and specifically *Christian*, dualistic metaphysics? As a student of philosophy during his university years, he knew the alternatives well enough. Why did he opt for a metalogic which, in effect, ontologizes the logic by making it isomorphic with real societal processes (as in Hegel), as exemplified in the spurious identification of "contradiction" (a logical conception with its locus in language) and "conflict" (a set of human relations), an identification which bedevils almost all neo-Marxist thinking?

What is seen as *logically* contradictory, according to some set of axioms underlying the logic, may or may not involve conflict, and conflict may or may not involve contradiction, unless one starts with the a priorism that they are identities. This decision was purely an axiomatic one, not justified by independent criteria at all. Marx was obviously cognizant of much of what was involved metaphysically in Hegel's work, as manifested in his attitudes toward and "inversion" of that great philosopher-historian, but Hegel's more deeply underlying commitment to dualism seems to have escaped Marx—and so many of his intellectual progeny.

This is no trifling matter since it is by no means self-evident that events occur in the universe in twos, much less in twos-in-opposition or "contradiction" (with a Trinitarian synthesis as outcome!). The notion of "contradiction," and even worse, its identification with conflict, is metaphysically a profoundly dualistic notion. I am convinced that the twoness, especially the oppositions, that we so often give ontological status can almost always be demonstrated to be a product of our axioms, categories, and logic, and to fly directly in the face of experience. Further, Marx's commitment to unfounded duality pervades his writings: any intensive reading, for example of *Das Kapital*, reveals uncalled-for and unjustified dualities on virtually every page.

Where this duality has created most problems for social science is in class analysis, because the criteria of class in the general theory of class—creators vs. appropriators of surplus value and internal organization of each aggregate of personnel so distinguished—*necessarily* leads to a two-class analysis. One can interpret much of recent neo-Marxan writing as an attempt to resolve this dilemma when confronted with social orders that "resist" (i.e., "enter into contradiction with the theory") being intellectually hammered into a two-class mold (see Serge Mallet's unsuccessful attempt, 1975). Several of my works have dealt with this problem (especially 1964b, and Chapters 4 and 5).

A related problem is that the dualistic, dialectical logic has led to treatment of the presence of class as axiomatic instead of as requiring, by Marx's own original correspondence rules, demonstration. This a priorism, which infests virtually all current social analysis in the Marxian or neo-Marxian tradition, instead of redefining and reordering class analysis by clarification of epistemic and methodological problems, has obfuscated the analysis of both structure and dynamics, because the axiom tends to preclude analysis of boundary-creating mechanisms and self-maintaining processes, as well as conflictual responses to both by other classes (see Leeds 1964a). Without spelling these mechanisms and processes out, one cannot understand "real" material outcomes, real political and social interaction, real group and individual motivation, real variations of ideology, let alone shifts in any of these over time.

My own work has increasingly involved the explicit attempt to work out, within a Marxian framework of historical materialism and a logic of multiplicities of concurrently interacting "social forces" (the term is Durkheim's, and suggests an implicit, undesirable Newtonian model of physical interaction, but will do for the moment), more refined and detailed substantive and theoretical approaches to these problems. As I indicate below, a number of my essays provide examples of this continuing effort.

We have inherited another difficulty from Marx: his identification of material foundations of society specifically with and only with production and, still further, with a relatively narrow conception of production and productive—both virtually isomorphic with these conceptions as they appear in classical and neoclassical economics. This identification is axiomatic, not empirical. One may question why Marx adopted it.

Where this difficulty emerges most strongly—early in Marx's own writings—is in the application of general Marxian theory to specific case analyses of the structure of power. It is very difficult to square Marx's general theory of power (largely based in the generic and necessarily two-class theoretical analysis of any society with private property) with a specific theory of the distribution of power in a given society at a given time and place, that is, in a concrete set of historical conditions, as Marx would say, for example, the France of *The 18th Brumaire of Louis Bonaparte* (1852). Despite Marx's warning in the *Grundrisse* against reified abstractions (e.g., 1857:18ff) and his adjuration to base all analysis in concrete realities, the general theory is full of abstractions whose application in the case analyses is, at best, ambiguously consistent, and, at worst, markedly inconsistent with the usage in the general theory, for example, the concept of "mode of production." At times his concept appears to characterize an entire society. In *The 18th Brumaire,* mode of production characterizes the foundations of various "classes" and "class fractions"—it is not even clear whether or not there were society-wide classes, which the differential appropriation of surplus value would seem necessarily to imply—sometimes looking more like ecologically based interest groups.

This ambiguous concept pervades all subsequent Marxian analysis and has been particularly noticeable in the recent resurgence of Marxian approaches, where, in extreme instances, any variation in organization of production becomes ipso facto "a mode of production" (e.g., Singer 1976). This appears to me a form of reductionism and a failure to see larger, more inclusive, and more compelling orders, not to mention the internal dynamics of such an order. For example, subsistence agriculture, one supposed "mode of production," does not exist in Brazil as a *separate* mode of production, any more than Appalachian marginal farming exists as a *separate* mode of production in the United States, but rather as a system of production generated by the capitalist mode of production itself under specifiable ecological conditions. Subsistence agriculture *is* an aspect of capitalist production when it occurs in the system of a capitalist economy and not in a tribal economy. Not only is it a form of marginalization related to capitalist profit mechanisms, but it is also a mechanism for creating more or less self-maintaining labor reserves outside the effective political centers, the cities.

To return to the problem of power. Most social science, including Marxian, not committed to a narrow or vulgar ideological Marxism

("Ich danke der liber Herr Gott dass ich kein Marxist bin," said Marx), has come to recognize sources of power other than those residing in production, that is, resources that can be used to control other actors against their will. *Any* form of organization can be used as a resource of power, even in the absence of control over or access to means of production; control of information, control over key decision-making points in a social system, mass mobilization with or without formal organization, and so forth, are all sources of power (see Chapter 7).

Marx is not unaware of this—as is obvious in his case analyses and, implicitly, in this theories concerning proletarian revolution which *must* occur by virtue of organization largely or entirely in the absence of control over, or access to, the means of production. But his dialectical theory of class with both its substantive two-class model and its two-value logic, and the assumption of their isomorphy, does not permit him to deal with this awareness systematically and theoretically. Most Marxian theory remains, rather, epiphenomenal, derivative, a product not a cause: the metaphysics of "structure" and "superstructure" (another expression of the underlying dualism).

I have over the years tried to break this impasse and develop a wider analysis of power, "its" (note the standard reification!) resources as they are distributed in society, and the dynamics of change inherent in such distributions. My first formulation of the approach (Chapter 7) was written in 1964. I have since refined and clarified it considerably, but not in systematic published form (see, however, Leeds and Leeds 1970, 1972, 1976, taken together). All the rest of the essays in Leeds and Leeds 1978, except Leeds 1964b, which preceded Chapter 7 and of which it is partly a formalization, developed from this essay. It should be noted that as soon as one specifies other sources of power one is able to escape the cul-de-sac of two-class analysis and produces a multiclass analysis, much like *The 18th Brumaire*. It might be argued that Chapter 7 is a crude statement of a general theory for which *The 18th Brumaire* provides a case history, in which the means of production and surplus value are only two of a number of resources of power.

Consistent with a materialist approach is the field of biosocial inquiry known as human ecology. This is a field in which I have done considerable research (1961c, 1964d, 1965a, 1980a; Leeds and Vayda ed. 1965) and human ecology is integrated with an elaborate description of the social organization and ideology of cocoa production in Bahia and other monoproductions of Brazil throughout its 450-year history in my dissertation (Leeds 1957). Though none of the essays [included in Leeds and Leeds 1978 or in this volume] are systematically ecological in approach, nonetheless, the ecological approach underlies several of them (especially Chapter 7 this volume; Leeds and Leeds 1970) in the grounding of their societal analyses in material, locational, topographical, physical, and climatic conditions. It should be noted that much contemporary ecological theory sees direct causal feedback from aims, goals, defined needs and wants, even esthetics— in short, ideology—to the material conditions which, in turn, have causal effects on conditions of living, hence, also, on ideology.

In a more abstract and formal form, this understanding of multiple, interacting causes is subsumed under an approach called General Systems Theory, which has developed in the last thirty to forty years out of problems of complexity in biology, engineering, meteorology, neurology, and other domains. Without going into detail here, General Systems Theory eschews two-valued logics, linear causality, unitary epistemologies imposed on phenomenally varied experience, fixed or reified categories treated as ontological entities, but accepts a much greater *degree* of variation and connectedness than most other social science paradigms. Surprisingly—or perhaps not so surprisingly— this approach is usually entirely consistent with Marx's application of his own theory to case analyses; two-valued logic largely disappears, causality emanates from many different loci in the socio-cultural system, including ideology, and runs in different directions; ideology becomes an active cause, not a relatively passive derivative; real people ideating are also actively causal; categories are, to a considerable extent, merely linguistic conventions or conveniences.

Admittedly much of what has appeared under the rubric of General Systems Theory has been merely programmatic (except in its cybernetic and information-theory subforms). Further, it has tended to be largely atemporal and ahistoric. This ahistoricity is not only *not* intrinsic, but is, in a sense, contrary to the very precepts of General Systems Theory. Since this approach conceives of systems as composed of variables which display different states at different times and occasionally, under specifiable conditions, shift to new ranges of states (a "change from quantity to quality"), temporal sequence—or history—is inherent in and essential to systems analysis, especially in so-called positive feedback or "system-amplifying" situations. Several of [my essays] are informed by a historical materialist general systems approach (especially 1969, 1973c, 1975, 1976a, 1976b, 1977a, 1980a, Chapter 7;

Leeds and Leeds 1976). Marxian writings are not as clear on different levels of system in hierarchies until the beginning of the latter third of this century, when the writings of Andre Gunder Frank appear (e.g., 1967). Frank's thinking has been fundamental to a whole generation of theorists, including myself, and was seminal in the development of Dependency Theory, which I have used occasionally (e.g., 1969, 1975) though not more than by implication in [other] essays.

In sum, all the essays concerning Brazil collected in Leeds and Leeds 1978, and including Chapter 7 in this volume, though almost without exception focused on some substantive issue in terms of specific ethnographic-sociological materials, are also theoretical attempts to clarify epistemological and methodological issues in the analysis of class and to establish specific and general modalities of class boundary formation and maintenance. They try to look at conflict in a broader frame of reference than merely class conflict, which is only one category of societal conflict. They try to develop a resource theory of power and consequent political behavior—a theory which, on one hand, subsumes the control of means of production and surplus value under a broader array of resources and, on the other, subsumes a theory of constraints of any actor upon any other actor. Finally, they try to develop a theory which allows one to deal with the entire range of actors, from individuals to international entities, in a single framework.

Thus I have been gradually merging various theoretical concerns into a more and more closely articulated theoretical system, one perhaps best articulated in Leeds and Leeds 1976. In general, the essays attempt to give tight definitions of key concepts in order to suggest rules of correspondence; the essays almost always indicate where quantification—as an epistemic procedure—is desirable or even available, even though detailed quantities are not frequently given. The situations I describe are situated in historical "contexts" which are not reified past settings, but continuous structured process whose current transect is the observed present. The analyses are committed to both a materialist understanding of the universe and a nondualistic dialectical understanding of the material world in history.

When the Gulls Fly, the Tempest Comes [1978]

This morning
between the clouds
and the torn patches of blue,
the gulls sailed up over the beach.

I went up to the shacks
where there are no gulls,
where still the tempest comes
grim and silent.

We have won our way
to each other,
my dearest friend.
I watched the policeman
go from your eyes,
their darkness become lucent
with their caring,
and your husband's
also my dear friend.

But he must go
to the mountains
to plant trees
for your new lives
while his mother's village
enslaves you
in the bald enclosure,
even among the shacks of Lisbon—
the tempest within,
against the malice
of the clipping of the wings.

When the Gulls Fly

Even the gulls find shelter
against the cutting
of the slanted rain
between our caring eyes,
the bleak grey wall of waiting.

This evening
on orange and purple wings
over a green and indigo sea,
I walked to the beach.
Your eyes were
the sea and the sky,
and the great swells
rolled up
on the beaches of my soul
to break.

São Martinho [1981]

We waited
in the dark shadows
of the kerosene candle
and the coals at the mouth of the oven
the talk threading among us quietly
as the bread baked
She swaddled the first loaves
out of the womb of the oven
in cloths to keep them soft
But soon she broke the bread—
pieces for each of us
still hot with birth
The bottle of wine
passed to all our mouths
We shared the bread
and drank the wine together
once again

Betrayals [1978]

I. There seemed to be
a growing
of light
together,
through so many
yesterdays.
But today
is today.

II. You promised
we should have,
at last,
supper
together.
But the bread
crumbled
from the drought
of our waiting.

III. In your garden
there seemed to be
so much fruit
to fill our cup.
But behind
the dead stones
of your wall
there was
so little.

IV. In time
you came to kiss me
on both cheeks—
our faith was sealed.

But to kiss
on both cheeks,
I must turn
the other.

V. On the paths
that cross
we came close.
But in the last hour
you closed
from me.
Why?

VI. The fire flamed
yesterday
for a time.
But it died
today,
or maybe tomorrow.

Localities in Urban Systems

[7]

Locality Power in Relation to Supralocal Power Institutions

This essay is an effort to develop some concepts and a model to deal with (a) the institutions of the territorial state, (b) the social unit—the community, and (c) the human-geographical unit—the locality, in a single frame of reference and as a single, systemic totality.[1]

In former days, anthropology dealt almost exclusively with sociocultural entities loosely called "tribes." These were "natural" units in the sense that they usually possessed a distinctive language or dialect; comprised socioeconomic systems or subsystems; had a series of discrete characterizing customs; and, finally, recognized themselves and were recognized by the use of some name as being separate. Such tribes are markedly constituted by autonomous locality groups (e.g., bands, villages, etc.), parallel as to ecology, institutions, culture content, and so on. The parallelism and autonomy permitted the intensive

---

[1] The essay stands essentially as written in 1964 with, however, expansion of theoretical considerations, clarification and tightening of definitions, and the like. The essay, elaborated deductively as a model, was intended as a theoretical work and a kind of position paper growing out of theoretical work on the nature of cities I had been doing for several years. It is also concerned, though this has not been underscored, with epistemological problems, particularly the status of our units of study. It was *not* intended as a data paper or abbreviated monograph. The *favela* material is only exemplary; it was not, then, properly field data at all, being based on three very brief visits to favelas combined with some reading. Subsequent fieldwork of about twenty months not only confirmed what I was arguing deductively from scraps of data but indicate that I underemphasized the argument. Data from the fieldwork are beginning to appear as indicated in the references but are not germane, in the mass, to the ends of this essay. The responsibility is mine for retaining the original form, despite criticism and several suggestions to build the theory out of the data. This was an inductive procedure I deliberately eschewed because I thought—and think—it has consistently tended to block fruitful theoretical vision.

study of one as a representative sample of all belonging to the same tribe (or so it was thought), because they were putatively complete communities.[2] From samplings of this sort, it was believed to be possible to describe a "total culture"[3] or a total society.

Anthropologists transferred this "method" to the study of complex societies when they were led to study them by the exigencies of the science and the times. They continued to focus on *localities*, a priori assumed to be communities and supposed to be representative samples of the total culture and society (e.g., Dollard 1937; Embree 1939; Lynd and Lynd 1929; Oberg and Jabiu 1960; Pierson 1949; Powdermaker 1939; Shirley 1971; Wagley 1953; Warner and Lunt 1941; West 1945; Willems 1947; and many others).

When it began to become clear that such "units" of study in complex societies are not analogs of the tribal local units and do not indeed give a picture of the totality,[4] anthropologists began to try treating sociocultural totalities in ways which were extensions of older methods, especially trait distribution and pattern analyses (cf. Benedict 1946a, 1946b; Embree 1945; Mead 1942; etc.). These, nevertheless (and necessarily), still failed to give descriptions of the functional dynamics of change and resistance to change.

For such problems of dynamics of change, resistance, and so forth, the older conceptions, models, and methods were inadequate because they did not in fact deal with the sociocultural "unit" of the complex society; that is, with the more or less clearly delimitable unit called a territorial state or country, the proper analog to the tribal locality-community.

Thus, neither anthropologists nor anyone else has presented models of an entity, for example, the United States, the community studies of

[2] The data on the Yaruro Indians, collected by Falla (personal communication), Le Besnerais (1954), Leeds (1964d), Petrullo (1939), and Rootes (personal communication) clearly demonstrate what appear to be microecological variations of some significance from village to village across a number of geographical gradients of the area; furthermore, the Yaruro are in interlocking relations with other linguistic groups or "tribes" which each have specialized ecological relations within the larger ecological system of the Llanos in which all of them exist. This sort of data, for which parallels may be found elsewhere in the world, suggest that the representativeness of single communities in "primitive" society should long have been questioned and sampling procedures used to control this kind of variation.

[3] For the concept of "total culture" see Kroeber 1948:316–18; also Leeds 1957.

[4] Cf. Steward 1950; Steward, ed. 1956; and the series of studies carried out by the Columbia University–State of Bahia project in 1950–52 (Harris 1956; Hutchinson 1957; Wagley, ed. 1952). In connection with this the following comments by Smith (1947:587) are striking: "the Brazilian rural community is not readily visualized and defined; . . . the village is by no means identical with the community; . . . the Brazilian countryman might have been called 'the man without a community.'" Cf. Leeds 1957.

which were supposed to constitute societal representatives or micro-cosmic reproductions of it. Far less have they presented what the relationships *among* the communities studied might be. For instance, what kind of structural, dynamic relationships might be said to exist between Plainville, U.S.A., and Yankee City or Middletown or Elm-town or even Hollywood? Where is the locus of such relationships? Are they to be studied in the respective localities? Are they, indeed, exemplified in the internal relationships of the ostensible "commu-nities?" If so, how? Are the only constraining parameters governing the organization and characteristics of these "communities" the local ecological conditions and the internally self-perpetuating cultural val-ues and options, or do the constraining parameters stem from a more comprehensive order, in fact, that order which *includes* locality A—Plainville, U.S.A.—and locality B–Yankee City, U.S.A.—in a single system? If the latter is the case, as this essay assumes, then we have, as anthropologists, virtually no extant methodological tools to deal with the relationships between Plainville and Yankee City, because we have not dealt anthropologically with the empirical social structure of the state and other large-scale orders in modern complex nations. This essay deals with certain aspects of these questions.[5]

The Community

By most common definitions or usages,[6] the community, especially as an object of study, is held to be a minimal social structural unit of some kind. It has generally been considered some sort of microcosm of

[5] I have dealt with other aspects elsewhere. Leeds 1964b gives a case study of how constitutive elements of social structure link localities of coordinate and hierarchic levels into national and even international networks as well, and construct social nodes of various scale which cross-cut all sorts of locality; Leeds 1964a relates local ecology, local political events, and national political events in an interactive system. Chapter 5 gives part of the theoretical framework underlying both. In Leeds 1957 the relationship between national legal systems and local social structure is extensively discussed. See also treatments of the connections of various "parts" and social loci, including "communities," in Adams 1970; Leeds 1969, 1971; Leeds and Leeds 1972.

[6] Note, for example, Murdock's statement (1949:79): "[The community] has been defined as 'the maximal group of persons who normally reside together in face-to-face association.'" Firth (1951:27–28) says, "The term community emphasizes the space-time component, the aspect of living together. It involves a recognition, derived from experience and observation, that there must be minimum conditions of agreement on common aims, and inevitably, some common ways of behaving, thinking, and feeling. Society, culture, community, these involve one another. . . ." It is interesting that Bredemeier and Stephenson (1964) do not even deal with the community!

some sort of macrocosm called the total-society, or an equivalent term. Thus, students doing community studies have assumed that the study of the community would of itself tell one about the total society.

A number of major fallacies are involved in these assumptions. First, it is not self-evident that the macrocosm is structured like the microcosm. Indeed, were anthropologists less illiterate in other social sciences, especially political science, economics, and geography, as well as the formidable political economy of the nineteenth century, it would be immediately evident on empirical grounds and impellingly clear on logical grounds that this could in no case be so. Also, on general axiomatic grounds, there would be every reason to suppose the opposite, at least for complex, state-organized societies.[7] It would seem more likely, *axiomatically,* that the localities studied in so-called community studies constitute specialized, differentiated, and variously interrelated entities of a total society possessing institutionalized mechanisms for tying them together. From such an axiom it is clear that the organization of the microcosm cannot be homologous with that of the macrocosm.

It would follow from this that the "community study" cannot possibly, in any usable definition of community, give us a description of the macrocosm; hence, that the ostensible ends of community studies were *always* off the mark. Herein lies the second great fallacy of the community study method.

It would follow, still further, that even if we had exemplary studies, one each from every category of community in a total-society or macrocosm, we would still not have such a description. A sampling from the community types of a nation, such as we now have for Brazil,[8] still gives us no picture of the interrelationships of these localities, that is, of macrocosmic *structures* and *dynamics*. All that can be derived from them are traits held in common. These may then be listed as an entirely static trait inventory characterizing the entire territorial unit of the macrocosm. On the basis of such an inventory, no prediction as to future conditions of either the macrocosm or the microcosm can be made. The inventory proves as sterile as most trait-listing, culture-

---

[7] But also, I think, for tribal societies, except perhaps for the simplest band-organized types whose locality units are, for the most part, largely autonomous.

[8] Cf. Forman 1970; Harris 1956; Hutchinson 1957; Leeds 1957; Oberg and Jabiu 1960; Pierson 1949; Shirley 1971; Wagley 1953; Wagley, ed. 1952; Willems 1947; Willems and Mussolini 1952; and from a historical point of view Morse 1951, 1958; Poppino 1953; Stein 1957.

area analyses, so common in the 1920s and 1930s, were to prove by the late 1940s when they substantially disappeared from modern anthropology as a major interest.

In short, the community study method is wholly inadequate to the study of state-organized societies, nations, complex societies, countries, or whatever one wants to call them.

We must, then, discover and analyze the direct and indirect forms of interrelationships among so-called communities or localities. This is not entirely virgin territory: political economy, political science, historical jurisprudence, and economics have been dealing with a number of such institutions for some centuries. These disciplines, however, have, for the most part, dealt only with the *forms* of interrelationship as such—with what I shall call here "supralocal institutions"—and then only with selected ones. For the most part, these have been considered without regard to the nature of their interdigitation with the "communities" and localities and without regard for the influence, in turn, of these latter on the institutions. Put another way, these disciplines have dealt with a restricted number of institutions which have been selected from among all social institutions and treated as if they operated entirely independently of local foundations. For example, economists deal with taxation, but I know of no instance in which the mobilization of local social organization to handle tax problems engendered by a given national taxation policy has been explored. I state the case extremely, but in the main the assertion is true.

Since it appears to be axiomatic among anthropologists that they are to deal with total societies or whole systems, they have been committed to attempting, and have indeed ventured, descriptions of the macrocosm.[9] But they have not been able to deal adequately with the supralocal institutions in themselves. Much less adequately, if at all, have they been able to deal with the interrelations between these institutions and the individual communities or localities with which they articulate. There are few descriptions of such relationships in the literature, with the possible exception of the sinological material, and virtually no general propositions, hypotheses, or models as to the nature of such interrelations (cf., however, Lopes 1964; Adams 1967). In what follows, I propose one such general model.

[9] Cf. Adams 1970; Adams et al. 1960; Benedict 1946b; Embree 1945; Lowie 1945; Mead 1942, 1955; Steward, ed. 1956; Wagley 1949.

The Locality

For present purposes, I shall use the term "locality" rather than "community" because of the prevailing confusions regarding the latter term as it has been used to designate the ethnographies of particular places. If one accepts Arensberg's definition (1961) or the rather different one given by Murdock (1949:79), it is clear that most so-called community studies are only dubiously studies of communities at all; they are rather studies of localities. The status of the locus of study in these field researches as an actual unit of the social order is most ambiguous in the sense of Arensberg's definition of community. In any case, he defines at best a unit conceived in isolation, not one which acts with respect to other units in a total system.

The term "locality," however, refers, in the context of human geographic distributions, to sensorily distinct loci of settlement characterized by such things as more or less stable aggregates of people or inventories of houses, generally surrounded by and including relatively empty, though not unused, spaces. Thus, what we ordinarily call a city, a town, a village, but also oil drilling platforms and mining camps, are localities. Visually distinct subareas of a city, sharply marked off like squatter settlements or a cathedral close, also fall under the definition. No matter how simple the locus, this still holds true. Even a farmstead, probably the simplest kind of locus of all, is a locality by the definition given.

It can be shown on theoretical grounds that localities comprise nodes of interaction (cf. Leeds 1976a), the points of greatest density and widest variety of categories of behavior in the area, but not necessarily having an exhaustive array of such categories of behavior as are required for the community by Arensberg's definition. This comment applies not only to towns and villages, but even to the cathedral close and to the farmstead mentioned above. They are places of greatest density and widest variety of categories of human behavior when seen in contrast to the space in between them and the next locality; economic, social, religious, and so on, transactions and behaviors all are concentrated there.

Long-term and customary face-to-face interaction and personalized relationships of all kinds are preponderantly locality interactions, but not exclusively so. It must be noted, however, that the definition does *not* imply that all relationships in localities are of these types; they may be impersonal and secondary ones. Indeed, it is the specific intent of the definition to be neutral in this respect so that the nature of the relationships becomes an empirical question rather than a definitional one; it may be the case, ideally, that *no* personalized relationships exist in the locality; that there are solely impersonal and secondary ones without community characteristics or feeling.

Thus, use of the term "locality" does not commit us to postulating a minimal or maximal unit of organization like the "community" (see McIver and Page 1949:281–309), nor to arguing about its ontological status. We need only develop adequate and relevant tools to deal with its empirical description.

It does not commit us to assuming that the locality in which we have lived and done research as anthropologists is also a community. It often is not or is only partially so. The fact that the localities anthropologists and sociologists have studied are so often not communities is, of course, another major ambiguity of the community study method in its attempt to deal with the macrocosmic society of which the communities are a part.

Characteristics of the Locality

Localities as loci of interaction, as I have noted above, are characterized, even in very simple localities, by a highly complex web of divers types of relationships. The most active kinship ties—those within the nuclear family and, often, those with close relatives—are largely to be found in the locality, especially a small one. The most immediate, numerous, and lively (if not the deepest) friendships tend to be in the locality. The majority of one's ritual kinfolk tend to be in the locality where they may be mobilized more or less instantaneously. One's neighbors whom one may call on for various ends are by definition in the locality. The ambience, as defined by Caplow (1955), is in great part necessarily a locality phenomenon. A plethora of informal groups such as cliques, gangs, work groups, and the like, as well as small associations whose interests and range of action are necessarily rather limited (e.g., a town band or a samba school) are phenomena of localities.

In contrast to kinship, ritual kinship, friendship, ambience, neighbor, informal group, and small associational personalized face-to-face relationships, countless impersonal face-to-face and secondary relationships also may characterize localities as loci of transaction and interaction (cf. Leeds 1976a, Chapter 5). The vast array includes mass services (such as are rendered by subway change-makers or restaurant cashiers), one-time services (like those of department-store sales clerks), buying and selling in the impersonal market, memberships in secondary groups (such as corporate bodies like a university or, more strikingly, mail-order book or record "clubs"), support from welfare agencies, and so on. Such relationships as these plainly do not fall under Murdock's definition of community and do not clearly relate to Arensberg's.

Inhabitants of localities interrelate by means of modes of action falling into many or all of these categories and hold them in readiness for meeting the contingencies and exigencies of daily life. Individuals choose among these modes, mobilizing now one, now another, as occasion and utility warrant. It is of greatest significance that, for most occasions or ends, two or more types of relationships might well be useful and mobilizable.

On one hand, to help in a moment of financial crisis one might call on friends, neighbors, kin, and ritual kin. To give support at sudden death, the same types of personnel might be called upon. To resist taxation or other external impositions, these types, as well as work groups and cliques, perhaps, may be called into play to serve as informal and undetectable distributive networks moving wealth away from the hand of the tax collector. All of these forms of organization may also facilitate the active preservation of valued cultural traditions and orientations against encroachments from outside.

On the other hand, localities, depending on size, may possess formal, institutional modes of action, in greater or smaller number, which may also be used to deal with such problems as financial crisis, sudden death, or others. Again, the question is an empirical one, not to be handled by assumptions which include or exclude these links from consideration.

The same kinds of relationships may be called upon to handle the extraordinary exigencies of life, especially those not arising from the daily routine characteristic of, or imposed by, the institutionalized economic, political, or social features of the locality. The most typical exigencies of this sort are external, imposed from outside the locality by supra-local agencies, and may include taxation, draft, military coercion, and others; these are discussed below. Among the most effective kinds of relationships to handle such exigencies are the informal and personalized ones, facilitated by proximity in the locality.

In sum, the social organization of the locality may be seen as a highly flexible system of human adaptation. Its very flexibility and looseness of organization, its unchartered and unspecified (or, one might say, unrationalized and unbureaucratized) complexity, permits it a wide range of responses to an almost infinite variety of events, contexts, and exigencies. Its flexibility permits rapid mobilization of its social and economic resources for different ends and in diverse forms, often under the most extreme stress, in a way not achievable by any other system of organization. It is limited only by the extent of the total available resources in land, matériel, personnel, and finances. These, of course, vary greatly in kind and among in different kinds of localities, as, for example, between a college town and a proletarian slum in Rio de Janeiro. The extent of the limitations is itself an important factor in giving form to the power and institutional interrelationships of locality and supralocal agencies.

In this connection, it is of utmost importance to note that all localities are also in some way ecological entities. That is, they are populations related to some tract of territory, possessing some resources, however minimal, including human labor. They are themselves differentially ordered into specialized areas and activities, often at least partly related to territorial differences and to the point of impingement of external influences (e.g., gas stations at the road entrances to towns, entry points of power lines, etc.).

Further, since the system of organization is so flexible, we should expect to observe not only long-term physical continuities of such localities, but also continuities of their characteristic orderings of the various types of ties, both internally and with respect to changing supralocal structures encroaching from the outside. Thus, though the government or even the state may change, the locality continues. Near Eastern villages, as Braidwood somewhere has remarked, Bolivian and other corporate communities, the Russian *mir,* the Indian village "community," and many other forms of locality are cases in point.

Two other features of localities may be noted. First, individuals are identified by their residence in and/or origin from some locality, for example, an Edinburgher living in Kensington, London, or a Recifense living in *favela* Tuiutí, in Rio de Janeiro. Residential identification involves no specification as to membership in a community or group, although such membership may actually exist. Again it is an *empirical* question, not a definitional one.

Second, the definition of locality allows for different levels of locality, one including the other; a kind of nested hierarchy, as for example in Rio de Janeiro: favela Babilônia, within the area called Lido, within the area called Copacabana, within the Regional Administration of Copacabana, within the area called the South Zone, within Rio de Janeiro City, within Greater Rio de Janeiro, and so on. Each of these levels is relevant to some set of supralocal institutions, which also occur as a nested hierarchy; or several levels of the one may be in relation to several of the other at the same time.

The amorphousness, multiplicity, and kaleidoscopic quality of the organization of localities, which give rise to the flexibility I have mentioned, are very difficult to grasp intellectually, even by the specially trained. By the same token, they are virtually impossible to legislate for (or against) or to control by uniform sets of sanctions. The only fully effective control over localities, one which would affect all forms of organization, would be total coercion through major application of force. Because of these conditions, localities are almost always found to be characterized by a certain autonomy from external agencies and institutions, a certain ability to enter into relationships with them as independent bodies. This independence is maintained by the "padding" provided by the complex of social relationships in the locality against the impact of these supralocal entities. In this independence and its social and ecological bases is found a locus of power for cooperation with—but especially for resistance against the encroachments of—the supralocal institutions, as will be seen. It is also the basis for the emergence of the true community: a cross-section of all major institutions of society transected by a local, self-maintaining boundary.

The Structure and Resources of Power

Before developing the argument further, we must turn briefly to the subject of power. The literature on power is monumental, but one thing appears to be increasingly clear. A definition of power which narrowly limits itself, on one hand, to the special prerogatives of the state or its personnel or to the institutions of state, or, on the other hand, to the control of strategic resources (which may also be wholly or partly state prerogatives) is entirely inadequate. The essential dimensions of the notion of power appear to be the exercise of some control, as individual or group, over one's own situation and the exercise of some effect on the situation of others. To speak of the *potential* to exercise such controls seems to me useless because it is neither observable nor measurable.

The only intelligible sense in which one might speak of power as potential is by considering the dimensions indicated above simply as the expression in action of a subset of empirically describable attributes among the many possible attributes that statuses, roles, or status and role networks may possess (see Chapter 5, for definition of these terms). The attributes in question appear to be of two main types: (a) an explicit right or privilege belonging to the status, role, or network by its cultural definition; and (b) a tactical location achieved by virtue of one's position in a status or role network (without any right being defined). Both the right and the tactical location are used to protect interests and prerogatives of the statuses and roles, and their networks and incumbents, by the application of sanctions, however these may be formulated.

The observation and measurement of power involve, then, on one hand, the description of situations in which controls are being exercised and for which the resources involved can be specified, and, on the other, the statuses, roles, and status and role networks, whose attributes are rights and privileges or tactical locations (see Mills 1956).

When such rights are differentially distributed among two (or more) groups, both of which agree to the right of one of the groups to exercise sanctions, a stable, peaceable arrangement exists. Where each group defines its own right of sanction, it is likely that conflict and opposition exist, and a constant tension and oscillation of power between the groups occur. If tactical locations are differentially distributed among two (or more) groups, relations may be peaceable or antagonistic, depending on whether the group controlling the locations and the noncontrolling group do or do not recognize the possession of the tactical location. Where the noncontrolling group does not cognize the existence of the tactical location, relations are likely to be peaceable (note, here, the role of ideology); where it does cognize the location, relations are likely to be antagonistic unless no countervailing rights or tactical locations are available to the group.

With respect to the resources of power, we may refer as a point of departure to Bierstedt (1967), who argues that power has three major sources: (a) the control of material resources; (b) the use of organization; and (c) mobilizable masses of persons. He argues that these three sources of power generally correspond to three great classes, respectively an upper, resource-controlling class; a middle class marked by endless arrays of large- and small-scale associations; and a lower class represented simply by quantity of personnel—the masses.

Extending Bierstedt's remarks, it is plain that each class in a class system possesses some degree of control over each source, though one of them may predominate. Thus, the groups of people who control strategic resources are also highly organized (e.g., the National Association of Manufacturers, the NAM; the Chamber of Commerce; the National Farm Bureau), probably *necessarily* so. The organized middle "classes," in the United States at least, are also extremely numerous, perhaps outnumbering the "masses" themselves, that is, those social levels supposedly characterized mainly by large numbers.

It is extremely useful to examine the distribution of Bierstedt's sources of power in the population at large in order to be able to map out power relations. Here we shall examine the distribution of such sources in localities and in the external, or supralocal, institutions which they confront.

Localities and the Sources of Power

The tenor of the preceding discussion has been that localities are in fact highly organized segments of the total population and are characterized by varying degrees of control over certain resources, especially those of territory and personnel, as well as a certain amount of capital, however small (Fried 1962). Most important, however, is that they are organized, indeed highly organized, but in the very special way I have described; that is, in a multifold, flexible, complex structure. By virtue of their possession of these sources of power, however limited, localities can be considered loci of power in the society at large, varying according to their unique histories, their geographical bases, their position in the locality hierarchy, and so on.

As loci of power, they can, therefore, enter into various sorts of interrelationships with other loci of power, characterized by different conjunctures of power sources. These relationships can be quite dynamic and may be of various sorts, for example, cooperative, hostile, competitive, autonomous, or *several of these at once*. Actual interrelationships observed between a locality and supralocal institutions are usually of several kinds at one time. The modalities of interaction obtaining at a given moment will depend on the various interests of both parties to the relationship and the social structure of the relationship itself. Where several different localities, especially if of different types, are interacting with several different types of supralocal structures in several different ways, the actual situation may be most complex and its description extremely difficult.

Supralocal Structures and Institutions

We may now turn to supralocal structures and institutions. The term "supralocal structures" refers to social bodies to whose organizational principles any given set of local and ecological conditions is irrelevant; that is, in their fundamental principles of action, supralocal structures confront any locality, any sociogeographical subunit of the total system or its subdivisions, with uniform, generalized, organizational, and operational norms or equipment. "Supralocal institutions" refers to principles and manners of operation of supralocal structures. Any structure whose form is not governed by, or related to, a given locality, and which confronts a number of localities identically, is a supralocal structure operating with supralocal institutions.

Among such supralocal structures and institutions are business organizations of national scale, the banking system, the price-making market or indeed the national economy itself, national political organizations (notably parties), labor unions, large-scale professional and private-interest associations (the NAM; the American Medical Association, the American Anthropological Association), paragovernmental associations (like the association of U.S. state governors or of secretaries of agriculture), and the state itself, including parts of the electoral system, the judiciary, the educational system, monetary agencies, administrative bureaucracies, and so on.

Together, the decision-making personnel of these structures comprise, either directly or indirectly, the major controllers of strategic resources—that is, of one of the significant sources of power. They are themselves highly organized, thereby utilizing another source of power, though availing themselves of only a narrow range of forms of organization. Many of the organizations involve significant masses of people, for example the large labor unions.

It should be noted, in terms of a general model, that supralocal structures such as national business organizations, labor unions, and political parties are recent evolutionary phenomena. Throughout recent evolutionary history, the most widespread supralocal structure has been the state (as opposed to sibs or age-sets, for example, which often would better be designated as "translocal"). For the present, I shall consider only the state and its generic relations to localities, especially in its hostile interactions, returning later to other supralocal institutions like national business organizations and parties.

The State and Localities

The state and its agencies, as social bodies or systems, exercise modes of control over their own situation and especially, of course, over the situations of others by means of a variety of institutions. The ends of state are dual: first, the public coordination, administration, and maintenance of order in the entire polity, and second, its own private self-maintenance as a special-interest group, usually composed of a dominating class or its representatives.

The first, the public end of state—that is, the supervision of the interests of the polity—is itself ambivalent because often the interests of the polity may correspond, for different reasons, to the private interest of the state in maintaining itself. This is the situation in contemporary Mexico where every sector of the polity—business, labor, peasantry, Church, and so on— each for its own reasons, works in the general interest of the polity to foster growth, increase consumption, widen distribution, and maintain order. But the state, in aggrandizing its own power, aims, and control as a private interest group, covertly operates just like the other sectors in the pursuit of its own goals by manipulating the overt–that is, public–ends of state so as to achieve those goals.

This duality of the ends of state entails, in its relationships with localities, a corresponding duality or perhaps, even better, polarity, one end of which involves clear-cut, cooperative relationships arising out of common interests and the other clear-cut antagonisms and struggle. Intermediate stages involve more ambiguous cooperations growing out of *different* goals which may be achieved by common means; rather neutral relations of ambivalent coexistence or generalized autonomy; resistance without overt antagonism, and so on.

These various types of relationship may be seen as a kind of scale. When the pressures of supra-local institutions on localities grow greater, relationships tend to drift toward the antagonistic end of the polarity. As the pressures of the supralocal institutions grow less vigorous or fewer, cooperation and autonomy tend to increase. The semi-autonomous villages or communities described for the Guatemala of twenty or thirty years ago, the Indian village community, and the Russian *mir* are perhaps examples of the latter. Though in each of these cases the pressures were doubtless considerable, yet for the most part they were restricted to a very narrow range of institutions, particularly taxation in money, kind, or labor. In other respects, the localities tended to be left to themselves to manage their own affairs internally. Only in special circumstances or at moments of crisis in the state or the locality did the state exert many and great pressures, including military sanctions, on the locality.

There is, then, always a dual tendency. On one hand, there is the pull toward common assent to the state's policy ends and their associated operations, simply because they contribute to the viability or well-being of the locality in terms of public order, welfare, relief, handling of foreign relations, and so forth. On the other hand, there is the tendency to antagonism toward the private ends of the state and their associated operations (which may merely be intensifications of the same operations that are used for the public policy ends but to a point beyond endurance), because they deny or curtail the interests, welfare, well-being, and so on, of the locality.

A word must be said about the emergence of national business and political structures as supralocal entities. Both of these, for intrinsic structural reasons, require access to large numbers of people for mass labor, memberships, votes, and the like, a condition *not* necessarily characteristic of the structures of the state. It becomes critical for the national business and political structures (though each in its own way) to have direct access to, control over, and use of masses of people. As the structures evolve, they require new forms of articulation between themselves, especially their supralocal decision-making bodies, and the masses of people, whose daily lives are largely locality-oriented in work, homes, schools, and so on. In other words, as society evolves, new types of complementary and dual relationships between localities and supralocal institutions emerge and old ones disappear. Any given historical situation displays combinations of both new and old types, but, of course, the kinds of combinations possible in a given society will vary sequentially as it evolves.

Further, the supralocal decision-makers of each of these types of national structures, while distinct from the mass of personnel of their own organizations, are linked with each other. The linkage is necessary because access to decision-making is itself a resource, and, for both value and operational reasons, must be kept among restricted groups of people.

Not only are the decision-makers linked with one another, even where they are competitive, but also they must, to some minimal degree, be channeled into the state in its role as coordinator of the polity. These linkings may pivot around common ends or around discrete goals—in general, cooperatively achievable. Both conditions are presently observable in Mexico in the relations between the state and parties, business, and labor, all of which tend to become supralocal structures in various complementary, multivalent relationships of opposition, cooperation, and neutrality with localities.

The state, therefore, occupies a key role as a set of supralocal institutions; first, because it is a channel and coordinator for the rest of the supralocal institutions of the society at large, and second, because it does not necessarily depend directly on masses for its resources but can exercise control over resources, numbers, and organizations by virtue of its public polity purposes, in a relatively autonomous and indirect way.

In general the evolution of society involves a continuous adjustment and readjustment between locality and supralocal power institutions. Any shift in resources or the institutions of control brings about shifts in the power relations, shifts which may be responded to by still further adjustments to compensate for the shifts. Power systems, as conceived here, may thus be seen as moving equilibria, occasionally passing into disequilibria or, through quantum leaps, from one equilibrium state to another.

State and Locality—The Favela Case

The dual or multiple relationships between the locality, on one hand, and the state and nonstate supralocal institutions, on the other, may be illustrated by the interactions between a special type of locality and a number of supralocal structures. I speak of the urban slum, and shall refer here especially to data on Brazilian favelas[10] and agencies of state.

In brief, the favela is a human-geographic unit, easily observable, possessing all of the forms of organization mentioned above as characteristic of localities. The favela has an ecology, that is, a distribution of social activities across its territory responding to topography, soils, and other geographic conditions. This distribution is often governed by, for example, the rain forests on the saddles of the hills dividing Rio de Janeiro into segments, which provide hideouts for criminals, while the thoroughfares at the base of the hills are sites for stores and other economic activities and for the entry of power lines and water supply. Thus, the territorial favela is subdivided into socially specialized zones which pattern daily activities.

On the whole favelas maintain their own order, a truly community-like endeavor. Bringing in the police—a supralocal organization—is rigorously avoided. Yet crime is not rampant in the favela, and even in the absence of the police, agents of the state, public order is generally well-established.

The favela is very complexly organized by kinship, pseudo-kinship, ambience, friendship, workgroup, clique, neighborhood, associational, and other ties. The social behavior of the favela consists of a constant flux among these, at least insofar as interaction takes place within the locality, a point I return to below. The importance of associational life is not to be underestimated, at least in Brazil. Recent evidence indicates that many favelas have an extraordinarily elaborate structure revolving about Carnaval clubs. Presently, many favelas, at least in Rio, also have favela civic associations which provide centralizing nodes of organization. All favelas have several kinds of church associations, as well.

---

[10] Strictly speaking favelas are not slums, but are discussed here as such because they are generally so conceived and treated. If one defines a slum as an area of a city with decaying housing, relatively high rents (in proportion to the salaries of residents), virtually no home ownership, substandard facilities, and high population density, where buildings are ordinarily officially docketed in the appropriate registry of titles, then a favela is not a slum. Favelas, for the most part, are areas of improvement occurring by means of the private investment of generally poor but independent homeowners who are squatters on the lands of others, on which, over time, the facilities tend to improve, though they tend also to be substandard. Population density, as in the slums, is quite high, but this is also true of some solid "middle" and "upper-middle" class areas of Rio de Janeiro, like parts of the south end of Copacabana, with up to about 3,000 persons per hectare (CEDUG 1965:152, 153). What is true of favelas in Rio is also true of Lima's barriadas (see Mangin 1967b; Turner and Mangin 1963) and squatter settlements in other parts of Latin America.

Nevertheless, it should be noted that the social relations occurring in a favela are preeminently of a face-to-face and personal sort, a fact which has led so many writers to speak of the urban "slums" (meaning squatter settlements) of Latin America as being "rural" in social and value structure (cf. Bonilla 1961, 1962; Pearse 1957; also Leeds and Leeds 1970). The attribute of rurality is made even though the "slum" dwellers have immigrated not from rural areas but from towns where, presumably, the immigrants *should* have learned urban ways. The attribution is even made in instances where the favela dwellers and the favela itself have been in situ for two, three, four, and more generations. Descriptions of Rio slums, or *cortiços*, from the mid- to late nineteenth century (cf. Azevedo 1891)[11] are remarkably like those of the mid-twentieth century. Observers have spoken of the favelas as rural enclaves in the city, despite much significant data which makes such descriptions misleading or entirely erroneous.

In this regard, I have already spoken of the existence of associational life in the favela, which is a feature not widely characteristic of rural or peasant areas of Brazil. I have mentioned a fair degree of ecological and social specialization. There are, however, other evidences against this rurality as well. For example, it seems that among those favela dwellers who have indeed come directly from rural areas a rapid shift of values in the direction of an urban orientation often takes place (cf. Cate 1962, 1963; Real 1967; and others). Second, there is much evidence that family structure changes (cf. Hammel 1961, 1964), for example, toward serial common-law marriages, toward matricentered family groups, toward a narrowing of the generational range (largely to two, rather than three or even four generations as in the country). Another way of saying this is that the demographic distribution according to age and sex is sharply changed from rural patterns. Other evidence will be discussed below in connection with the external relations of the favela.

[11] The cortiço no longer exists in Rio, with one or two exceptions. It was a multiunit rooming house, built by building speculators for low-income rentals, laid out, usually, in a double row with a group of toilets at one end or in the middle of the courtyard where, too, were found the water faucets and laundry tubs which serviced the entire set of rooms. A good deal of community life centered in these rooming house-enclosures and around the wash tubs and water faucets. The cortiço residents appear to have been one of the pools of people from which the favela populations began to be drawn around the turn of the century and afterward as the decaying cortiços were gradually destroyed, mostly to be replaced by higher-rent housing. With respect to the question of the urbanness of the favela residents, see Leeds and Leeds 1970.

Under all these circumstances, the question arises why the face-to-face—the ostensibly "rural" relationships—exist, or, according to current thinking, persist, in the favela. It seems to me that part of the answer to this question lies not in origins (i.e., persistences), but in the fact that these relationships, given the ecology and demography of the favela, must perforce be face-to-face. The other part of the answer, the more important one, lies in the relationships of the favela to its supralocal environment. I am, then, arguing that the long-term continuity of those aspects of the favelas that observers have called "rural" is a functional question and only incidentally a question of origins (or history), and especially so when the favela is considered in the context of supralocal structures and institutions, as I shall try to show.

Favelas as Localities vs. Supralocal Structures and Institutions

How shall we look at these ecological, social, and legal characteristics of the favela (or also of a slum) which we have been discussing? The conceptions of locality power, supralocal power institutions, and their relationships are useful here.

Favelas, as well as slum localities, in Brazil and undoubtedly generally in Latin America and other parts of the world, confront a highly organized set of structures which control strategic resources, make decisions, and operate with respect to the nation as a whole, that is, supralocally. The structures operate both singly, in their own right, and linked together, especially through the state.

The supralocal demands on the favela appear in the form of taxes, ground rents, charges for utilities, draft, police pressure or interference, and, of course, vote solicitation and labor recruitment. Taxes, rents, utility charges, and like institutions are all supralocal institutions which drain notably scarce resources from the locality, whether favela or slum. As a rule, favela social organization apparently mitigates—that is to say, exerts a certain power of resistance against—these drains, unless the demands are too oppressively enforced. Unbeknownst to the supralocal agencies, the social organization may serve to redistribute the meager resources among the favela and slum dwellers by means of mutual aid devices and the like, in such a way as to decrease the take of the agencies. It may operate to make "illicit" uses of utilities. It may help to reduce or evade the payment of rents by keeping all information about unapproved construction tightly

[227]

within the favela community, entry into which by rentier types for inspection purposes is difficult or unsalutary.

Favela and slum social organization serves as a highly complex but effective communication system which, however limiting the conditions under which it operates, helps to maximize the advantages to be extracted from the external agencies and their personnels, and to reduce stress. These and a host of other procedures can only be carried out by forms of organization operating specifically within the local ecological units.

However, favela and slum resistance may be more active, as in Brazil today, where favelas, often through their favela civic associations, have moved judicially against unjustified rent practices. The law has also been used for other purposes in recent times. That is, the favela, as a locality, acts as a juridical person against outside pressure. To do so, it makes use of institutions arising from the polity ends of state, against both nonstate supralocal interests and against the interests of the state-as-private-person.

However, from an external point of view, the most important resource of the favela or slum locality is, of course, masses of people: in a place like Rio, where perhaps 20–25 per cent of the city's population lives in "unsightly" favelas, they constitute significant parts of the electorate and of the labor force. They also comprise potentially large forces of riot and rebellion. As an electorate and labor force, from the point of view of the supralocal structures, they are to be mobilized as means to achieve ends of supralocal personnel; as a potential force for riot and disorder, they are to be contained or actively repressed—contradictory tasks of the supralocal agents, between which these agents must necessarily oscillate. These relationships are characteristic of certain types of societies in which mass exploitation is important to the economy and polity—capitalist societies, and possibly others based on private gain from resource control.

These contradictory tasks enjoin a series of relationships with the locality which the locality, in turn, exploits as much as possible or evades by means of its own forms of organization and by use of its available power resources, extremely limited as most of them may be. Thus, for example, the parties, on one hand, and the state in its polity role, on the other, are brought into the position of doing favors for, carrying out public works in, providing public welfare and relief to, the residents of the favelas. In other words, a distribution of resources of the supralocal structures to the locality occurs, which, however limited it may be, nevertheless helps insure the viability of the locality whose sanctions are riot, disorder, noncooperation or opposition by means of voting, legal recourse, and so on. A response to both status attributes and tactical location—in other words, to power—is made.

On the other hand, when supralocal agencies attempt actively to repress, stress may be minimized by using the flexible organization of the favela or slum. The locality can, for example, use its social structure to spirit away the person or persons sought by the police, make wanted goods and material disappear, withhold information, deceive and mislead with great consistency, and so forth. No one and nothing can be found. The only solution for the supralocal agency is the elimination of the locality itself. In Brazil, there have been instances of this, as when a Rio favela was burned to the ground on the grounds that it was harboring criminals.

In sum, with respect to favela locality organization, it may be said that the viability and long-term continuity of favelas as phenomena can, in considerable part, be accounted for in terms of their effectiveness as loci of power in countering, evading, or making use of pressures of supralocal institutions in the interests of the locality, especially under highly stressful conditions. It may be said, too, that their so-called rural attributes are not necessarily rural at all but the functionally most effective organizational adaptations in the *urban* context in view of their economic, social, and institutional resources and the constraints operating on them. Any other organizational alternative for the larger mass of favela dwellers is likely to put most of them in much worse condition, given the exploitative foundations of the society referred to above, than that which they are constrained to when living in the favela—a fact that must be kept in mind in all development and housing or urban renewal schemes.

Generalizations and Conclusions

Generalizing from the favela material, I would propose that many, if not all, long-term continuities of localities (such as Bolivian corporate communities, the Near Eastern villages Braidwood speaks of as being continuous with ancient times, or the village communities of India), in contrast with the relative changeability of states which have come and gone, may be accounted for in terms of the conception of locality power presented here. The explanation seems to me the more powerful when land resources for food production and military action are involved in the locality situation.

In this regard, as an example, it seems easier to understand the slowness of Soviet agricultural development despite (or better, because of) constant, vigorous, and sometimes violent supralocal pressures. The agricultural populations which have been developing so slowly are locality groupings under pressure, variously resisting supralocal blandishments while preserving their own interests (as yet undescribed[12]). Real revolution in agriculture involves demolition of old forms of locality power and their replacement either by new forms or by total supralocal control.[13] The institution of the Chinese communes by the Red Chinese supralocal agencies was just such a demolition of old forms and replacement by new, just as the Cultural Revolution destroyed locality features and translocal extensions of the archaic, patriarchal, capital-holding extended family. The implications of this sort of analysis for agrarian reform and community development seem to me numerous but cannot be developed here.

In sum, localities may be looked at as loci of certain forms of power, often in highly attenuated condition: supralocal structures as loci of other forms of power whose intensity of concentration and application may vary greatly over time. Localities and supralocal structures, with their respective forms of power, enter into a variety of oppositional, cooperative, complementary, and other types of relationship which constitute some of the most important structures of the total society, though they have largely been neglected in the literature. They require a great deal of fundamental research. Doing such research requires specification of those forms of national structures and institutions which are almost always, at best, treated peripherally in anthropological studies, though it is specifically the supralocal or national character of these entities that ties communities or localities into

[12] Soviet social scientists have only in the past few years begun to recognize that there is indeed a need here and that "value" and "psychological" aspects play a more active role in society than they had been willing to allow. The German Democratic Republic early recognized this and permitted more local interest openly to operate in agriculture by attempting to preserve, at least in part, the local social arrangements of work even though property was made largely collective (interview with collective farm administrative committee, near Leipzig, G.D.R., August 1964).

[13] Most schemes for agrarian reform are not revolutionary in this sense at all but tend rather to foster the ossification of old forms of locality organization. Most of the schemes seem to me, then, preordained to fail from the very beginning. Since the schemes are almost entirely formulated by personnel of the supralocal agencies, one may well ask about the function of such failures.

a single system. One needs, then, conceptually well-formulated anthropological descriptions of national institutions, of localities and communities, and of the arrangements of their interrelationships. Only then will we be able to develop adequate theories of change and resistance to change.

Rio demolition, 1976. The irony of urban development. (photo by Anthony Leeds)

[8]

The Anthropology of Cities:
Some Methodological Issues

This essay is concerned with what an anthropologist is to do in a field situation when carrying out ethnography in any given city, that is, with what knowledge is to be acquired about a city rather than with the theory of cities. The two are intimately connected since the latter specifies what knowledge is to be sought, but, nevertheless, they involve quite different concepts and thoroughly different methodologies. The essay, then, is concerned with some theoretical considerations regarding the content of cities, rather than the theory of cities.[1]

The considerable amount of anthropological or closely related fieldwork dealing with social and cultural phenomena observed in cities has done mainly one of two things.

On one hand, it has dealt with social phenomena which, like kinship, are not restricted to the city or even to urban society (including its country aspect). In such studies,[2] the question asked has generally been, "How is kinship operating in this city?", not, "What is the effect of cityness on the operation of kinship?", that is, what systemic and characteristic aspects of kinship—if any—are elicited or forced into being in the city, and only in the city, as a function of specifiable features, or variables if you will, characteristic of the city. They have

---

[1] I have dealt with some theoretical aspects in Leeds 1968c.

[2] See Bott 1957; Clifton, 1966; DESAL 1966; Epstein 1961; Firth, ed. 1956; Goldrich 1965; Leacock 1969; Leeds 1964b; Lewis 1966a, 1966b; Mangin 1959; Meillassoux 1960; Patch 1967; Pearse 1957; Warner and Lunt 1941; Whiteford 1960; Willmott and Young 1960; Young and Willmott 1957.

been studies of kinship in the city, not of the city in kinship. Generally, they have been (a) particularistic; (b) in the mold of kinship studies carried out in the country areas and among "primitives"; and, (c) evasive of dealing with the urban ambience as such, to which the kinship organization is related. Studies of other kinds of social life—networks, associations, and so on—have tended to take the same approach. In short, all such studies have, as far as the city aspect is concerned, tended to be nongeneralizable, not related to generalizable theory, models, or hypotheses, and hence not generative of broader theory as to cities, urban society, or the social evolution of urbanized societies.

On the other hand, anthropological work has been the kind of community study approach exemplified by Leeds, Lewis, Mangin, Padilla, Patch, and others.[3] Here, some segment of the society, like the Puerto Rican minority, which is not even necessarily a city phenomenon, or some specialized housing settlement type like Lewis's or Patch's *vecindad* or *callejon,* or Clifton's, Leed's, Lewis's, or Mangin's squatments (*caillampa, favela, arrabal, barriada,* respectively) is chosen for study and treated as if it were a self-contained, more or less autonomous community. It may indeed be such a community in the city, but this cannot be *assumed* a priori as these studies have tended to do. Rather, the fact that it *is* a community must be *empirically* shown, and the mechanisms which create and maintain the boundaries of that community as over against the rest of the city empirically analyzed in detail as part of the total social process. Failure to do this has led to a thorough failure to justify the units of study used and failure to show mutual effects between the asserted "units" of study and the city in which they are immersed.

Further, it has led to the creation or perpetuation of prevalent myths concerning the continuity of the entity of study for autonomous cultural reasons (e.g., "culture of poverty," "marginalidad") rather than to the achievement of insights as to the continuity of the entity as a socio-economic and political reflex, dependent variable, or coordinate subsegment of the larger city and national society of which it is part.[4]

[3] Banton 1957; Bonilla 1961; Cardona G. 1968a, 1968b; Clifton 1966; Leeds and Leeds 1970; Lewis 1959a, 1959b, 1961; Lynd and Lynd 1929, 1937; Mangin 1967a, 1967b, 1967c; Matos 1960, 1961, 1967, 1968; Mayer 1961; O'Neil 1966; Padilla 1958; Patch 1961; Pearse 1958, 1961; Seminário 1967; Southall 1956; Turner 1965, 1966, 1967; Warner and Lunt 1941.
[4] Abrams 1966; Bonilla 1961, 1964; Cardona 1968c; Cardona and Simonds 1968; DESAL 1965, 1966; Goldrich 1965; Goldrich, Pratt, and Schuller 1967–68; Lewis 1959a, 1959b, 1961, 1966a, 1966b; Patch 1961; Pearse 1957, 1958, 1961; Seminário 1967.

Finally, there is the failure to see, or even look at, the city as an entity.[5]

In sum, anthropologists have tended to perpetuate traditional concerns of kinship, the community, child training, study of associations, and so on—transferring these, first, forty to fifty years ago, to the quite different societal context of rural communities and then, more recently, to the drastically different context of the city in large-scale society. Some of the methodological problems regarding tribal societies were never resolved, and sometimes never even raised, though they closely involved both theoretical models and fieldwork procedures. In this transference of traditional concerns from tribal experience to city studies, these problems were perpetuated and intensified.

Perhaps one of the most important of these was the implicit mental model, accompanied by its explicit fieldwork practice, which treated the tribe or the "rural" community as if it were an autonomous unit. Its role as merely one of a population of tribes in a larger ecology (cf. Leeds 1964d) or as a constituent element of a larger society was treated as more or less an epiphenomenon while its autonomy was conceived of as a necessary result of its essential, unique, internal characteristics. That this "essence" itself might be a result or function of its place in a population or as a constituent element is a hypothesis which has scarcely been formulated, let alone investigated theoretically, methodologically, or empirically in the field.

The failure even to raise this question in tribal and "community" studies has been transferred to the city studies, where it has become a yet greater failure because the justification for treating the units under description as autonomous is still less self-evident, while the blindness to the complexity of interrelation within the encompassing social entity or entities (e.g., city, nation) which includes the unit as one of its variables is even vaster. In the case of the city, the blindness leads to its atomized treatment, as if these variables (kinship, associations, housing, etc.) were separable, discrete, and unrelated elements—as it were, *accidents* of the city rather than caused and linked manifestations *of* the city (and national) process.

Essentially what is involved are the methodological and theoretical issues inherent in such questions as "Why the city at all?", and, at a lower level of generalization, "Why *this* city?" The answer to the first

[5] In my experience, the persons with the clearest view of the city as an entity, a system, are some of the urban planners (cf. Modesto 1968).

[235]

question would have the form of a general law whose content, I believe, would refer to hypothesized universal functions of cities in the context of a consideration of the range of major socio-cultural and ecological variables of human populations and their societal units.

The answer to the second question involves this general law and some corollary or corollaries of limiting reference which should predict the characteristics of this city, or, possibly, at least a class of such "This Cities," for example, a class of administrative cities (nonindustrial capitals like Brasília or Canberra) or a class of heavy-industry towns in "developing" countries (like São Paulo). Additional questions such as "Why this city *here*?" introduce additional variables, relating to the entire city system, which have relevance to the study of any given variable *in* that city system.

These questions have not been asked in anthropology and its urban field studies, except in the most obvious and everyday sort of way, as, for instance, in the writings about the "urban revolution" (Childe 1942, 1948). Even this broad and rather shallow kind of generalization is not used, or the questions themselves are simply not asked, in the empirical city studies so that it is impossible to assess whether the data observed are caused by, related to, affected by, or independent of, other variables at work in the city system.

For example, in the city of Lattakia, Syria,[6] it seems clear that the shape-up procedure for employing dock workers through kinship and hometown ties was obviously related to the town's location at the seaside and causally related to residence patterns and location of workers, many of whom were rural immigrants. In the system of exchange which ties the Syrian polity to many other polities, Lattakia operates as a point of both physical and juridical transfer. Policies with respect to both types of transfer, set both by the national and municipal governments and conditioned by the geographical-ecological considerations, as well as foreign interests, have direct and indirect effects on the patterning of kinship behavior. To describe kinship behavior without reference to these potent variables of the national and local institutional and geographical conditions is to fail to see the dynamics of the social process and of change.

Another example is afforded by *favelas* in Rio de Janeiro. Almost without exception, all literature on favelas treats them as enclaves

[6] These comments are based on Baggett (1965) who got her ethnographic information from Ghassan Arnaoot, a former resident of Lattakia, and on my own subsequent interviews with him and his draft of a study of that city.

having their own unique internal characteristics in all respects: they are self-maintaining, culturally autonomous outsiders; strangers to the city; in fact, they are rural migrants who have squatted in the physical confines of the city, remaining isolated in it, but not of it.[7]

Virtually none of the studies of favelas (or *barrios, barriadas, ranchos, cortiços, callejones, vecindades,* etc.) deal systematically with the relationships of the favela or *cortiço* to a series of variables which describe the city system, and, quite as important, to the state or condition of those variables. This failure is due to the absence of adequate sociological models, theoretical and descriptive of the city as such, when analytically or empirically examining the favelas or other delimitable entities in the field or in the library. Such variables include the interests of the social and political elites of the city and the mechanisms for their fulfillment, the intensity of action of such mechanisms and the threats, if any, to them; the conditions of the labor market with special reference to pressures varying the rates of unemployment and underemployment and to barriers to attainment of specialized training; the structure and operation of the rent and labor laws, especially the salary structure, including differential pay rates; the structure, accessibility, and costs of the metropolitan transportation system, and so on.

Boundary conditions which delimit a favela population and give it some coherence as an aggregate or as a subcommunity are created and maintained by variables such as these. They also define the kinds of action which take place over boundaries: which are impossible, which are possible, and which are probable and likely to be frequent. In general, these variables delimit, either directly or indirectly, the parameters of action and relationship inside the favela or other unit of study.

Variations over time of certain basic variables, such as national salary structures and national salary policy (e.g., prohibiting or delaying salary increases in an inflationary situation; cf. O'Neil 1966), as these are manifested in the city labor market, govern, on the one hand, the

---

[7] On theoretical grounds, had these facts been developed or even had very undeveloped theory been brought to bear on the favela phenomena, these views should have been considered, at the very least, doubtful. I would say that with any reasonable development of city theory, they should have been thrown out altogether. But they were not, and data collection, including, to some degree, the first stages of my own, went on in the framework of the myth outlined above. In other words, the myth perpetuated the questions asked, which perpetuated the reception of only certain kinds and interpretations of data, which perpetuated the myth.

relations of favela residents to the economy generally and specifically. Thus, for example, national salary policy sets minimum wages and the entire wage scale based on it, as well as schedules for different types of professions and occupations. Obviously such scales correspond to jobs in the labor market absorbing workers from the favelas as well as from the rest of the city. Depressed wage structures, especially under inflationary pressure, are chiefly and specifically related to residence in favelas. In turn, there is some evidence that residence in favelas tends to make more difficult the tasks of job-hunting and job-holding, because of the discriminatory and abusive practices of employers against favela residents who are "illegal," "marginals," "squatters," "irresponsibles," "untrustworthy," and so on. There are specific institutions or customs to circumvent such discriminations. Again, there is also some evidence that the existence of favelas per se helps reduce the general wage level of the city by making possible the more successful maintenance of a pool of cheap labor for a labor-intensive production system.

On the other hand, these basic variables also govern discrete and predictable relationships inside the favelas, describable with game theory models, such as a series of dyadic, triadic, or similar reduced types of groupings. These include the paternalistic creditor-debtor relationship, the matricentered mother-child household, a series of types of martial relationships, reciprocal friendships, dyadic or small pluradic neighbor groups, patron-client/client-subclient, and other chained dyadic relations (cf. Leeds 1964b).

In sum, the states of the variables relevant to the city as a whole (viz., the labor market and its intracity variations; the transportation system and its differential costs and accessibilities inside the city; the distribution, costs, and accessibilities of urban facilities such as light, water, sewerage; the intracity topography; special legislation, decrees, and ordinances referring to the city as a whole, and so on) have direct and indirect institutional effects—indeed molding effects—on the internal characteristics of the unit of study which cannot be understood at all without reference to these variables.

All the foregoing considerations have major implications for the anthropologist carrying out fieldwork in cities. Given the general precepts of anthropology and its methods regarding all fieldwork (e.g., participant-observation, thorough ethnography), the anthropologist working in the city is logistically constrained to working at most in two or three sites given any standard amount of time that he is likely to have. This constraint is the more severe, the larger the city and the fewer the coworkers he has, and especially if he is alone.

I can, perhaps, exemplify these points with my own case. I found myself—a single fieldworker with thirteen months of field time ahead of me for the study of favelas in Rio de Janeiro (1965–66)—confronted with 300 highly differentiated possible units of study. My previously developed hypotheses indicated I should pick four, each with certain characteristics. Given (a) the vast number from which to choose these four; (b) the virtually total lack of any useful information for Rio's favelas regarding the characteristics which interested me; (c) the cost in time entailed by Rio's transportation, which would have had to be used while trying to identify the appropriate favelas, the universe of which is spread over the length and breadth of a topographically very difficult city; and (d) a number of other considerations involving time, my own manpower, available information, and so on, I decided to focus ethnographically on three or four favelas and attempt to control the variation in the entire population of favelas by other means, primarily through thorough documentation (such as it might be).[8] It should be noted here that one's resources tend to set the limits for one's field strategies, but also that changes in resources, even during the field session, may permit one to shift strategies advantageously.

It might be asked of me "Why did you insist on studying favelas in a city as large as Rio de Janeiro whose metropolitan area contains about 7,000,000 people? Why did you not choose a city of perhaps 100,000 like Ilheus or Itabuna, which, in any case, you have known for fifteen years since doing your initial Brazilian fieldwork?" The answer is that, except for particular hypotheses that might revolve about specified city sizes, a somewhat unlikely possibility at present, I was con-

[8] That, in fact, this latter policy was only partially adhered to is irrelevant to the present argument and has to do with accidents of the local situation, especially with the presence of the Peace Corps volunteers, selected Brazilian social workers, and sociologists working in the favelas, and the emergence of a working field seminar among all of these. Ethnographically, I did, indeed focus intensively on only five favelas—a study carried further in the summers of 1967 and 1968 and by my wife in February of the latter year. My wife and I also carried out the documentation (40,000 microfilm frames of all sorts of published and unpublished materials, statistical and qualitative, plus acquisition of books, magazines, journals, and newspapers). At the same time, these accidents of the local situation permitted me sufficient freedom to move away from the five favelas in order to make visits of varying duration to a total of fifty other favelas as well as to other types of housing-settlements. This gave me an additional direct experiential control over the range of variability within the class of entities on five of whose exemplars I was concentrating.

strained by the theoretical conceptions underlying my research, especially regarding power distributions (cf. Chapter 7). These indicated the desirability of a fieldwork site which presented various politico-economic and administrative levels of organization at one and the same time. Rio de Janeiro is ideal: it is still, partially, the de facto national capital; it is the capital of the city-state of Guanabara; it has subdivisions called regional administrations, equivalents of the standard Brazilian municipalities; and finally, it has semiconventionalized, nonofficial subdivisions, the *bairros*, the favelas, and the like, more or less equivalent to natural localized "community" entities. I was able, therefore, to get a cross section of the entire hierarchy of power-distribution, based on different resources of power and reflecting a larger variety of power relations growing out of the differentiated kinds of power.

As I remarked above, unless he has indefinitely long time, almost unlimited resources, and a large personnel, the anthropologist in the city must limit himself, ethnographically, to one locus or a very few loci of intensive fieldwork. But, as can be deduced from the comments in the first pages and was quite clear from my actual field experience (indeed from all my field experience in quite different kinds of situations), no one locus can be understood without reference to (a) the other examples of the same type of locus, that is, in my study, other favelas; (b) other loci of related types, for example, the other types of intracity settlements or other proletarian housing aggregates; (c) other examples of the same class of locus contexts, in my case other Brazilian, Latin American, and similar "underdeveloped" cities.

It is only with reference to each of these crosscutting sets of comparisons that one can confirm theoretically indicated variables or discover empirically the most significant variables affecting the locus of ethnography. It is only by reference to the other examples from the same and related classes and the city context of the fieldwork site and comparisons with other cities that one can determine the range of variation of the variable, discover the pressures which bring about or the factors which causes the variations, and establish the essential relationships among the variables.

Put another way, the study of a single example or a very few examples of the class of entities chosen is methodologically erroneous. It either prohibits or limits examining similarities and differences to be found in the full *range* of examples, an examination of which allows one to isolate the relevant fundamental features of the system of which they are manifestations. Thus, even the study of an entire class of entities, such as the entire universe of favelas of Rio, is inadequate, because it is, in fact, a single example of several larger universes: that of differentiated and interdependent settlement types, that of differentiated and interdependent power aggregates and groups, that of differentiated and interdependent economic aggregates, and so on, in the city.

Because of the differentiation and interdependence, no one example from any of these universes can be fully understood alone. They are all variables of the system which is the city under study for which the field-worker, before and during his study, must develop a special model. This model will indicate the fundamental features, referred to above, which relate all the kinds of entities, their characteristics, and their mutual effects.

Even this cannot be adequately done unless the ethnographer has some comparative or contrastive foundation for designating the fundamental features. He must keep in mind such usually unasked questions—Whiteford (1960) being a rare exception—as "How and why are such-and-such two cities different from each other as a whole or with respect to some specified feature?"—a question to be asked in the context of the generic question, "How is one to account for the difference of any two cities from each other?"

For example, the ethnographic fact, which the field ethnographer studying a favela in one city, Rio, must know both by reading and some minimal ethnographic observation, is that in São Paulo, a city somewhat larger than Rio (8,000,000 in the metropolitan area), there are about one-sixth the number of favelas in Rio, and these are on the average about one-fourth to one-third the size of those in Rio. This fact raises some extremely interesting questions as to the relationship between those variables which generate favelas—the labor market, migration, housing conditions, and so on—and other variables comprising the city, for example, the prior history of the city growth, the degree of industrialization, the skill level and educational facilities for the working population, and the overall role of the city in the inclusive body politic.

Again, apropos of my general theme and the foregoing example, the field ethnographer must ask himself specific questions about his city of study as a whole: "Why does *this* city have such-and-such characteristics?" Such a question is, in fact, a comparative or contrastive question in the same way that those mentioned above are, and the answer helps determine significant features of his locus of study.

By way of what may seem a rather esoteric example, he may ask a question such as "Why the intense level of sexuality of Rio de Janeiro society (as contrasted with, say, São Paulo or Belo Horizonte)?" The answer to this specific question, I believe, lies in the role that the city of Rio de Janeiro—and, by contrast, the role that the city of São Paulo—plays in the body politic as a whole. Rio, I believe, constitutes an institutional nexus for a privileged, patrimonial, governing elite occupying public positions whose symbols of office must constantly receive overt validation as part of the mechanism of maintaining power, authority, influence, and prestige. The sexuality and sensuality seem to me part of a complicated system of mate selection through public offering mediated by a subtle cue system which indicates both availability and social status exclusiveness. The resort-town atmosphere and economy (beaches, Carnaval, vistas, and outlooks) are both physical arenas for the specialized social drama of Rio and part of the actual economy of the courtly patrimonial elitism which permeates all sectors and activities of Rio's population.

São Paulo's role, in contrast, is that of an institutional nexus of *private* governing elites occupying private positions in big business and big industries, most of whose basic operations, interests, knowledge, and so on, are enhanced by privacy. The operations of home life, courtship, sexuality, are correspondingly private.

These differentiated roles relate to the historical origins and continuities of each city including the institutional conditions of its founding. It is interesting, in this connection, that, in 1890, Rio and São Paulo had about 523,000 and 64,000 people respectively, while today São Paulo is larger than Rio, as the figures cited above indicate. In other words, Rio, as capital during 100 years of the colonial status and throughout the empire, was already a very substantial city at the end of the nineteenth century, while São Paulo, founded at about the same time as Rio, was still a provincial capital beginning its surge of growth about the explosive expansion of coffee and early industrialization. Though Rio, too, has since then industrialized heavily, it has also maintained much of its original administrative role and ethos in contemporary Brazil.

The various social classes and other possible entities of study (e.g., favelas) orient themselves with respect to the differentiated roles in the national society about which the two major cities are focally structured. Such differential orientation is reflected in a variety of ways. One example is the absolute and relative size of the body of public functionaries in Rio. Until 1960 when the official capital was removed to Brasília (although Rio for many purposes continues as the de facto capital), public employees were about 40 percent of the labor force in the city! Anybody working for any public body, especially if he has one tenure (*estabilidade*), considers himself a *funcionário público,* a prestigeful status even for the tenured janitors of a ministry or the pickup drivers of a *repartição pública* (a public agency), especially if compared with their nontenured equivalents in private employ. Though there is a large public bureaucracy in São Paulo, it is relatively much, much smaller, and the ethos of being a funcionário público much less important. The ethos and its action manifestations permeate all associational life in favelas and other delimitable aggregates.

Another example is the difference in intensity and elaborateness of the Carnaval in the two cities, and the extreme imitation, among the lower "classes" in Rio, of elite public privilege and prestige in the popular carnaval, especially the *blocos* and *escolas de samba* with their themes (*enrêdos*) dealing with public, literary, or artistic personages, the Academy of Letters, the 400th anniversary of the founding of Rio; with their bewigged, bejeweled Louis XIV–XVIth baroque parade figures; with their imitations of wealth, splendor, courtliness, and elitism. São Paulo has its Carnaval, but it is no parallel to Rio's in its much more plebeian and unstructured *kermesse* (cf. Morocco 1966).

The point is that the highly differentiated roles in the nation of these two cities (here used simply as particular examples of the generic problem in question) seen as total systems significantly affect what happens to the specific variables or entities under study. The field ethnographer is obligated to ask himself, therefore, "What are the generic and particular variables affecting, and the generic and particular relationships among, any of the entities of study (mentioned in the opening paragraphs) for *all* cities, for designated classes of cities, and especially for the city I am now studying?" He must have some ethnographic control over all these variables and the different kinds of entities involved because he cannot understand the ethnographic data of his particular entity of study without such control.

Thus, one cannot properly understand, that is, give an account of, the favelas without understanding the dynamics of migration; residence in other types of proletarian housing such as rooming houses, housing projects, backyard favelas, tenements, and so on; rent patterns; land tenure; inheritance; litigation; and so on. That this methodological point is *not* self-evident is amply demonstrated by the great majority of the documents on favelas which do not touch on these subjects at all. Since the favela populations mostly hail from, and frequently return to, such other forms of housing-settlement types, respond to rent laws and conditions, and are involved directly with land tenure and litigation problems, the omission of these considerations contributes drastically to the mythology already extant about favelas, as in the works of Bonilla, Pearse (to some extent), Goldrich, and any number of Brazilian writers.[9] These remarks apply, with very few exceptions, to the literature on housing-settlement types in urban centers for México, Perú, and Puerto Rico, including such well-known works as those by Oscar Lewis, except his article of 1952 from whose stance he subsequently departed.

The questions raised above, in their generalized form, require the generation of a general theory of the relationship between the structure of society in all its aspects and its nucleated settlements, on one hand, and, on the other, from such theory, the generation of differentiated models describing different categories of cities. From among such differentiated models (e.g., as unsystematized and incipient examples: the industrial city, the preindustrial city, the parade city, the administrative city; see Mumford 1938, 1961; Sjoberg 1960) the ethnographer must choose the appropriate one from which to generate a specific model relevant to the description of his city of study.

The appropriate category model and the specific model together will guide him in his ethnographic fieldwork, indicating to him the significant variables to be examined, desirable quantifications, types of evidence for relationships among the variables, and so on. The models

---

[9] Bonilla 1961; Goldrich 1965; Pearse 1957, 1958. Seminário 1967 provides a typical if extreme version of the myth. This astonishing publication was produced by the magnificent rectors of six of the major universities in and around Rio de Janeiro with the assistance of a number of professionals such as geologists and others. The following quotation from this "authoritative" statement about favelas will illustrate the remarkable persistence of the myth, in one of its most virulent forms, as late as 1967: "The favelas leap out at the eyes of all not only as a social cancer—incubators of rebels and gangsters—but also as urbanistic monstrosities destroying one of the most beautiful landscapes of the planet. Rio de Janeiro, with its bay, its beaches, its belt of steep, verdant slopes, is universally considered the most beautiful city of the world, a patrimony for humanity which we have in custody without the right to mutilate it. "Cidade Maravilhosa" was its nickname before the invasion of the barbarians. . . . [The favelas] appeared evilly, expanded, and proliferated like the true cancers that they are" (1967:76–77, translation mine).

will set forth the hypothesized relationships and effects, mutual or otherwise, in a total system, among the entire range of entities and variables that have been mentioned above. They will indicate, too, the pressures, the constraints, the demands, which, it seems to me, have largely been disregarded in the studies of cities so far carried out by anthropologists and for which quantitative measures are desperately needed.[10]

[10] It is too early yet to present such models. However, a sketchy sort of thing of what I have in mind may be useful for discussion. In "developing societies," at least those whose central organizing principle is capitalistic, the following appear to be the fundamental characteristics of the total society: (a) the society as a whole is undergoing a basic reorganization of the institutions of the economy, e.g., by introduction of price-making markets, of planning, of new forms of finance, of new transaction procedures, etc.; (b) concomitantly, sharp changes in the system of property and its inheritance are taking place, eliciting extensive confusion and concurrent litigation with respect, for example, to land claims, usufructs, tenure systems, rent forms, etc., themselves linked with new transaction procedures; (c) extensive elaboration, revision, recasting, and experimentation with law and the legal system occur, producing very considerable confusion and contradiction which provide a basis for quite characteristic abuses and manipulations; (d) centralization of the power system accompanied by breakdown of ecological localism (cf. Leeds 1964b:1321–22), a process usually referred to as "integration," unfortunately, because it implies that prior states were *not* integrated; (e) institution of national (total-societal) systems of taxation (e.g., imposts, income tax), social welfare, administration, etc.; (f) shift in basic technology, toward increasing mechanization, capital-intensiveness, large-scale operations, "efficiency," and "rationalization"; (g) increasing specialization and linkage among specializations, necessitating rapid and short-distance transportation and communications, i.e., localization as in cities which are also the locales for providing the welfare services, the transactional services, the information circulation for the ever more complicated economy and for the power system, etc. (cf. Leeds 1968c).

These conditions generate surplus labor throughout the society, tending to draw it toward the sites of welfare distribution, authority (which may solve problems), economic elaboration (which may provide jobs), and population growth (which may provide better possibilities for marginal types of work such as peddling), i.e., toward the cities. The surplus labor itself reduces wage levels and depresses and restricts the markets, setting limits on production and productivity levels—hence on the job markets in the cities. A partial response to this is the hypertrophy of welfare systems. The hypertrophy of the unskilled labor force, of low-paid domestic services, of marginal peddling, odd-jobbing, and the like, in confrontation with the changes, confusions, and manipulative opportunisms of the property systems, especially in landed property, land payments, real estate, and so on, and of the employment system, particularly under a legislative and juridical system controlled by the propertied elites, generates such phenomena as squatter settlements and a considerable number of their internal characteristics, e.g., factionalism, patron-clientism, and others.

Specific historical and ecological conditions should permit us to specify the distinctive states of the variables more closely. Thus, the recency of São Paulo's growth—*after* it had already begun to develop an extensive industrial base and *after* sizable European immigration, but without a history of extensive use of slaves in the production system—contrasts with the much earlier, imperial and patrimonial growth of Rio with its sizable slave population freed as late as 1888, a reduced immigrant population, its courtly life, and its fundamentally administrative rather than productive economy. These conditions appear to have pro-

In conclusion, I think the future of anthropological studies of cities lies in dealing with the multiple variables of the city system in a single synthetic framework. In any case, the ethnographer dealing with some specific aspect of the city must keep this framework in mind and, to some extent, attain some ethnographic control over all the significant entities to which it refers. In the generation of such a synthetic framework and, more sophisticatedly, the theory behind it, the anthropologists' evolutional, ecological, and holistic perspectives should contribute significantly.

---

found influences on the demography and subsequent settlement characteristics, especially the favela pattern mentioned above in the text. It should be predictable from these specific models that the cultural characteristics of the favelas of Rio and those of São Paulo should be different in important respects, proletarianized versions of elitism and the patrimonial attitudes prevailing in the former; plebian and industrial types of proletarianization prevailing in the latter. At this time, preliminary inspection seems generally to confirm these predictions.

Bibliography

Abbot Irminon [fl. 800 A.D.]. 1946. The Polyptich of Saint Germain des Prés. In *Introduction to Contemporary Civilization in the West,* ed. Contemporary Civilization Staff, Columbia College, I:34–38. New York: Columbia University Press.

Abrams, Charles. 1964. *Man's Struggle for Shelter in an Urbanizing World.* Cambridge: M.I.T. Press.

——. 1966. *Squatter Settlements: The Problem and the Opportunity.* Washington, D.C.: Division of International Affairs, Department of Housing and Urban Development.

Acosta, M., and J. E. Hardoy. 1972. Urbanization Policies in Revolutionary Cuba. *Latin American Urban Research* 2:167–78.

Adams, Richard N. 1967. *The Second Sowing: Development in Latin America.* San Francisco: Chandler.

——. 1970. *Crucifixion by Power: Essays on Guatemalan National Social Structure, 1944–1966.* Austin: University of Texas Press.

Adams, Richard N., John P. Gillin, Allan R. Holmberg, Oscar Lewis, Richard W. Patch, and Charles Wagley. 1960. *Social Change in Latin America Today.* New York: Vintage.

Adams, Robert McC. 1966. *The Evolution of Urban Society.* Chicago: Aldine.

——. 1974. Anthropological Perspectives on Ancient Trade. *Current Anthropology* 15:239–58.

Almquist, Eric. 1975. Domestic Industries and Irish Rural Society, County Mayo, 1950–1974. Research Progress Report to the Social Science Research Council, European Program. New York. [Photocopy]

Amado, Jorge. 1942. *Terras do Sem Fin.* Rio de Janeiro: Editora Martins.

Antonil, João Antônio. 1711 [1950]. *Cultura e Opulencia do Brasil.* Bahia: Livparia Progresso Eitora.

Bibliography

Arensberg, Conrad M. 1937. *The Irish Countryman: An Anthropological Study.* New York: Peter Smith.
——. 1961. The Community as Object and as Sample. *American Anthropologist* 63:241–64.
Azevedo, Alusio. c.1891 [1965]. *O Cortiço.* São Paulo: Martins. [*A Brazilian Tenement,* trans. Harry W. Brown. New York: Robert M. McBride, 1926.]
Baggett, Susan. 1965. The City as Transactional System: A Case Study of Lattakia, Syria. Department of Anthropology, University of Texas, Austin. [Typescript]
Banton, Michael. 1957. *West African City.* London: Oxford University Press.
——. 1973. Urbanization and Role Analysis. In *Urban Anthropology,* ed. Aidan Southall, 43–70. New York: Oxford University Press.
Barker, Roger G., and Herbert F. Wright. 1954. *Midwest and Its Children: The Psychological Ecology of an American Town.* Evanston, Ill.: Row, Peterson.
Baxter, Ellen, and Kim Hopper. 1980. *Private Lives/Public Spaces: Mentally Disabled Adults on the Streets of New York City.* New York: Community Service Society.
Benedict, Ruth F. 1946a. Thai Culture and Behavior. New York: Institute for Intercultural Studies. [Mimeographed]
——. 1946b. *The Chrysanthemum and the Sword: Patterns of Japanese Behavior.* Boston: Houghton Mifflin.
Bierstedt, Robert. 1967. Power and Social Class. In *Social Structure, Stratification, and Social Mobility,* ed. Anthony Leeds, 77–83. Studies and Monographs VIII. Washington, D.C.: Pan American Union, General Secretariat, Organization of American States.
Birdsell, Joseph. 1953. Some Environmental and Cultural Factors Influencing the Structuring of Australian Aboriginal Populations. *American Naturalist* 87:169–207.
Blau, Peter M. 1964. *Exchange and Power in Social Life.* New York: John Wiley.
Bohannan, Paul. 1963. *Social Anthropology.* New York: Holt, Rinehart, and Winston.
Bonilla, Frank. 1961. Rio's Favelas: The Rural Slum within the City. *Reports Service,* East Coast of South America Series, 8(3):1–15. New York: American Universities Field Staff.
——. 1962. Rio's Favelas: The Rural Slum within the City. *Dissent* 9:383–86.
——. 1964. The Urban Worker. In *Continuity and Change in Latin America,* ed. John J. Johnson, 186–205. Stanford: Stanford University Press.
Bookman, Ann, and Sandra Morgen, eds. 1988. *Women and the Politics of Empowerment.* Philadelphia: Temple University Press.
Bott, Elizabeth. 1957. *Family and Social Network: Roles, Norms, and External Relationships in Ordinary Urban Families.* London: Tavistock.
Bradfield, Stillman. 1973. Selectivity in Rural-Urban Migration: The Case of Huaylas, Peru. In *Urban Anthropology,* ed. Aidan Southall, 351–72. New York: Oxford University Press.
Braidwood, R. J., and G. R. Wiley, eds. 1962. *Courses toward Urban Life: Archeological Considerations of Some Cultural Alternatives.* New York: Wenner-Gren Foundation.

Bray, David. 1989. Letter to Elizabeth P. Leeds, 3 March.

Bredemeier, Harry C., and R. M. Stephenson. 1964. *The Analysis of Social Systems.* New York: Holt, Rinehart, and Winston.

Bruner, Edward M. 1973. Kin and Non-Kin. In *Urban Anthropology,* ed. Aidan Southall, 373–92. New York: Oxford University Press.

Burnham, James. 1942. *The Managerial Revolution.* London: Putnam.

Caplow, Theodore. 1955. The Definition and Measurement of Ambiences. *Social Forces* 34:28–33.

Cardona Gutierrez, Ramiro. 1968a. Barrio de Invasión Juan XXIII. Bogotá: Asociacion Colombiana de Facultades de Medicina, División de Estudios de Población, Bol. 19. [Mimeographed]

———. 1968b. Barrio de Invasión Policarpo Salivarrieta. Bogotá: Asociación Colombiana de Facultades de Medicina, División de Estudios de Población, Bol. 20. [Mimeographed]

———, ed. 1968c. Migración, Urbanización, y Marginalidad. Bogotá: Asociación Colombiana de Facultades de Medicina, División de Estudios de Población. [Mimeographed]

Cardona Gutierrez, Ramiro, and Alan Simonds. 1968. Investigación Nacional Sobre Urbanización y Marginalidad. Bogotá: Asociación Colombiana de Facultades de Medicina, Division de Estudios de Población. [Mimeographed]

Caro, Robert. 1974. *The Power Broker: Robert Moses and the Fall of New York.* New York: Vintage.

Cate, Katherine Royal. 1962. Final Report to the Technical Secretary of the O.A.S. Fellowship Program, 15 July. [Typescript]

———. 1963. Letter to Dr. Vera Rubin, Director, Research Institute for the Study of Man, 11 September.

CEDUG. 1965. *Guanabara: A Plan for Urban Development.* Athens: Doxiadis Associates, for the Commissão Executiva Para o Desenvolvimento Urbana, Guanabara, Brasil.

Childe, V. Gordon. 1942. *What Happened in History.* Harmondsworth: Penguin.

———. 1948. *Man Makes Himself.* London: Watts.

———. 1950. The Urban Revolution. *Town Planning Review* 21:3–17.

Clifton, James A. 1966. A Study of Processes of Urbanization and Adaptation in a Chilean Callampa Community: A Petition for a Grant-in-Aid of Research to Wenner-Gren Foundation. Lawrence: University of Kansas. [Cited with author's permission]

Cohen, Abner. 1971. The Politics of Ritual Secrecy. Man 6:427–48.

———. 1981. *The Politics of Elite Culture: Explorations in the Dramaturgy of Power in a Modern African Society.* Berkeley: University of California Press.

Crevenna, Theo, ed. 1950–51. *Materiales para el estudio de las clase media en la América Latina,* 6 vols. Washington, D.C.: Pan American Union.

Curtin, Philip D. 1986. *Cross-Cultural Trade in World History.* Cambridge: Cambridge University Press.

Dahl, Robert A. 1961. *Who Governs? Democracy and Power in an American City.* New Haven: Yale University Press.

D'Antonio, William V., and Eugene C. Erickson. 1962. The Reputational Technique as a Measure of Community Power: An Evaluation Base on Comparative and Longitudinal Studies. *American Sociological Review* 27:362–76.

D'Antonio, William V. et al. 1962. Further Notes on the Study of Community Power. *American Sociological Review* 27:848–54.

D'Antonio, William V., and Howard Ehrlich, eds. 1961. *Power and Democracy in America*. Notre Dame: University of Notre Dame Press.

Davis, Kingsley, and Wilbert E. Moore. 1945. Some Principles of Social Stratification. *American Sociological Review* 10:242–49.

Delhi Pradesh, Bharat Sevak Samaj. 1958. *Slums of Old Delhi: A Report on the Socio-Economic Survey of the Slum Dwellers of Old Delhi City.* Delhi: A. Ram.

DESAL. 1965. *Poblaciones Marginales y Desarollo Urbana, el Caso Chileno.* Santiago: Centro Para el Desarollo Económico y Social de América Latina.

———. 1966. *Antecedentes para el Estudio de la Marginalidad en Chile.* Santiago: Centro Para el Desarollo Económico y Social de América Latina.

Dobzhansky, Theodosius. 1962. *Mankind Evolving: The Evolution of the Human Species.* New Haven: Yale University Press.

Dollard, John. 1937. *Caste and Class in a Southern Town.* New York: Harper.

Duncan, Kenneth, ed. 1976. *Land and Labour in Latin America.* London: Cambridge University Press.

Eckstein, Susan. 1989. Comments at Memorial Service for Anthony Leeds. Latin American Studies Association, Miami, December.

Eddy, Elizabeth, ed. 1968. *Urban Anthropology: Research Perspectives and Strategies.* Southern Anthropological Society Proceedings 2. Athens: University of Georgia Press.

Embree, John. 1939. *Suye Mura: A Japanese Village.* Chicago: University of Chicago Press.

———. 1945. *The Japanese Nation: A Social Survey.* New York: Rinehart.

Epstein, A. L. 1958. *Politics in an Urban African Community.* Manchester: Manchester University Press.

———. 1961. The Network and Urban Social Organization. *Rhodes-Livingstone Institute Journal* 29:28–62.

Evans-Pritchard, E. E. 1940. *The Nuer.* Oxford: Oxford University Press.

Feder, Ernest. 1968 [1971]. Latifundia and Agricultural Labour in Latin America. In *Peasants and Peasant Societies,* ed. Teodor Shanin, 83–97. Harmondsworth: Penguin.

Firth, Raymond. 1946. *Malay Fishermen: Their Peasant Economy.* London: Routledge.

———. 1951. *Elements of Social Organization.* London: Watts.

———, ed. 1956. *Two Studies of Kinship in London.* London: Athlone.

Fisher, Humphrey. 1972–73. "He Swalloweth the Ground with Fierceness and Rage": The Horse in the Central Sudan. *Journal of African History* 13:369–88, 14:355–79.

Form, William H. 1945. Social Stratification in a Planned Community. *American Sociological Review* 10:605–13.

Forman, Shepherd. 1970. *The Raft Fishermen: Tradition and Change in the Brazilian Peasant Economy.* Bloomington: Indiana University Press.

Fox, Richard G. 1977. *Urban Anthropology: Cities in Their Cultural Settings.* Englewood Cliffs, N.J.: Prentice-Hall.

Frank, Andre Gunder. 1967. *Capitalism and Underdevelopment in Latin America: Historical Studies of Chile and Brazil.* New York: Monthly Review Press.

Fried, Morton. 1962. Power Relations between Local and Translocal Institutions: Centrifugal and Centripetal Tendencies in Chinese Society. Paper read at American Anthropological Association annual meeting, Chicago.

Geertz, Clifford. 1980. *Negara: The Theatre State in Nineteenth-Century Bali.* Princeton: Princeton University Press.

Gilderbloom, John. 1980. *Moderate Rent Control: The Experience of U.S. Cities.* Washington, D.C.: Conference on Alternative State and Local Policies.

Gilderbloom, John, and Friends. 1981. *Rent Control: A Source Book.* Santa Barbara, Calif.: Foundation for National Progress, Housing Information Center.

Goldrich, Daniel. 1965. Toward the Comparative Study of Politicization in Latin America. In *Contemporary Cultures and Societies of Latin America,* ed. Dwight B. Heath and Richard N. Adams, 361–78. New York: Random House.

Goldrich, Daniel, Raymond B. Pratt, and C. R. Schuller. 1967–68. *The Political Integration of Lower Class Urban Settlements in Chile and Peru.* Studies in Comparative International Development 3(1). St. Louis: Social Science Institute, Washington University.

Goodenough, Ward H. 1964. Lectures on the Componential Analysis of Whole Systems of Terms. University of Texas, Austin.

Goody, Jack. 1971. *Technology, Tradition, and the State in Africa.* London: Oxford University Press.

Gottman, Jean. 1961. *Megalopolis: The Urbanized Northeastern Seaboard of the United States.* New York: Twentieth Century Fund.

Greenwood, Davydd J. 1973. *The Political Economy of Peasant Family Farming: Some Anthropological Perspectives on Rationality and Adaptation.* Rural Development Occasional Paper 2. Ithaca: Cornell University, Center for International Studies, Rural Development Committee.

Gross, Neal C., Ward S. Mason, and Alexander W. McEachern. 1958. *Explorations in Role Analysis: Studies of the School Superintendent's Role.* New York: Wiley.

Gugler, Josef, and William G. Flanagan. 1978. *Urbanization and Social Change in West Africa.* Cambridge: Cambridge University Press.

Hall, Peter. 1966. *The World Cities.* New York: McGraw-Hill.

Hammel, Eugene A. 1961. The Family Cycle in a Coastal Peruvian Slum and Village. *American Anthropologist* 63:989–1005.

———. 1964. Some Characteristics of Rural Villages and Urban Slum Populations on the Coast of Peru. *Southwestern Journal of Anthropology* 20:346–58.

Hardie, Graeme. 1980. Tswana Design of House and Settlement—Continuity and Change in Expressive Space. Ph.D. thesis, Boston University.

Hardoy, J. E. 1964. *Pre-Columbian Cities.* New York: Walker. [1973.]

———. 1968. *Urban Planning in Pre-Columbian America.* New York: George Braziller.

Hardoy, J. E., and R. P. Schaedel, eds. 1969. *El proceso de urbanazación en*

Bibliography

América Latina desde sus orígens hasta nuestros dias. Buenos Aires: Instituto Torcuato di Tella.
——. 1975. *Las ciudades de América Latina y sus áreas de influencia a través de la historia.* Buenos Aires: SIAP.
Harris, Marvin. 1956. *Town and Country in Brazil.* New York: Columbia University Press.
——. 1959. Caste, Class, and Minority. *Social Forces* 37:248–54.
——. 1964. *The Nature of Cultural Things.* New York: Random House.
——. 1967. The Classification of Stratified Groups. In *Social Structure, Stratification, and Social Mobility,* ed. Anthony Leeds, 298–324. Studies and Monographs VIII. Washington, D.C.: Pan American Union, General Secretariat, Organization of American States.
——. 1989. Comments at Memorial Service for Anthony Leeds. American Anthropological Association annual meeting, Washington, D.C., November.
Hoebel, E. Adamson. 1958. *Man in the Primitive World: An Introduction to Anthropology,* 2d ed. New York: McGraw-Hill.
Homans, George C. 1942. *English Villagers of the Thirteenth Century.* Cambridge: Harvard University Press.
Hunter, Floyd. 1953. *Community Power Structure: A Study of Decision Makers.* Chapel Hill: University of North Carolina Press.
Hutchinson, Bertram. 1960. *Mobilidade e Trabalho: um estudo na cidade São Paulo.* Rio de Janeiro: Centro Brasileiro de Pesquisas Educacionais, Instituto Nacional de Estudos Pedagógicos, Ministério Nacional de Educação e Cultura.
——. 1962. Social Mobility Rates in Buenos Aires, Montevideo, and São Paulo: A Preliminary Comparison. *América Latina* 5:3–20.
Hutchinson, Harry W. 1957. *Village and Plantation Life in Northeastern Brazil.* Seattle: University of Washington Press.
Jacobs, Jane. 1963. *The Economy of Cities.* New York: Random House.
John of Salisbury [fl. 12th century]. 1949. The Body Social. In *The Portable Medieval Reader,* ed. J. B. Ross and M. M. McLaughlin, 47–48. New York: Viking.
Johnson, John J. 1958. *Political Change in Latin America: The Emergence of the Middle Sectors.* Stanford: Stanford University Press.
Johnson, Marion. 1980. Polanyi, Peukert, and the Political Economy of Dahomey. *Journal of African History* 21:395–98.
Julião, Francisco. 1972. *Cambão—the Yoke: The Hidden Face of Brazil,* trans. John Butt. Harmondsworth: Penguin.
Kahl, Joseph. 1957. *The American Class Structure.* New York: Holt, Rinehart, and Winston.
Kemper, Robert V. 1977. *Migration and Adaptation: Tzintzuntzan Peasants in Mexico City.* Beverly Hills, Calif.: Sage.
Koestler, Arthur, and J. R. Smythies, organizers. 1969. *Beyond Reductionism: New Perspectives in the Life Sciences.* New York: Macmillan.
Kornhauser, Ruth R. 1953. The Warner Approach to Social Stratification. In *Class, Status, and Power: A Reader in Social Stratification,* ed. Reinhardt Bendix and Seymour M. Lipsset, 224–55. Glencoe, Ill.: Free Press.

Kraeling, C. H., and R. McC. Adams, eds. 1960. *City Invincible.* Chicago: University of Chicago Press.

Kroeber, Alfred L. 1923. *Anthropology.* New York: Harcourt Brace.

———. 1948. *Anthropology.* New York: Harcourt Brace.

Lamphere, Louise. 1987. *From Working Daughters to Working Mothers: Immigrant Women in a New England Industrial Community.* Ithaca: Cornell University Press.

Langness, L. L., and Gelya Frank. 1981. *Lives: An Anthropological Approach to Biography.* San Francisco: Chandler and Sharp.

Law, Robin. 1977. Royal Monopoly and Private Enterprise in the Atlantic Slave Trade: The Case of Dahomey. *Journal of African History* 18:555–77.

———. 1986. Dahomey and the Slave Trade: Reflections on the Historiography of Dahomey. *Journal of African History* 27:237–67.

Leacock, Eleanor. 1969. *Teaching and Learning in City Schools: A Comparative Study.* New York: Basic Books.

Le Besnerais, Henri. 1954. Contribution à l'Etude des Indiens Yaruro. *Journal de la société des Américanistes* 43:109–22.

Leeds, Anthony. 1957. Economic Cycles in Brazil: The Persistence of a Total Culture-Pattern: Cacao and Other Cases. Ph.D. diss., Columbia University.

———. 1960. The Ideology of the Yaruro Indians in Relation to Socio-Economic Organization. *Antropologia* 9:1–10.

———. 1961a. Considerations Regarding Anthropology in High School Curricula. *Human Organization* 10:134–40.

———. 1961b. The Port-of-Trade in Pre-European India as an Ecological and Evolutionary Type. In *Symposium: Patterns of Land Utilization and Other Papers,* ed. Viola Garfield, 26–48. Proceedings of the 1961 Annual Spring Meeting of the American Ethnological Society. Seattle: University of Washington Press.

———. 1961c. Yaruro Incipient Tropical Forest Horticulture—Possibilities and Limits. In *The Evolution of Horticultural Systems in Native South America: Causes and Consequences—A Symposium,* ed. Johannes Wilbert, 13–46. Antropologia Supplement Publication No. 2. Caracas: Editorial Sucre.

———. 1962a. Ecological Determinants of Chieftainship among the Yaruro of Venezuela. *Acts of the 34th International Congress of Americanists,* 597–608. Vienna: F. Berger, Horn. [Reprinted in *Environment and Cultural Behavior: Ecological Studies in Cultural Anthropology,* ed. Andrew P. Vayda, 377–94. New York: Natural History Press.]

———. 1962b. Genetic Composition and Cultural Structure. *Science* 137:914–17. [Letter]

———. 1962c. "Microinvention" as an Evolutionary Process. *Transactions of the New York Academy of Sciences* 24:930–43.

———. 1962d. Borderlands and Elite Circulation: Locality Power Versus Central Power Institutions. Paper read at American Anthropological Association annual meeting, Chicago.

———. 1963. The Functions of War. In *Violence and War with Clinical Studies,* ed. Jules H. Masserman, 69–82. Science and Psychoanalysis Volume VI. New York: Grune and Stratton.

Bibliography

——. 1964a. Brazil and the Myth of Francisco Julião. In *Politics of Change in Latin America*, ed. Joseph Maier and Richard W. Weatherhead, 190–204. New York: Praeger.

——. 1964b. Brazilian Careers and Social Structure: An Evolutionary Model and Case History. *American Anthropologist* 66:1321–47.

——. 1964c. Cultural Factors in Education: India, Brazil, The United States, The Soviet Union; Some Problems of Applied Anthropology. In *Contemporary India*, ed. B. N. Varma, 271–318. New York: Asia Publishing House.

——. 1964d. Some Problems of Yaruro Ethnohistory. *Acts of the 35th International Congress of Americanists*, 157–75. Mexico: I.C.A.

——. 1965a. Reindeer Herding and Chukchi Social Institutions. In *Man, Culture, and Animals: The Role of Animals in Human Ecological Adjustments*, ed. Anthony Leeds and Andrew P. Vayda, 87–128. Washington, D.C.: American Association for the Advancement of Science.

——. 1965b. Some Preliminary Considerations Regarding the Analysis of Technologies. *Kroeber Anthropological Society Papers* 32:1–9.

——. 1967. Some Problems in the Analysis of Class and the Social Order. In *Social Structure, Stratification, and Mobility*, ed. Anthony Leeds, 327–61. Studies and Monographs VIII. Washington, D.C.: Pan American Union, General Secretariat, Organization of American States. [Chapter 5, this volume]

——. 1968a. The Anthropology of Cities: Some Methodological Issues. In *Urban Anthropology: Research Perspectives and Strategies*, ed. Elizabeth M. Eddy, 31–47. Southern Anthropological Society Proceedings No. 2. Athens: University of Georgia Press. [Chapter 8, this volume]

——. 1968b. Comment on D. P. Byw's "Instability in Latin America: The Cross-Cultural Test of a Causal Model." *Latin American Research Review* 3:79–87.

——. 1968c. Specialization, Transaction, Location, and Power—Some Theoretical Considerations Regarding Towns and Cities. Paper read at Seminar on Urban Studies, Rutgers University.

——. 1969. The Significant Variables Determining the Character of Squatter Settlements. *American Latina* 12(3):44–84.

——. 1970. Thales de Azevedo's Influence on Brazilian Studies by North Americans: A Personal Note. *Universitas* 6/7:21–27.

——. 1971. The Concept of the "Culture of Poverty": Conceptual, Logical, and Empirical Problems, with Perspectives from Brazil and Peru. In *The Culture of Poverty: A Critique*, ed. Eleanor Leacock, 226–84. New York: Simon and Schuster.

——. 1972. Urban Anthropology and Urban Studies. *Urban Anthropology Newsletter* 1(1):4–5.

——. 1973a. Economic-Social Changes and the Future of the Middle Class. In *Proceedings of·the Experts Conference on Latin America and the Future of Its Jewish Communities*, 48–72. London: Institute of Jewish Affairs. [Chapter 4, this volume]

——. 1973b. Locality Power in Relation to Supralocal Power Institutions. In *Ur-*

ban Anthropology: Cross-Cultural Studies of Urbanization, ed. Aidan Southall, 15–41. New York: Oxford University Press. [Chapter 7, this volume]

———. 1973c. Political, Economic, and Social Effects of Producer and Consumer Orientations toward Housing in Brazil and Peru: A Systems Analysis. In *Latin American Urban Research Volume 3. National-Local Linkages: The Interrelationship of Urban and National Polities in Latin America*, ed. Francine F. Rabinowitz and Felicity M. Trueblood, 181–215. Beverly Hills, Calif.: Sage.

———. 1974a. Darwinian and "Darwinian" Evolutionism in the Study of Society and Culture. In *The Comparative Reception of Darwinism*, ed. Thomas F. Glick, 437–85. Austin: University of Texas Press.

———. 1974b. Housing-Settlement Types, Arrangements for Living, Proletarianization, and the Social Structure of the City. In *Latin American Urban Research Volume 4. Anthropological Perspectives on Latin American Urbanization*, ed. Wayne A. Cornelius and Felicity M. Trueblood, 67–99. Beverly Hills, Calif.: Sage.

———. 1974c. "Subjective" and "Objective" in Social Anthropological Epistemology. In *Philosophical Foundations of Science*, ed. R. J. Seeger and R. S. Cohen, 349–61. Boston Studies in the Philosophy of Science. Boston: D. Reidel.

———. 1975. Capitalism, Colonialism, and War: An Evolutionary Perspective. In *War: Its Causes and Correlates*, ed. M. A. Nettleship and D. Givens, 483–513. The Hague: Mouton.

———. 1976a. Urban Society Subsumes Rural: Specialties, Nucleations, Countryside, and Networks;—Methatheory, Theory, and Method. *Acts of the 40th International Congress of Americanists*, 4:171–82. Genoa: Tilgher.

———. 1976b. "Women in the Migratory Process": A Reductionist Outlook. *Anthropological Quarterly* 49:69–76.

———. 1976c. Institutions; Technology; Technology and Subsistence. In *Encyclopedia of Anthropology*, ed. D. E. Hunter and P. Whitten. New York: Harper and Row.

———. 1976d. Review of George M. Foster and R. V. Kemper, eds. *Anthropologists in Cities. American Anthropologist* 78:448–49.

———. 1977a. *Brazil as a System*. Program in Latin American Studies Occasional Paper Series No. 5. Amherst: International Area Studies Programs, University of Massachusetts at Amherst.

———. 1977b. Mythos and Pathos: Some Unpleasantries on Peasantries. In *Peasant Livelihood: Studies in Economic Anthropology and Cultural Ecology*, ed. Rhoda Halperin and James Dow, 227–56. New York: St. Martin's Press. [Chapter 3, this volume]

———. 1977c. Sociobiology, Anti-Sociobiology, and Human Nature. *Wilson Quarterly* 1(4):127–39.

———. 1978. Introduction. In Anthony Leeds and Elizabeth Leeds, *A Sociologia do Brasil Urbano*. Rio de Janeiro: Zahar Editora. [English version, typescript; Chapter 6, this volume]

———. 1979. Forms of Urban Integration: "Social Urbanization" in Comparative Perspective. *Urban Anthropology* 8:227–47.

Bibliography

———. 1980a. Systems Levels Interactions in the Texas Hill Country Ecosystem: Structure, History, and Evolution. In *Beyond the Myths of Culture: Essays in Cultural Materialism*, ed. Eric Ross, 103–38. New York: Academic Press.

———. 1980b. Towns and Villages in Society: Hierarchies of Order and Cause. In *Cities in a Larger Context*, ed. Thomas W. Collins, 6–33. Southern Anthropological Society Proceedings No. 14. Athens: University of Georgia Press. [Chapter 2, this volume]

———. 1980c. Process, Structure, and Differentiation in Cities and Society. [Typescript]

———. 1981a. Lower-Income Urban Settlement Types: Processes, Structures, Policies. In *The Residential Circumstances of the Urban Poor in Developing Countries*, United Nations Centre for Human Settlements (HABITAT), 21–61. New York: Praeger.

———. 1981b. Letter from Anthony Leeds to Ernesto Meneses, Universidad Iberoamericana, Mexico City, 2 January.

———. 1981–82. The Language of Sociobiology: Reduction, Emergence, History, Social Science, Normativeness. *The Philosophical Forum* 13(2–3):161–206.

———. 1982a. Presidential Address. *Urban News: Newsletter of the Society for Urban Anthropology* 3(1):4–8.

———. 1982b. "To Live in Wonder": On Seeing and Photographs as Seeing. Exhibit Program Notes, Bentley College.

———. 1982c. Loci of Conflict between Agriculture and the City Sectors of Urban Societies. [Typescript]

———. 1982d. Letter from Anthony Leeds to Timothy Weiskel, Department of Anthropology, Yale University, 16 October.

———. 1984a. Cities and Countryside in Anthropology. In *Cities of the Mind: Images and Themes in the Social Sciences*, ed. Lloyd Rodwin and Robert M. Hollister, 291–311. New York: Plenum Press. [Chapter 1, this volume]

———. 1984b. Minha Terra, Portugal: Lamentations and Celebrations—the Growth of an Ethnography and a Commitment. [Unpublished manuscript]

———. 1984c. Through Selfethnography to Human Nature: Continuous Diversity as Escape from Categories of Unity. [Unpublished manuscript, 84 pp.]

———. 1985a. [Thirteen Poems.] In *Reflections: The Anthropological Muse*, ed. J. Iain Prattis, 141–52. Washington, D.C.: American Anthropological Association.

———. 1985b. Career History. Guggenheim Foundation grant application, 2 pp.

———. 1986. Urban Anthropology. In *Urban Anthropology in the 1980s*, ed. Risa S. Ellovich and Carol B. Stack, 10–13. Washington, D.C.: American Anthropological Association.

———. 1987. Work, Labor, and Their Recompenses: Portuguese Life Strategies Involving "Migration." In *Migrants in Europe: The Role of Family, Labor, and Politics*, ed. Hans C. Buechler and Judith Maria Buechler, 9–59. Westport, Conn.: Greenwood Press.

———, ed. 1965. Texas Villages: Sixty-Three Short Studies of Texas Rural Villages. Austin: University of Texas, International Office. [Mimeographed]

———, ed. 1967. *Social Structure, Stratification, and Mobility*. Studies and Monographs VIII. Washington, D.C.: Pan American Union, General Secretariat, Organization of American States.

Leeds, Anthony, and Valentine Dusek. 1981–82. Editors' Note: Sociobiology: A Paradigm's Unnatural Selection through Science, Philosophy, and Ideology. *The Philosophical Forum* 13(2–3):i–xxxv.

Leeds, Anthony, and Elizabeth Leeds. 1968. System Continuity in Brazil. Paper read at Conference on Urbanization and Work in Modernizing Societies, St. Thomas, Virgin Islands.

——. 1970. Brazil and the Myth of Urban Rurality: Urban Experience, Work, and Values in "Squatments" of Rio de Janeiro and Lima. In *City and Country in the Third World: Issues in the Modernization of Latin America*, ed. Arthur J. Field, 229–85. Cambridge, Mass.: Schenkman.

——. 1976. Accounting for Behavioral Differences: Three Political Systems and the Responses of Squatters in Brazil, Peru, and Chile. In *The City in Comparative Perspective: Cross-National Research and New Directions in Theory*, ed. John Walton and Louis H. Masotti, 193–248. Beverly Hills, Calif.: Sage.

——. 1978. *A Sociologia Urbana do Brasil.* Rio de Janeiro: Zahar Editora.

Leeds, Anthony, and Andrew P. Vayda, eds. 1965. *Man, Culture, and Animals: The Role of Animals in Human Ecological Adjustments.* Washington, D.C.: American Association for the Advancement of Science.

Leeds, Elizabeth. 1972. Forms of "Squatment" Political Organization: The Politics of Control in Brazil. M.A. thesis, Department of Government, University of Texas, Austin.

Leeds, Elizabeth, and Anthony Leeds. 1972. *Brazil in the 1960's: Favelas and Polity, The Continuity of the Structure of Social Control.* LADAC [Latin American Development Administration Committee] Occasional Papers Series 2, No. 5. Austin: Institute of Latin American Studies, University of Texas.

Lewis, Oscar. 1952. Urbanization without Breakdown. *Scientific Monthly* 75(1):31–41.

——. 1959a. *Five Families: Mexican Case Studies in the Culture of Poverty.* New York: Basic.

——. 1959b. La Cultura de Vecindad en la Ciudad de México. *Ciencias Políticas y Sociales* 5:349–64.

——. 1961. *The Children of Sanchez.* New York: Random House.

——. 1966a. *La Vida: A Puerto Rican Family in the Culture of Poverty.* New York: Random House.

——. 1966b. The Culture of Poverty. *Scientific American* 215(4):19–25.

Little, Kenneth. 1973. Urbanization and Regional Associations: Their Paradoxical Function. In *Urban Anthropology*, ed. Aidan Southall, 407–23. New York: Oxford University Press.

Lopes, Juarez R. B. 1964. *Relações Industriais na Sociedade Tradicional Brasileira; Estudo de duas Comunidades Mineiras.* Ph.D. thesis, Faculdade de Filosofia, Ciências, e Letras de São Paulo. [Mimeographed]

——. 1965. *Desenvolvimento e Mudança Social: A Formação da Sociedade Urbana-Industrial no Brasil.* São Paulo: Companhia Editôra Nacional.

Louis the Pious [fl. 795 A.D.]. 1946. Capitulare de Villis. In *Introduction to Contemporary Civilization in the West*, ed. Contemporary Civilization Staff, Columbia College, I:25–33. New York: Columbia University Press.

Lovejoy, A. O. 1937. *The Great Chain of Being: A Study in the History of an Idea.* Cambridge: Harvard University Press.

Lowie, Robert H. 1945. *The German People: A Social Portrait to 1914.* New York: Rinehart.

Lynd, Robert S., and Helen M. Lynd. 1929. *Middletown: A Study in American Culture.* New York: Harcourt Brace.

——. 1937. *Middletown in Transition: A Study in Cultural Conflict.* New York: Harcourt Brace.

Machado da Silva, Luiz Antonio. 1971. *Mercados Metropolitanos de Trabalho Manual e Marginalidada.* M.A. thesis, Universidade Federal do Rio de Janeiro, Programa de Pos-Graduação em Antropologia Social.

McIver, Robert M. 1937. *Society: A Textbook of Sociology.* New York: Farrar and Rinehart.

McIver, Robert M., and Charles H. Page. 1949. *Society: An Introductory Analysis.* New York: Rinehart.

Mallet, Serge. 1975. *Essays on The New Working Class.* St. Louis, Mo.: Telos Press.

Mangin, William. 1959. The Role of Regional Associations in the Adaptation of Rural Populations in Peru. *Sociologus* 9:21–36.

——. 1967a. Latin American Squatter Settlements: A Problem and a Solution. *Latin American Research Review* 2:65–98.

——. 1967b. Squatter Settlements. *Scientific American* 217(4):21–29.

——. 1967c. Political Implications of the Barriadas in Perú. Paper read at Latin American Colloquium, Brandeis University.

——. 1973. Sociological, Cultural, and Political Characteristics of Some Urban Migrants in Peru. In *Urban Anthropology*, ed. Aidan Southall, 315–50. New York: Oxford University Press.

Mangin, William, and John C. Turner. 1968. The Barriada Movement. *Progressive Architecture*, May, 154–62.

Marcuse, Peter. 1981. *Housing Abandonment: Does Rent Control Make a Difference?* Washington, D.C.: Conference on Alternative State and Local Policies.

Margolies, Luise, and R. H. Lavenda, Eds. 1979. Social Urbanization in Latin America. *Urban Anthropology* 8(3–4).

Marx, Karl. 1850–52 [1971]. Peasantry as a Class. In *Peasants and Peasant Societies*, ed. Teodor Shanin, 229–37. Harmondsworth: Penguin.

——. 1852. [1963]. *The 18th Brumaire of Louis Bonaparte.* New York: International Publishers.

——. 1857 [1971]. *Grundrisse*, trans. David McLellan. New York: Harper Torchbooks.

Matos Mar, José. 1960. *La Urbanización "Simon Rodriguez".* Caracas: Banco Obrero de Venezuela.

——. 1961. Migration and Urbanization: The Barriadas of Lima—an Example of

Integration into Urban Life. In *Urbanization in Latin America*, ed. Philip Hauser, 170–89. New York: UNESCO.

———. 1967. *Estudio de las Barriadas Limeñas*. Lima: Instituto de Estudios Peruanos.

———. 1968. *Urbanización y Barriadas en América del Sur*. Lima: Instituto de Estudios Peruanos.

Maxwell, Andrew. 1988. The Anthropology of Poverty in Black Communities: A Critique and Systems Alternative. *Urban Anthropology* 17:171–91.

———. 1991. Personal Communication to R. Timothy Sieber.

Mayer, Philip. 1961. *Townsmen or Tribesmen*. Cape Town: Oxford University Press.

Mayntz, Renate. 1967. Methodological Problems in the Study of Class. In *Social Structure, Stratification, and Social Mobility*, ed. Anthony Leeds, 8–26. Studies and Monographs VIII. Washington, D.C.: Pan American Union, General Secretariat, Organization of American States.

Mead, Margaret. 1942. *And Keep Your Powder Dry: An Anthropologist Looks at America*. New York: Morrow.

———. 1955. *Soviet Attitudes toward Authority: An Interdisciplinary Approach to Problems of Soviet Character*. New York: Morrow.

Meillassoux, Claude. 1968. *Urbanization of an African Community: Voluntary Associations in Bamako*. Seattle: University of Washington Press.

———. 1972. The Social Organization of Peasants. Seminar on Peasants, Centre for International and Area Studies, University of London. [Mimeographed]

Mills, C. Wright. 1951. *White Collar: The American Middle Classes*. New York: Oxford University Press.

———. 1956. *The Power Elite*. New York: Oxford University Press.

Mitchell, J. Clyde. 1956. Urbanization, Detribalization, and Stabilization in South Africa: A Problem of Definition and Measurement. In *Social Implications of Industrialization and Urbanization in Africa South of the Sahara*, ed. Daryll Forde, 693–711. Paris: UNESCO.

———. 1973. Distance, Transportation, and Urban Involvement in Zambia. In *Urban Anthropology*, ed. Aidan Southall, 287–314. New York: Oxford University Press.

———, ed. 1969. *Social Networks in Urban Situations*. Manchester: Manchester University Press.

Modesto, Hélio. 1968. Favelas: Reflections Regarding the Problem. [Unpublished paper]

Morocco, David. 1966. Carnaval Groups—Maintainers and Intensifiers of the Favela Phemomenon in Rio de Janeiro. [Unpublished paper]

Morse, Richard M. 1951. A Cidade de São Paulo no Período 1855–1870. *Sociologia* 13:230–51, 341–62.

———. 1958. *From Community to Metropolis: A Biography of São Paulo, Brazil*. Gainesville: University of Florida Press.

———. 1965. The Sociology of San Juan: An Exegesis of Urban Mythology. *Caribbean Studies* 5(2):45–55.

Bibliography

——. 1973a. Las ciudades latinoamericanos. 1. Antecedentes. *Ediciones SepSe-tentas* No. 96.

——. 1973b. Las ciudades latinoamericanos. 2. Desarrollo histórico. *Ediciones SepSetentas* No. 97.

——. 1974. Trends and Patterns of Latin American Urbanization, 1750–1920. *Comparative Studies in Society and History* 16:416–47.

Mullings, Leith, ed. 1987. *Cities of the United States: Studies in Urban Anthropology.* New York: Columbia University Press.

Mumford, Lewis. 1938. *The Culture of Cities.* New York: Harcourt, Brace.

——. 1961. *The City in History: Its Origins, Its Transformations, and Its Prospects.* New York: Harcourt, Brace, and World.

——. 1967. *The Myth of the Machine.* New York: Harcourt, Brace, and World.

Mundy, J., and P. Riesenberg. 1948. *The Medieval Town.* Princeton, N.J.: Van Nostrand.

Murdock, George P. 1949. *Social Structure.* New York: Macmillan.

Nash, June. 1989. *From Tank Town to High Tech: The Clash of Community and Industrial Cycles.* Albany: State University of New York Press.

Nelson, Benjamin. 1964. Actors, Directors, Roles, Cues, Meanings, Identities: Further Thoughts on Anomie. Revised version of paper read at Seminar on Structural Approaches to the Study of Meaning Systems, American Association for the Advancement of Science, Section H, 1962.

Nutini, Hugo. 1972. The Latin American City: A Cultural-Historical Approach. In *The Anthropology of Urban Environments,* ed. T. Weaver and D. White, 89–95. Boulder, Colo.: Society for Applied Anthropology.

Oberg, Kalvero, and Thomas Jabiu. 1960. *Toledo: um Município da Fronteira Oeste do Paraná.* Rio de Janeiro: Serviço Social Rural.

Olson, Everett C., and Robert L. Miller. 1958. *Morphological Integration.* Chicago: University of Chicago Press.

O'Neil, Charles. 1966. Problems of Urbanization in Rio Favelas. [Unpublished paper]

Osmundsen, Lita. 1991. Personal communication to R. Timothy Sieber.

Padilla, Elena. 1958. *Up from Puerto Rico.* New York: Columbia University Press.

Pappas, Gregory. 1989. *The Magic City: Unemployment in a Working-Class Community.* Ithaca: Cornell University Press.

Parsons, Talcott. 1951. *The Social System.* Glencoe, Ill.: Free Press.

Patch, Richard. 1961. Life in a Callejón: A Study of Urban Disorganization. *Reports Service,* West Coast of South America Series, 8(6). New York: American Universities Field Staff.

——. 1967. La Parada, Lima's Market—A Study of Class and Assimilation. I: The Villager Who Met Disaster; II: Serrano and Criollo, the Confusion of Race with Class; III: Serrano to Criollo, A Study of Assimilation. *Reports Service,* West Coast of South America Series, 14(1–3). New York: American Universities Field Staff.

Payne, James L. 1965. *Labor and Politics in Peru: The System of Political Bargaining.* New Haven: Yale University Press.

Pearse, Andrew. 1957. Integração Social das Famílias de Favelados. *Educação e Ciências Sociais* 2:245–77.

——. 1958. Notas Sobra a Organização Social de Uma Favela do Rio de Janeiro. *Educação e Ciências Sociais* 3:9–32.

——. 1961. Some Characteristics of Urbanization in the City of Rio de Janeiro. In *Urbanization in Latin America*, ed. Philip Hauser, 191–205. New York: UNESCO.

Petrullo, Vincenzo. 1939. The Yaruros of the Capanaparo River, Venezuela. *Bureau of American Ethnology Bulletin* 123:161–290.

Pierson, Donald. 1949. *Cruz das Almas: A Brazilian Village.* Smithsonian Institution Institute of Social Anthropology Publication 12. Washington, D.C.: Government Printing Office.

Pirenne, Henri. 1925 [1956]. *Medieval Cities.* Garden City, N.Y.: Anchor.

Polanyi, Karl. 1945. *The Great Transformation: The Origins of Our Time.* London: Gollancz.

Polanyi, Karl, Conrad M. Arensberg, and Harry W. Pearson, eds. 1957. *Trade and Market in the Early Empires: Economies in History and Theory.* New York: Free Press.

Pollock, F., and F. W. Maitland. 1895 [1968]. *The History of English Law before the Time of Edward I.* Cambridge: Cambridge University Press.

Polsby, Nelson W. 1959. Three Problems in the Analysis of Community Power. *American Sociological Review* 24:796–803.

——. 1960. How to Study Community Power: The Pluralist Alternative. *Journal of Politics* 22:474–84.

——. 1962. Community Power: Some Reflections on the Recent Literature. *American Sociological Review* 27:838–41.

Poppino, Rollie. 1953. Princess of the Sertão: A History of Feira de Santana. Ph.D. thesis, Stanford University.

Poulantzas, N. 1976. *The Crisis of Dictatorships.* London: New Left Books.

Powdermaker, Hortense. 1939. *After Freedom: A Cultural Study in the Deep South.* New York: Viking.

——. 1950. *Hollywood, the Dream Factory.* Boston: Little, Brown.

Radcliffe-Brown, A. R. 1952. *Structure and Function in Primitive Society: Essays and Addresses.* Glencoe, Ill.: Free Press.

Real, Katherina [Katherine Royal Cate]. 1967. *O Folclore no om Carnaval no Recife.* Rio de Janeiro: Ministério da Cultura e Educação, Divisão da Cultura Popular.

Redfield, Robert. 1930. *Tepotzlan, A Mexican Village: A Study of Folklife.* Chicago: University of Chicago Press.

——. 1941. *The Folk Culture of Yucatan.* Chicago: University of Chicago Press.

——. 1947. The Folk Society. *American Journal of Sociology* 52:293–308.

——. 1953. *The Primitive World and Its Transformations.* Ithaca: Cornell University Press.

——. 1955. *The Little Community: Viewpoints for the Study of the Human Whole.* Chicago: University of Chicago Press.

Bibliography

———. 1956. *Peasant Society and Culture.* Chicago: University of Chicago Press.
Sahlins, Marshall. 1958. *Social Stratification in Polynesia.* Seattle: University of Washington Press.
Saint-Louis, Loretta. 1989. Comments at Memorial Service for Anthony Leeds, Boston University, 10 March.
Samuelson, Paul. 1955. *Economics: An Introductory Analysis,* 3d ed. New York: McGraw Hill.
Sanjek, Roger. 1984. *Crowded Out: Homelessness and the Elderly Poor in New York City.* New York: Coalition for the Homeless.
———. 1990a. On Ethnographic Validity. In *Fieldnotes: The Makings of Anthropology,* ed. Roger Sanjek, 386–418. Ithaca: Cornell University Press.
———. 1990b. Urban Anthropology in the 1980s: A World View. *Annual Review of Anthropology* 19:151–86.
———. 1991. The Ethnographic Present. *Man* 26:609–28.
———. 1995. Politics, Theory and the Nature of Cultural Things. In *Science, Materialism and the Study of Culture: A Reader in Cultural Materialism,* ed. Martin Murphy and Maxine Margolis. Gainesville: University of Florida Press. [in press]
Saul, John, and Roger Woods. 1971. African Peasantries. In *Peasants and Peasant Societies,* ed. Teodor Shanin, 103–14. Harmondsworth: Penguin.
Schaedel, R. P. 1972. *Urbanización y proceso social en America.* Lima: Instituto de Estudios Peruanos.
Schaedel, R. P., J. Hardoy, and N. S. Kinzer, eds. 1978. *Urbanization in the Americas from the Beginnings to the Present.* The Hague: Mouton.
Schneider, Jane. 1977. Was There a Pre-Capitalist World-System? *Peasant Studies* 6:20–29.
Schwartz, Norman B. 1977. *A Milpero of Peten: Autobiography and Cultural Analysis.* Newark, Del.: University of Delaware Latin American Studies Program.
Scott, James. 1975. Exploitation in Rural Class Relations: A Victim's Perspective. *Comparative Politics* 7:489–532.
Seminário Interuniversitário. 1967. *Seminário Interuniversitário para o Exame das Consequências das Chuvas e Enchentes de Janeiro de 1966 na Região da Guanabara e Áreas Vizinhas.* Rio de Janeiro: Universidade Federal de Rio de Janeiro.
Shanin, Teodor. 1966. The Peasantry as a Political Factor. *Sociological Review* 14:5–27.
———, ed. 1971. *Peasants and Peasant Societies.* Harmondsworth: Penguin.
Sheehan, J. Brian. 1984. *The Boston School Integration Dispute: Social Change and Legal Maneuvers.* New York: Columbia University Press.
Shirley, Robert W. 1971. *The End of a Tradition: Culture Change and Development in the Municipio of Cunha, São Paulo, Brazil.* New York: Columbia University Press.
Sieber, R. Timothy. 1990. Selecting a New Past: Emerging Definitions of Heritage in Boston Harbor. *Journal of Urban and Cultural Studies* 1:101–22.

——. 1991. Waterfront Revitalization in Post-Industrial Port Cities of North America. *City and Society* 5:120–36.

Silva Campos, João da. 1947. *Cronica da Capitania de São Jorge dos Ipheus.* Bahia: Imprensa Vitoria.

Simpson, George Gaylord. 1961. *Principles of Animal Taxonomy.* New York: Columbia University Press.

Singer, Paul. 1976. *Desenvolvimento Económico e Evalução Urbana,* 2d ed. São Paulo: Companhia Editora Nacional.

Sjoberg, Gideon. 1960. *The Preindustrial City: Past and Present.* New York: Free Press.

Skidmore, Thomas. 1967. *Politics in Brazil, 1930–1964: An Experiment in Democracy.* Oxford: Oxford University Press.

Skinner, George William. 1964–65. Marketing and Social Structure in Rural China. *Journal of Asian Studies* 24:3–43, 195–228, 25:363–99.

Smith, Adam. 1776 [1906]. *The Wealth of Nations.* New York: Macmillan.

Smith, Carol A. 1975. Examining Stratification Systems through Peasant Marketing Arrangements: An Application of Some Models from Economic Geography. *Man* 10:95–122.

Smith, T. Lynn. 1947. *Brazil: People and Institutions.* Baton Rouge: Louisiana State University Press.

Southall, Aidan. 1956. Determinants of the Social Structure of African Urban Populations, with Special Reference to Kampala. In *Social Implications of Industrialization and Urbanization in Africa South of the Sahara,* ed. Daryll Forde, 557–78. Paris: UNESCO.

——. 1967. Kampala-Mengo. In *The City in Modern Africa,* ed. Horace Miner, 297–332. New York: Praeger.

——. 1973. The Density of Role-Relationships as a Universal Index of Urbanization. In *Urban Anthropology: Cross-Cultural Studies of Urbanization,* ed. Aidan Southall, 71–106. New York: Oxford University Press.

——. 1989. Comments at Memorial Service for Anthony Leeds, Boston University, 10 March.

——,ed. 1973. *Urban Anthropology: Cross-Cultural Studies of Urbanization.* New York: Oxford University Press.

Southall, Aidan, and Peter C. W. Gutkind. 1957. *Townsmen in the Making.* Kampala: East African Institute of Social Research.

Stavenhagen, Rodolfo. 1967. Las Relaciones entre la Estratificacion Social y la Dinamica de Clases. In *Social Structure, Stratification, and Social Mobility,* ed. Anthony Leeds, 126–51. Studies and monographs VIII. Washington, D.C.: Pan American Union, General Secretariat, Organization of American States.

Stein, Stanley. 1957. *Vassouras: A Brazilian Coffee County, 1850–1900.* Cambridge: Harvard University Press.

Stein, William W. 1961. *Hualcan: Life in the Highlands of Peru.* Ithaca: Cornell University Press.

Steward, Julian H. 1950. *Area Research: Theory and Practice.* New York: Social Science Research Council.

———,ed. 1956. *The People of Puerto Rico: A Study in Social Anthropology.* Urbana: University of Illinois Press.

Strassmann, W. Paul. 1958. *The Urban Economies of Southern Michigan.* Institute of Community Development Series, Bulletin 3. East Lansing: Michigan State University Press.

Sumner, William Graham. 1906 [1959]. *Folkways: A Study of the Sociological Importance of Usages, Manners, Customs, Mores and Morals.* New York: Dover.

Theodorson, George A., and Achilles G. Theodorson. 1969. *A Modern Dictionary of Sociology.* New York: Crowell.

Thorner, Daniel. 1962 [1971]. Peasant Economy as a Category of Economic History. In *Peasants and Peasant Societies,* ed. Teodor Shanin, 202–18. Harmondsworth: Penguin.

Turner, John C. 1965. Lima's Barriadas and Corralones: Suburbs vs. Slums. *Ekistics* 19.

———. 1966. Uncontrolled Urban Settlements, Problems and Policies. Paper for the U.N. Interregional Seminar on Development Policies and Planning in Relation to Urbanization, Pittsburgh.

———. 1967. Autonomous Urban Settlements, Problems or Solutions. Paper read at Latin American Colloquium, Brandeis University.

Turner, John C., and William Mangin. 1963. Dwelling Resources in South America: Urbanization Case Study in Peru. *Architectural Design,* August, 360–93.

Vayda, Andrew P., Anthony Leeds, and David B. Smith. 1961. The Place of Pigs in Melanesian Subsistence. In *Symposium: Patterns of Land Utilization and Other Papers,* ed. Viola Garfield, 69–77. Proceedings of the 1961 Annual Spring Meeting of the American Ethnological Society. Seattle: University of Washington Press.

Velho, Gilberto. 1991. An Intellectual Pioneer. [Unpublished manuscript, trans. Elizabeth P. Leeds]

Wagley, Charles. 1949. Brazil. In *Most of the World: The Peoples of Africa, Latin America, and the East Today,* ed. Ralph Linton, 212–70. New York: Columbia University Press.

———. 1953. *Amazon Town: A Study of Man in the Tropics.* New York: Macmillan.

———, ed. 1952. *Race and Class in Rural Brazil.* Paris: UNESCO.

Wagley, Charles, and Marvin Harris. 1958. *Minorities in the New World.* New York: Columbia University Press.

Wallerstein, Immanuel. 1974. *The Modern World-System: Capitalist Agriculture and the Origins of the European World-Economy in the Sixteenth Century.* New York: Academic Press.

Warner, W. Lloyd, and Paul S. Lunt. 1941. *The Social Life of a Modern Community.* New Haven: Yale University Press.

———. 1942. *The Status System of a Modern Community.* New Haven: Yale University Press.

Weatherford, J. McIver. 1985. *Tribes on the Hill.* South Hadley, Mass.: Bergin and Garvey.

Weber, Max. 1921 [1958]. *The City.* Glencoe, Ill.: Free Press.

West, James. 1945. *Plainville, U.S.A.* New York: Columbia University Press.

Westermann, William Linn. 1929. *Upon Slavery in Ptolemaic Egypt.* New York: Columbia University Press.

———. 1955. *The Slave Systems of Greek and Roman Antiquity.* Philadelphia: American Philosophical Society.

Wheatley, Paul. 1975. Satyanrta in Suvarnadvipa: From Reciprocity to Redistribution in Ancient Southeast Asia. In *Ancient Civilization and Trade,* ed. Jeremy A. Sabloff and C. C. Lamberg-Karlovsky, 227–83. Albuquerque: University of New Mexico Press.

Whiteford, Andrew H. 1960. *Two Cities of Latin America: A Comparative Description of Social Class.* Beloit, Wisc.: Logan Museum.

Willems, Emilio. 1947. *Cunha: Tradição e Transição em uma Cultura Rural do Brasil.* São Paulo: Secretaria da Agricultura do Estado de Sao Paulo, Directoria de Publicidade Agrícola.

Willems, Emilio, and Giaconda Mussolini. 1952. *Buzios Island: A Caiçara Community in Southern Brazil.* Locust Valley, N.Y.: J. J. Augustin.

Williams, Brett. 1988. *Upscaling Downtown: Stalled Gentrification in Washington, D.C.* Ithaca: Cornell University Press.

Willmott, Peter, and Michael Young. 1960. *Family and Class in a London Suburb.* London: Routledge and Kegan Paul.

Wolfinger, Raymond E. 1960. Reputation and Reality in the Study of "Community Power." *American Sociological Review* 25:636–44.

———. 1962. A Plea for Decent Burial. *American Sociological Review* 27:841–47.

Woodham-Smith, Cecil. 1962. *The Great Hunger: Ireland 1845–49.* London: New English Library.

Young, Michael, and Peter Willmott. 1957. *Kinship and Family in East London.* London: Routledge and Kegan Paul.

Index

Index

Leeds, Anthony (*cont.*)
  study groups and, 5, 11, 15–17
  University of Texas and, 9, 11–12
Leeds, Arthur, 6, 19
Leeds, Elizabeth P., 11–12, 13, 15, 26, 40
Liberalism, 61
Localities. *See also* Nucleations; Societal
    system of localities
  specialization and, 53, 55
  urban analysis and, 41–45
Logic, dualistic/dialectical, 195–196
Lower-Income Settlement Types: Processes,
  Structure, Policies (Leeds), 42
Lowrey, Jo Alice, 10
Luxury items, imported, 35

Mankind Evolving (Dobzhansky), 28
Marxism, 8–9, 25
  class system and, 39, 40, 193, 195–196,
    198
  logic and, dualistic/dialectical, 195–196
  power and, 197–198
  production and, 196, 197
Medieval European system, 59, 63–68
Microinvention, 29
Middle class
  Argentina and, 157–158, 162
  assumptions about, 145–147
  organizational boundaries and, 148–151,
    153–154
  supralocal institutions and, 42
  United States and the, 38, 148–151
Minhua Terra, Portugal: Lamentations and
  Celebrations—the Growth of an
  Ethnography and a Commitment
  (Leeds), 14, 24
Mobility and nodal analysis, 187–188
Monetarization, 64
Multimedia presentations and fieldwork,
  23–24
Museu Nacional of the Universidade
  Federal do Rio de Janeiro, 12

National networks/policies/resource flows,
  94
Nelson, Benjamin N., 9
Nexuses, 176–182, 242
Nodal networks, 39–40, 71
  analysis and, 187–191
  boundaries and, 179–184
  differential distribution and, 184–187
  identifying, 169–173
  nexuses and, 176–182, 242
  structure of, 173–176
  urban renewal projects and, 43–44

Nucleations, 71
  differentiation/specialization and, 82–86
  exchange and, 86–89
  externalities and, 79–82, 89–94
  specialization/linkage and, 74–77
  theorems dealing with, 77–79

Ontological view of class, 39
Organization:
  agrarian labor and, 116–125
  boundaries and, 54–55, 148–151, 152–
    154
  control and, 42
  nodal analysis and, 189–190, 191
  squatter settlements and, 227, 228, 229
  strategic resource control and, 220

Palerm, Angel, 10–11
Pan-American Union (PAU), 4, 10–11, 147
Parallelism, 184
PAU. *See* Pan-American Union
Peasant society, 36. *See also* Agrarian
    social orders
  attributes of, 117–119
  capital and, 138
  capitalist urbanism and, 63
  cocoa production in Brazil and, 132–133
  criteria for preserving concept of, 115–
    116
  feudalism and, 65
  Latin America and, 142
  role alters and, 136–137
  scientific validity and, 109–115
  specialization and, 56
  tribalizing, 57
Pennhurst State School for Mental
  Defectives, 19
Photography, 5, 23
Plantations, 132–133, 135–136,
  139
Poetry, 5, 20
  complex truths and, 21–22
  ethnographic, 14
  fieldwork and, 22–23
Policies, national, 94
Political activism, 5, 19–20
Poor (masses) and power, 42
Population and specialization, 78
Ports-of-trade, 34–35
Portugal:
  capitalist urbanism and, 61
  demonetarization and, 64
  IMF and, 22–23
  kin networks in, 90–94
  labor and, 14, 89–90

Index

Subjective and Objective in Social Anthropological Epistemology (Leeds), 30
Supralocal structures and institutions, 41–42, 221–224, 227–229
Symbol systems, 28, 30
Syria and kinship behavior, 236

Teaching and Leeds, 24
Technology, 35–36, 53
Tenancy, 121–122, 128, 141
Texas, systems analysis of, 12, 31
Third World societies and labor, 37–38
Three-class social orders, 38
Through Selfethnography to Human Nature: Continuous Diversity as Escape from Categories to Unity (Leeds), 25
Thursday Night Group, 3, 16, 26
Total system. See Societal system of localities
Towns contrasted with cities, 76–77. See also Nucleations
Trade, 34–35, 80
Trade and Market in the Early Empires (Polanyi, Arensberg, and Pearson), 34, 35
Traditional inductivist approaches, 20, 24
Transnodal networks, 179–182
Tribes, 57, 209
Two-class systems, 38, 42, 153, 159–160
Typicality of sample, 82–83, 88

United States
blockage of access in, 154
Canada's relationship with, 96–97
middle class in, 38, 148–151
University of Texas and Leeds, 9, 11–12
Urban analysis, 4
Brazilian social science and, 12–13
interdisciplinary approach to, 9
localities and, 41–45
methodological issues in, 233–246
misconceptions about, 51–57
Urban centers. See also Capitalism: urbanism and; Nucleations
defining, 43–44
differential integration and, 58–59
feudalism and, 64–66
renewal projects and, 43–44
rural living interconnected with, 17–18, 73–74
Urban socialization. See Social urbanization

Validity, 31
Velho, Gilberto, 13, 26
Villages. See Nucleations
Visual documentation and fieldwork, 23–24

Walden School, 6
Wealth distribution, 158
Weber, Max, 33
Weil, Edmund, 6
Weil, Polly L., 5, 6, 19
Wirth, Louis, 57
Workers. See Rural proletariat

Yaruro people (Venezuela), 10

Anthropology of Contemporary Issues

A SERIES EDITED BY

ROGER SANJEK

www.ingramcontent.com/pod-product-compliance
Lightning Source LLC
Chambersburg PA
CBHW030644270326
41929CB00007B/198